JENNIFER JUNIPER

A journey beyond the muse

JENNIFER JUNIPER

A journey beyond the muse

Jenny Boyd

Urbane
PUBLICATIONS

urbanepublications.com

First published in Great Britain in 2020 by Urbane Publications Ltd
Unit E3 The Premier Centre Abbey Park Romsey SO51 9DG

Copyright © Jenny Boyd, 2020

A CIP catalogue record for this book is available from the British Library.

ISBN 978-1-912666-61-4
MOBI 978-1-912666-62-1

Design and Typeset by Michelle Morgan

Cover design by Larry Vigon

Cover photo by Eric Swayne

Printed and bound by MultiPrint Ltd

Urbane
PUBLICATIONS

urbanepublications.com

FOR
WOLF & IZZY

COURAGE
STARTS
WITH
SHOWING
UP AND
LETTING
OURSELVES
BE SEEN

Brené Brown

CONTENTS

INTRODUCTION

JENNIFER JUNIPER

When George Harrison and my sister Pattie invited me to join them, along with the rest of the Beatles and their wives, on their trip to Maharishi's ashram in India, I asked, "But how can I ever repay you?"

"Just be yourself," George replied.

And that's it. As I realized many years later, that's all we ever have to do, just be ourselves.

This is my journey.

It is the story of people I spent time with and what I learned from being part of a unique time in history, when young people changed and shaped our culture forever. Having a certain look that reflected this new era was pure luck; it took me to places I might never have gone. In my thinking and feeling I epitomized what was going on in my generation. I lived and breathed this new world before I became aware of the dramatic shifts we were making.

From the age of sixteen I found myself in the center of the 'Swinging 60s' with all its innocence and wonder. Being a house model for up-and-coming young fashion designers Foale and Tuffin brought me into the heart of Carnaby Street, to witness the beginnings of what was to become the center of 60s fashion and pop culture in London.

I wore all the latest and innovative Foale and Tuffin designs for owners of boutiques and editors of glossy magazines; magazines I was later to find myself in once I became a photographic model, including newspapers, fashion catalogues and a couple of short films. I represented the look of that time as I cat walked and had fashion photographs taken in New York, along with my sister and two other models, for the "Youthquake" movement. We were the first contingent of the huge "British Invasion" in fashion that was about to sweep across America.

I danced with my boyfriend, Mick Fleetwood, at all the latest clubs: The Ad Lib, Crazy Elephant, and The Scotch of St James, where we'd go with my sister Pattie

3

and her boyfriend George Harrison and the rest of The Beatles.

I was enchanted by the spirit of our age. I breathed it in before I knew it was there, it became part of me, and I followed its call. I was a natural 'Flower Child' and all it represented; fairy-like and whimsical, and so it was no surprise to find myself inadvertently in San Francisco at the beginning of 'Flower Power' in 1967. I was deeply immersed in the counter culture and feel privileged to have been part of a generation that made such an impact on the world, from our outlook on life, to the sexual revolution, mind-opening drugs, metaphysics, and most of all, music. Musicians became the spokespeople of our time; they represented this new age and spoke for the masses.

I worked in The Beatles shop, Apple, the first of its kind, and was interviewed by journalists to describe what the shop represented. We were all idealists and believed we could change the world.

I went to India to study meditation with The Beatles and witnessed their creativity at work while writing songs later to appear on the White Album. I found myself in these pivotal places at a pivotal time in history, living my life without any awareness that one day we would look back at this time as an inspirational decade.

Although I was at the center of the spiritual bloom and innocence of the 60s, I was also part of the turmoil and decadence of the 70s and 80s. My marriage to Mick Fleetwood, founder member of Fleetwood Mac, brought me to the forefront of rock and roll, of fame, money, drugs and heartache. I struggled in the darkness searching for my own voice, before finding a light at the end of the tunnel. Aged 37, I went to college and studied psychology where I gained a better understanding and came to terms with my life and my actions. Having spent so much of my life in the company of many of the greatest musical legends, those who influenced our culture to this day, I finally found my own creative ability, my own sense of self and purpose. This is what I learned along the way.

A journey beyond the muse

1

SIXTIES LONDON

I remember vividly the first time I heard of The Beatles. It was a normal Saturday in November 1962 and I had recently turned 15. My friends had given me a lift home after a morning of walking around Wimbledon and listening to our favorite 45s in the local record shop. Just before I opened the door, *Love Me Do* came on the radio. That was it!

"Turn it up," I shouted, my hand still resting on the door handle of the car.

It was a never-to-be forgotten moment; something new and completely different had just arrived. Everyone stopped what he or she was doing or saying, the music was turned up and we all stared at the radio. The sound of voices singing in harmony and the wail of a harmonica pinned me to my seat. A wave of happiness ran through my veins. Everything about this song, even the simple words, ignited my imagination.

"Who are they?" I asked.

"The Beatles," someone answered. I smiled, enchanted with the idea of a group being named after an insect. Little did I know then that I was listening to a band of musicians who were to go down in history as defining the 60s. Nor could I have imagined that in just over a year, my sister would play a part in The Beatles film, *A Hard Day's Night*, or that she would become George Harrison's girlfriend.

Pattie had left home the year before and I missed her dreadfully. I had four other siblings, but she and I were the closest. Pattie now worked as an apprentice at the Elizabeth Arden beauty salon. This meant that she could afford to leave home and share a flat with one of her girlfriends. We were frequently in touch and I would visit her in Chelsea, or she would come home for Sunday lunch with her photographer boyfriend. It was while Pattie was working at Elizabeth Arden's salon that a client had suggested she should get an agent and become a model. She sprung to fame after being seen on a television commercial, (directed by Richard Lester who was later to direct the Beatles film *Hard Day's Night*) advertizing Smiths

Crisps. "Smiths have crispness in the bag," she said, her eyes wide open, and blonde bouffant shoulder length hair flicking up at the ends. Now that her modeling career was launched, she became increasingly busy, frequently appearing in magazines and catalogues.

One afternoon, I was in the sitting room at home, when I heard the phone ring. I could hear my mother's voice in the kitchen and knew at once it must be Pattie. Her voice got higher and louder, finishing off with, "That's so exciting, I'll tell the others." She appeared in the doorway, smiling. "Pattie's been asked to audition for a small part in the Beatles film. And, not only that," she said, looking at my younger sister, Paula, and me, her eyes glistening as she held her breath. "She's got the part! She has to be a fan and dress up like a schoolgirl."

Photographs of The Beatles filming appeared in every newspaper throughout the weeks that followed, including Pattie with a smile on her face, her long blonde hair and wearing a school uniform either on set during Hard Day's Night or standing behind George's chair with a comb in her hand. It was during this time she told me that George had asked her out. She was in a dilemma and didn't know what to do, since she already had a boyfriend, but the pull was strong, and the feelings were mutual and so she and George began their love affair.

One afternoon, Pattie invited me to her flat after school so I could meet George. When I walked inside and saw him leaning against the wall beside the door, my first reaction was surprise - how small and slim he was! He was much smaller in person than the larger-than-life pictures I'd seen of him. I don't know what I expected but he seemed so normal. I shook his slender hand and looked into his dark brown eyes and smiling familiar face, a face I knew so well yet had never met. I wanted to give him a hug, as though he were an old friend. Shaking hands seemed so unnaturally formal.

A few months later, after George had returned from The Beatles US tour, our sister brought her famous boyfriend home for a Sunday lunch. They arrived in George's E-Type Jaguar, which he parked outside what looked like an empty suburban street. It was the most exciting thing that anyone on that street had seen on a Sunday, or any other day, as they peeked through their net curtains. My mother opened the glazed front door that led into a red brick, tiled, porch, and invited them into the sitting room. She had already put her favorite song onto the record player, *My Boy Lollipop*, having seen them sitting in the car outside. It was now blaring out to greet him.

And so our family met one of the four most popular men in the country. The couple sat next to each other, taking up very little space on the crushed strawberry-colored '50s sofa. I noticed how they held hands the whole time, and how George's eyes stayed glued to Pattie.

George was easy to be with. It felt no different than any older sister bringing home her latest boyfriend to meet the family, except for bits of the conversation relating to The Beatles. It was hard to equate this person in our midst with the world-famous icon. He talked to us about Liverpool, about the film, and their recent trip to America which had been unexpectedly frightening. The police had failed to cope with, what had been dubbed as 'Beatle Mania', and at times had resorted to using fire hoses to hold back the unexpected crowds. Everyone, including the police, had been taken by surprise as fans climbed up drainpipes trying to break into their hotel rooms. Coping with this 'Beatle Mania' would become part of their world as their fame grew.

I showed George my acoustic guitar that afternoon and he taught me how to play the three basic chords needed for my favorite Buddy Holly songs. He must have noticed me squinting as I looked at my fingers holding down the strings and told me I should try wearing contact lenses.

"John wears them now," he said, "and he's as blind as a bat."

I had to wait a year before I could buy contacts, but his thoughtful words stayed with me. I discovered, as I got to know him better, how caring George was, and he would share that side of himself with our family. To me he was always like a very kind older brother.

Without realizing it at the time and looking back on it now, 1964 was the year that changed my life and increasingly brought me into the beginning of what was soon to be known as the 'Swinging 60s'.

The significance of Pattie and George's relationship was not in the forefront of my mind; I was too involved with having crushes on the sixth form boys at school, feeling the excitement of youth and the beginnings of independence. I had become part of a group of friends who went to parties on Saturday evenings, sometimes linking up with the college boys nearby. If I missed my last train home, I often stayed the night with my friend Dale and her family in Notting Hill Gate. This seemed to happen quite frequently, and I began to feel accepted as part of her family.

I'd noticed Dale earlier in the year as I made my way hurriedly down the stairs from one class to the next. She had long, straight, blond hair with a fringe and was the first girl in the school to wear knee length, black leather boots made by a theatrical boot maker in Charing Cross Road, called Annello and Davide.

She looked like Honor Blackman in The Avengers, a weekly television series we all watched. This show exemplified the spirit of our time, wacky and eccentric, with Patrick Macnee playing the part of a tweed-suited, bowler-hatted, umbrella-sporting spy, in complete contrast to his judo-kicking co-star Honor Blackman known as the youthful, beautiful and confident Mrs. Gale. She dressed in the latest fashion, often clothed from head to foot in leather, including her black boots that were given the nickname, 'kinky boots'.

I lusted after those boots. I loved the look, I thought they were the ultimate in everything that was cool, but I knew they came with a price that touched the stars. It was Dale who introduced me to a sixteen-year-old Mick Fleetwood, the very person who told me later that when he first spotted me had told himself I was the girl he would marry one day. It was very like Mick, having known him now for over fifty years, to recognize certain people who were destined to play a significant part in his life.

I was first introduced to Mick through a sculpture Dale had made. I was sitting at my desk one afternoon in July, waiting for the English class to begin and idly watching the minute particles of dust lit up by the sun streaming in through the window. Feeling hot and while doodling in my notebook, I heard the door close with a bang followed by a scraping of the chair next to me. I knew it was Dale. She slapped her books on the desk, sat down, and then brought out of her bag a small figure made of thin copper wire. As the teacher began talking, she adjusted this piece of sculpture and sat it on the edge of her desk with its long legs dangling over the side.

"Who is it?" I whispered.

"It's this boy called Mick, who's gorgeous," she replied. "He's got long hair, long legs and plays in a group called The Cheynes." As she spoke, she re-arranged the sculpture, still whispering about Mick, her head facing me, and her hand cupped over her mouth until a shout from the English teacher made us both jump.

"Will you two stop talking!" his voice bellowed out from across the room. "Or you'll stay in after class and write an essay."

I froze. The wrath of Mr. Steadman-Jones was not to be taken lightly. We both put our heads down and continued reading from Macbeth, but every now and then I stole a glance at Dale's wire figurine, sitting silently beside me.

"Come with me and meet him," Dale whispered as she bent down, pretending to look for something in her bag. "I'm going to his bedsit after school with some grapes. He's got flu."

Glimpsed from the doorway, my first impression of this young man, who would one day become my husband, was a rather blurred pale face poking up from under the bedclothes with big eyes and unkempt brown hair. I watched Dale stride over to this sorry sight, say a few words, put the grapes on his bedside table and then, as I walked back along the corridor, she said,

"He's not feeling well. He'll be at the Coffee Mill tomorrow, so he'll see us then."

I was later to find out that sixteen-year-old Mick Fleetwood was only six months older than me but had left school and his home in Salisbury the previous year filled with dreams of living in London and becoming a drummer. Every day he practiced drumming in the basement where he lived with his sister and her husband in Notting Hill Gate, just around the corner from the Coffee Mill and not far from my school. A young keyboard player living in the same mews, heard him one day and asked him to join his group called The Cheynes.

The Coffee Mill was situated on a bend in the road, very close to Portobello Market. This café had become our meeting place after school where we'd take over the upstairs room; a group of teenagers sitting at tables in a haze of cigarette smoke and drinking hot chocolate from glasses encased in metal frames. I loved the atmosphere – it was our place. I met Dale at the Coffee Mill on this particular Saturday afternoon, and that was where I first officially met Mick Fleetwood. He walked into the cafe with one of the band members, also his roommate, Roger.

They both wore what seemed to be a band uniform; black mohair trousers with a pink shirt and white collar and cuffs. Mick was tall, skinny, with brown shoulder length poker-straight hair, which was parted on the side and hid most of his pale narrow face. When he did sweep his curtain of hair aside the most enormous eyes looked directly at me, before taking another sip of his hot chocolate. He appeared very gentle, and softly spoken in comparison to Roger, who was swarthy looking with black frizzy hair. Dale and Roger did most of the talking while Mick and I sat quietly, like two little peas locked in the same silent pod.

The sound of a horn beeping outside interrupted their conversation. The boys stood up, and after Roger had left the cafe, and just before walking out the door Mick turned around to face Dale, saying,

"Why don't you both come to Brentwood tonight? We're playing a gig in the Town Hall and we can catch the train up. It's not that far."

"We'd love to," Dale said, as she nudged my leg with her foot.

The Town Hall was completely empty. Its bare wooden floorboards were scuffed from people dancing and stained with spilt drinks and stubbed-out cigarettes.

Chairs were lined up next to each other against the whitewashed walls, leaving the rest of the floor for the crowds to occupy.

After setting up his drums Mick leaped off the stage and sat between Dale and me. He spread his long spidery legs in front of him and then brought them back with his elbows resting on his knees. I felt his foot on top of mine but as I tried to move it, the pressure got stronger. I felt conflicted. I liked Mick, but my loyalty to Dale stopped me from allowing myself to enjoy the attention.

Rhythm and blues filled the Town Hall that night as Roger's rasping voice belted out songs by Bo Diddley, Howlin' Wolf, and Chuck Berry. These were the songs I'd listened to over the last year and loved them. It was the first live band I'd ever seen and having met the musicians before they went on stage added to the feeling of excitement. I noticed that every time I looked at Phil, the guitar player, he winked and smiled at me. His smiles continued throughout the show, over the crowds and smack bang into my sixteen-year old heart. It was my first introduction to the fickleness of flirting from the stage. It was also my introduction to the world of musicians.

A few weeks after that evening, much to my surprise, Dale and Roger came to visit me in hospital. I was under surveillance for a suspected appendicitis and was waiting to be given the all clear. Roger handed me some flowers, as I sat up in bed, and Dale brought a bunch of grapes. Little did I suspect Roger would ask me out a few days later, having had no idea that he felt anything for me and seeing him with Dale much of the time took me off guard.

Although I felt attracted to Mick, I ended up going out with Roger for almost a year. There was something that drew me to him; he was charismatic, dark and brooding. I was aware that he'd been adopted and had a tough and lonely childhood. Knowing this made me feel sad for him. Although I hadn't had much in the way of parenting, I did at least have a family.

Whenever we spent an evening together, I always left before eleven o'clock to catch the train for the 45-minute journey back home, but not before being made to backcomb and blow-dry his hair ready for whatever party he was going to later that night. Sometimes, after saying goodbye I would bump into Mick, holding the banister as he climbed the narrow staircase to the room he shared with Roger. Our eyes would meet halfway down, hold each other's gaze, and then, without a word we'd continue in opposite directions. I felt tongue-tied in his presence, my insides would flutter, and I longed to talk to him. During that time, I frequently saw Mick after school with Peter Bardens, the keyboard player, either in the Coffee Mill or the restaurant next door, his face usually hidden by his hair as he leaned over a plate of omelet and chips, but he rarely spoke to me.

While The Beatles were on tour, Pattie had temporarily moved into Whaddon House, a flat in Knightsbridge where George and Ringo had set up residence. I would often visit her after school and we'd spend evenings together, sitting on a plush sofa in front of a glass coffee table, drinking scotch and coke, smoking Gitanes, often unfiltered, and listening to music turned up to full volume. The Beatles had bought or were given all the latest LPs and 45s while in the States, singles by Mary Wells, The Supremes, Marvin Gaye, Smokey Robinson, and other Motown records. I loved listening to these records, they were so different to anything I'd heard in England and made me want to dance.

The flat was luxurious. Thick onyx ashtrays were everywhere with a gold Dunhill lighter nearby, guitars leaned against the wall, looking beautiful but untouchable. I met Paul McCartney's girlfriend, Jane Asher there one Saturday morning. It was a hot day and I remember her wearing what I thought was a very cool-looking cotton dress made out of Liberty Print. I didn't have the money to buy clothes at that time but even so I was curious to know more about the latest fashions. I asked her who the designer was. "Foale and Tuffin," she said. We didn't have very much more to say to each other after that. She seemed quiet and slightly withdrawn and I was just Pattie's younger sister. The name Foale and Tuffin stood out to me as I remembered seeing a photograph of my sister in a magazine wearing a very stylish raincoat made by the same designers.

The first thing I noticed when Pattie introduced me to Cathy McGowan was that she was wearing the same dress. Cathy McGowan was a young woman who hosted the popular *Ready Steady Go* television show where all the latest groups of that time played live in front of a room full of dancing teenagers. She had long brown hair with a fringe that hid most of her eyes. We'd been invited to the television show one Friday afternoon and chatted to her backstage while she put on her make-up alongside her friend Sandie Shaw, whose song *Always Something There To Remind Me* had recently become a hit. The dressing room was filled with excitement, the smell of powder, lively chatter, and bright lights. Singer, Dusty Springfield, sat with us. Her make-up glistened and sparkled, looking as though it could be scraped off with a knife.

Once the show started, I went out to where the audience was waiting, my 'Dancer' badge pinned to my dress, and danced with about twenty-five other teenagers, our heads bobbing up and down in time to the music. Television cameras were wheeled across the floor, missing us by inches, while each singer or group performed under the bright lights. At the end of the show Cathy told me I could come again any time, and so after school I would make my way to the loo in Notting Hill Gate tube station, change out of anything resembling a school uniform, and then catch the Central Line to Holborn wearing my trendiest clothes. I was in heaven! It didn't matter to me whether we were being televised or not, being able to watch my favorite performers and dance to their music was quite enough on its own. Over the weeks, I was to see Eric Burdon and the Animals, The Zombies, Dave Clark Five, Peter and Gordon, Dusty Springfield, and many others.

There were positive and negative implications to having a Beatle as my sister's boyfriend. Each time I left the *Ready Steady Go* studio, I came across a large group of young girls outside the door. They would wait for hours, in hopes of catching someone, no matter who, that knew The Beatles. Waving their books, they would crowd round me, calling my name, and asking for an autograph. Signing autographs for fans was the positive part of being associated with The Beatles, but then there were those who harassed me because they hated them, like some of the girls at my school. Dale and I came across a group of Mods walking along the pavement towards us in their signature style clothing, leather coats and shortly cropped hair, with cigarette smoke billowing out of their nostrils. As they came closer, one of them gave me a strong push with her leather-clad arm and shoved me into the road as they shouted in unison, "Beatle Lover," followed by peals of laughter. "Sister's got a new boyfriend." This sort of behavior had become part of my world, although usually not as violently. Other girls at school had whispered and pointed in my direction.

The Mods were a sub-culture that focused on music and fashion. Unlike their rivals, the Rockers, the Mods dressed in smart tailor-made suits and listened to rhythm and blues. They liked groups such as The Who, The Small Faces, and The Kinks. What they didn't like were The Beatles.

Around this time, Pattie and George moved to a bungalow in Esher, not far out of London. One evening after supper, while the three of us were sitting around a little table in the kitchen, George introduced me to a few puffs of a joint. It was early days of pot smoking for us, and that night was innocent and giggly. While we sat there chatting, I was aware of them looking at me, waiting for a reaction but I didn't feel anything. Then George reached over and picked up a wooden cat or cow that sat on the red-tiled windowsill and held it in front of me, bouncing it up and down and speaking in a funny voice trying to make me laugh.

I must have been a slow starter as far as feeling the effects of pot, but that was to change pretty soon. For me, the consequence of smoking pot became far more heady, my brain would go into overdrive as one thought after another scrambled for attention, desperately seeking the meaning of life. Even though I didn't get high with them that evening, I loved being with Pattie and George, they were so gentle, so generous and kind, but most of all they were my first steadying influence in what had been a disruptive upbringing.

I still lived at home but without any thought of what I wanted to be as I continued my day-to-day treks to school. The idea of going to college was never discussed, the closest thing to any conversation regarding my future was my mother suggesting I learn to type, the thought of which I dismissed straight away. I wanted to do something that inspired me like my English class, but I didn't know what that could be.

The Cheynes had disbanded and Roger and Mick both, independently, looked for house painting jobs while waiting for a new group to join. Instead of his smart mohair suit, Roger now sauntered around Notting Hill with work clothes, showing off his new trade with specks of colored paint all over his face and in his black wiry hair.

It wasn't until many years after my relationship with Roger that I came to the realization that each relationship can be a gift. Often at the time it might not feel like that, but there is something to be learned, some outcome, either physical or emotional, that comes of this meeting. And so, it was that Roger played a crucial part in me securing my first job, my introduction to the world of modeling and ultimately everything that represented the swinging sixties.

He got the job of redecorating Foale and Tuffin's new showroom in Carnaby Street and while he was there, they told him that they were looking for a house model. He suggested me. It had never occurred to me to become a model, but as arranged, I went with him a few days later to meet Sally Tuffin and Marion Foale. I was still very shy and had never been to any kind of interview before but made my way along Carnaby Street and into their showroom.

In the middle of the room stood two young pattern cutters bending over a large table. They looked up and smiled as I walked towards the sofa. Marion and Sally were in their mid-twenties, both with Vidal Sassoon haircuts; and both very friendly. As soon as we sat down they said, "You would definitely be a size six, and we've never made anything so small." I answered questions about my availability and about myself, feeling horribly self-conscious each time I looked at Roger, sitting on a chair opposite me, rolling his eyes at my every word. Later, he made fun of the way I'd conducted the interview, told me that I didn't speak loud enough or had given confusing answers. And so I didn't think for a minute I had the job, and made my way back to school ready to continue my education with the thought of one day becoming a journalist.

Those plans came to an abrupt halt the following evening when Marion Foale called to offer me the job. She told me I would be expected to model their latest designs in their showroom for the fashion editors from *Vogue, Harper's Bazaar, Queen, Elle*, and other glossy magazines. I would also be expected to help in the office when they didn't need me to model and to serve customers in the boutique they were soon to open. I would be paid £5 a week after tax. I was thrilled! Without a moment's hesitation, I took the job. I left school at the end of the week without even discussing this new turn of events with my mother. She was too busy looking after my unruly younger sister and my two brothers to take any notice of what I did. The following Monday, I caught the train to Carnaby Street and arrived at the Foale and Tuffin office at 9am ready to see where this might lead.

I had never heard of Carnaby Street up until that time, and nor had many others, except for the fashion-conscious Mods who swarmed around the flamboyant, brightly colored but affordable clothes inside a men's boutique called John Stephen or another newly opened clothes shop, Lord John. Carnaby Street was just starting to come alive and into its own; its run-down buildings and cheap rents soon to give way to trendy shops and bars. There was no way of guessing that within a very short time it would become the epicenter of men's fashion and would define the swinging 60s, attracting not only teenagers but also pop stars such as Jimi Hendrix, The Beatles, The Rolling Stones, and the Kinks. It was an exciting place to be.

I walked through the door of the old brick building and up the narrow rickety staircase to the Foale and Tuffin office in Marlborough Court. It was smaller than I'd expected. I was greeted by a friendly face sitting behind a large desk surrounded by a stack of papers, but it wasn't long before Sally and Marion arrived, full of smiles and bustling with energy. They whisked me across the road to their showroom where they immediately set to work, sifting through the black satin dresses and mustard-colored trouser suits, pulling out their designs one after another and telling me to try them on. At the end of the session I tried on a double-breasted pillar-box red trouser suit with silver buttons on the jacket. It fit me perfectly. It was as though I'd suddenly found myself, as if these trousers and jacket had been made just for me. Their clothes felt free and comfortable and the relief of knowing

I would never have to wear the restrictive suspender belt and stockings my mother had encouraged as she tried to prepare me for life as a young woman, filled me with joy.

"You're tiny," Sally and Marion said, almost in unison, "much smaller than our last model." They both looked at me in the red trouser suit. "It's yours," they said.

That was the beginning to not only my first job, but also to having a wardrobe filled with clothes that many young women would have given anything to own. Everything I wore were samples made to fit me. Sally and Marion were the hippest designers in London. They were the first designers to make sharply tailored trouser suits for women; everything they created was for the young and epitomized the Sixties. I was fortunate to have them as my first employers. They knew how to get the best out of people and made everyone who worked for them feel like part of the family. Being one of six children, I had never experienced such individual attention. These two highly respected designers saw something in me that enabled me to live up to their expectations. Their encouragement helped me build my confidence as I began showing their collection, walking up and down the showroom in front of one fashion editor after another, a photographer or buyers for boutiques and department stores. The atmosphere was always friendly and relaxed.

Marit Allen was editor of *Vogue* magazine. She was a gentle, smiling woman, softly spoken and great friends with Sally and Marion. She always looked very smart with short hair and thin wire-framed glasses on the end of her nose.

"I would like to use Jenny in a photographic session for Brides magazine. She's perfect," she said, not long after we'd met. This was to be my first taste of photographic modeling. When I look at that photograph now, I see a young woman standing straight, no poses, wearing a full-length empire line dress, hands down loosely beside her body, silver daisies perched on top of her head, long hair and with a coy smile looking straight into the camera. Most of the photographers I began working with were fun, young, upbeat and encouraging, with a clever knack of putting me at my ease. Although I continued to work for Foale and Tuffin for another year or so, because I was asked to do more photographic jobs, they suggested I get an agent.

"You look just like Pattie," photographers, agents or editors would often say. "You could almost be twins."

I was flattered in some ways, knowing how pretty Pattie was and I was used to being compared to her, even as a child. When I appeared in newspaper articles or magazines modeling the latest fashion, it was inevitable that the description would refer to me as Pattie's younger sister, or a little later, as sister-in-law to Beatle,

George Harrison. We became known as the 'Boyd Sisters'. Even so, we approached modeling from different perspectives; Pattie was more strategic, more pragmatic, whereas I tended to be more happy-go-lucky in my outlook. Although I wasn't a trained model, like so many girls were, I started to create my own style, my own unique way of expression.

Sally and Marion came into the office one day with exciting news. An American called Paul Young had seen their clothes and wanted a collection made to launch Youthquake, his company in the States. As well as Foale and Tuffin and Mary Quant, he had asked a few other up-and-coming designers who were also transforming British fashion in the 60s, including Mick's sister, Sally Jesse, designer of soft leather handbags with clear Perspex handles, and a new shoe designer called Moya Bowler, who's black snakeskin ankle boots I now owned after paying a week's wages. This event was to be called 'The British Fashion Invasion'. Pattie and I were chosen to wear Foale and Tuffin designs, and two other women were chosen to model the Mary Quant collection. The first step towards this venture was for the four models to go out to New York and begin the publicity campaign.

This was to be the first time of doing a catwalk in front of so many people, and the first time of doing photographic modeling with Pattie, neither of which fazed me. I was excited to be chosen as part of the team, but mostly I went along with whatever was asked of me, believing it to be part of my job.

An Englishman called Terry met us at the airport in New York, full of smiles and enthusiasm. The noise, the heat, and the humidity hit me as he herded us towards a waiting limo. While sinking into the soft black leather seats, feeling the cool bursts of air-conditioning and listening to the latest Motown songs on the car radio I had my first glimpse of New York and my memorable journey to Manhattan.

Photographs for *American Vogue* were taken of us that evening as we danced hour after hour under the bright lights at one of Manhattan's new celebrity nightclubs called Arthur. Sybil Burton, ex-wife of actor Richard Burton and founder of the nightclub, had named it Arthur in honour of a George Harrison quip in The Beatles film, *A Hard Day's Night*. When asked the name of his hairstyle he had replied, "Arthur". We danced the night away in our wide satin black and white zigzag print trousers, mini skirts and dresses, everything we wore designed to be youthful and fun, I'm sure we were seen by many people in the audience as outrageous and daring.

Apart from being seen at Arthur's most evenings wearing our trendy clothes and being photographed by the press, there was not quite the same enthusiasm in more conventional places such as the Algonquin Hotel where we were staying. It was my first morning in Manhattan and after my wake-up call from Terry I was told we were to meet downstairs for breakfast, before going off to the Youthquake office on Broadway. I stood with him and Pattie as well as the two sophisticated Mary Quant models while we waited for a table, but as soon as the maître di saw me in my red trouser suit he looked at Terry and then pointed at me.

"She can't come in here wearing trousers," he said. "It's not allowed."

I felt myself go scarlet. I was incensed and horribly embarrassed as Terry tried to sooth my fragile ego in front of the others, telling me to go upstairs and put on a dress. This was 1965 and I was seventeen, but it was indicative of how conservative people still were at that time. The Algonquin was one of the oldest New York City hotels and it had been home to a gathering of literary writers and artists in the 20s known as the Algonquin Round Table. For ten years writers, critics, and actors would meet there for lunch every day, establishing a reputation across America for being very creative and witty. And yet, the very place that housed them was now throwing me out for wearing trousers.

The Youthquake office was right in the heart of the garment industry, 1400 Broadway. One by one, we met Paul Young and his partners in their office. It was still very much a man's world in the fashion business, and I had been used to working mostly for women since leaving school. I stood in front of these three, large, middle-aged men, as they sat behind a desk talking and laughing amongst themselves while every so often glancing my way and looking me up and down. I felt uneasy. It disturbed me to see them acting as if they were a bunch of overgrown kids in starched white shirts and ties, playing at being businessmen. I suddenly felt trivialized by them, made to look small and insignificant, and I could feel myself getting tearful as I closed their door after the meeting, a mixture of disgust and exhaustion. "Don't take it to heart," Pattie told me later. "Treat it as a game."

Pattie and I had photographs taken for *Seventeen Magazine*, both in our Foale and Tuffin clothes and long, blond hair. Each day of the first week was filled with either modeling or going back for yet more fittings at 1400 Broadway, a place that became increasingly chaotic and disorganized as the days went by.

We were under the spotlight from early in the morning until late at night; either being photographed for magazines and newspapers, dancing at Arthur's, or showing up for dinners and receptions. Throughout our stay in New York City, we represented the British Invasion, the new era of fashion. We were the messengers of what was to come.

Vidal Sassoon also played a large part in representing the British Invasion and was there at the same time as us. We were all invited to his opening party to celebrate his first salon in New York, which was an historic moment. He had changed the world of hair and become one of the major players in fashion at that time, creating a style that complimented the new designs and epitomized what became known as the 'Swinging Sixties'.

After an intense few days, Pattie and I were invited to spend the weekend at a house in the Hamptons where Paul Young had friends who were curious to meet us. Cocktails were served throughout the day as more and more guests arrived, obviously summoned to look at and talk to the young English dollybirds. By the end of our stay I felt as if we'd arrived from another planet. They did everything except poke us to see if we were real.

Finally, after our week of publicity and fittings, Sally and Marion arrived for the big day. It was to be their first fashion show to this large an audience and in America. As I walked along the four-foot-high platform in front of a hall full of people, including the press, fashion editors, and merchandisers I realized that a layer of shimmering, white, silk cloth had been draped over the catwalk since our rehearsal. Keeping my balance in heels was a feat in itself, let alone without my glasses. I couldn't make out where the platform ended and where the drop to the white carpet began. Even so, with the help of the loud thumping music I pulled it off but vowed never again to do a traditional catwalk.

I was in the company of models who had completed numerous catwalks and knew exactly how to do the exaggerated walk; twisting and gliding along the platform, feet moving on an invisible straight line, hands on hips, and all the time smiling confidently. But for someone who was inherently shy, walking along a slippery platform with the disadvantage of being near-sighted, in front of hundreds of people was a nerve-wracking experience. I was younger, inexperienced, and had jumped in at the deep end. It was my baptism of fire.

From then on, whenever I went to catwalk auditions, much to the annoyance of other models who had spent a small fortune on training to walk professionally, I just danced. I would get the job. This became my identity. I couldn't be compared to Pattie or my brother-in-law. I had found my passion, my own self-expression.

When I left New York carrying a blonde-haired doll I'd been given at one of the press interviews and wearing a pair of white Courreges-style calf-length boots, I felt that getting through the challenges of this trip had given me more self-confidence. So much so that when I arrived back in England and saw Roger, I knew instantly the relationship had changed, he had lost his hold on me.

A short time later, as I sat in the new Foale and Tuffin shop, putting records on the turntable and serving customers, I looked out of the window and to my surprise, there was Mick standing on the pavement, looking up at the Foale and Tuffin sign above the shop. His hair had been cut in the same Vidal Sassoon shape that was so fashionable and for the first time I could see his face. He stood with a couple of friends, looking very stylish in a long white cardigan and black flares. I walked outside and was introduced to members of the new group he'd recently joined, The Bo Street Runners. As the others waved goodbye and drifted off, Mick followed me into the shop.

We hadn't seen each other for a few months, and by this time, he and Roger had moved into separate flats. I felt very happy to see him. His gentle ways were like cool running water compared to the dark brooding quality of Roger.

He stayed with me for the rest of the afternoon while I served customers. Little did I know then how pivotal this reconnection was to be; it was the beginning of a long and at times painful journey we were destined to embark on together. Ever since I met Mick, I'd always had a sense of something familiar about him, either we recognized parts of ourselves within each other or it was because we'd come from similar backgrounds and had similar temperaments. He had, like me, been brought up in other parts of the world and his father, a Wing Commander, had also flown planes, just as my father had. We were both also cripplingly shy with each other. No matter how strong and innocent our love was, we never knew how to voice it when the going got tough.

Now, though we had my New York trip to talk about, a lot of the time we sat in silence. I didn't mind, I liked him being close by and breathed in the coolness of his presence. I stood up periodically as people came into the shop but after a while Mick stood up. "I have to meet the others," he said, his hands dug deeply into the pockets of his cardigan. "We're playing tonight." And off he went. I didn't know when I'd next see him, but I did know he knew how to find me now. A few days later, unexpectedly, he came in again. This time, he sat in the shop until it was time to close.

Sometimes it is the first kiss one remembers that seals the new relationship, or maybe one doesn't remember what happened when, but for me, what sticks in my memory is the first time Mick held my hand. We were in Notting Hill Gate about to cross the road when he did something that felt perfectly natural, without looking at me he held his hand out behind his back. I remember putting my hand in his for the first time, feeling the gentle contact of our skin together as we crossed the road and on to our destination.

Mick shared a large flat in Finchley with Pete, his friend and keyboard player from The Cheynes who was now playing with Them, a Belfast band led by the dynamic singer, Van Morrison. The flat had one enormous room where everyone congregated, a small bedroom big enough for two single beds at one end and a kitchen and bathroom at the other. There were always people coming and going, smoking dope or going out to score. Music played continuously.

One evening, Mick and I walked into the flat and for the first time we were alone. After putting on some records, he sat on a chair opposite me and began rolling a joint. Bobby Bland's voice came blaring out of the speaker: Further on up the road, he sang, rich and soulful. I remember wishing we could dance around the room together - it would have stopped me feeling so shy, but instead I inhaled deeply on the joint he offered me and sat in silence.

Silence was often the expected response to getting stoned and listening to music, but we were still new to each other as a couple, and I found it agonizing. Finally, Mick broke through our wall.

"I've been asked to go on a three-month tour of Europe," he said, his voice barely audible, his eyes holding mine. "A singer in France, Johnny Hallyday, has asked me to join his band." He took another drag of the joint.

I dug deep inside, looking for my voice, feeling almost paralyzed. Our relationship was so new, so fragile, and anything could happen. He might find someone else.

"Are you going to go?" I whispered.

"I don't know," he said. "I haven't decided."

I Put a Spell on You, Nina Simone began singing; it made me want to cry. I wanted to be held in Mick's arms and plead with him not to go. But I couldn't find the words and felt as though I was stuck to the sofa. The more stoned we became the more deafening the silence between us, even through the music.

Fortunately, at that moment, the front door opened and in walked Peter Bardens with Van Morrison behind him. Van the Man we would call him, because he was The Man. He had a commanding presence and was respected by fellow musicians. His recent hit, Here Comes the Night, showed what a powerful voice and deliverance he had.

Mick sat down beside me and held my hand, giving it a squeeze, while the two men dragged a couple of chairs closer around the coffee table and began rolling a joint. This was the second or third of many evenings I spent with Mick in that flat, with the loud music and people coming and going throughout the night. We would sleep in one of the single beds in the bedroom, either with Peter in the bed next to us, or with Peter and his latest girlfriend. There was no privacy, but somehow, because we were young, it didn't seem to matter.

I would usually arrive at Foale and Tuffin's boutique exhausted, having had very little sleep after spending the night at the flat. No one went to bed before dawn and not long afterwards I would wake up, get dressed, step over sleeping bodies slumped around the big room and make my way off to work.

One afternoon, while I was sitting in the shop, Mick rang. "Listen to this," he said, in a quiet voice. I loved listening to his voice; it was gentle, always softly spoken. What followed was a drum solo that didn't end! I hung on as long as I could so as not to hurt his feelings, put the phone down, served a customer, got back to the phone and he was still playing. He was obviously stoned and had lost himself in his own musical world.

Another phone call I received in the shop, much to my surprise, was from Gary Walker, one of the Walker Brothers. They were three Californian boys who'd become famous over the last year through their hit record, *Make it Easy on Yourself*.

"Is this Jenny?" he asked.

"Yes." I replied.

And then he said, "Because you look so much like Pattie, and I look just like George, would you go out with me?"

I had to resist my impulse to laugh and told him sweetly that I already had a boyfriend.

Pattie and I continued to work together on a few photographic shoots. We'd sit side by side in the dressing room, start putting on our makeup and chatting to each other in front of a large mirror surrounded by naked light bulbs. We liked working together and instinctively knew where the other was about to move, placing our arms, legs or head in whatever direction the photographer asked. One of these shoots was for a spread in *Vogue*, photographed by David Bailey. I had seen him many times before on Saturday mornings in Hennekeys, the very popular pub on Portobello Road, often frequented by models, photographers, and musicians. During this session, Pattie whispered to me that George had asked her to marry him. She had a dreamy expression when the pictures of her as Mrs. Pattie Harrison were published in *Vogue* three months later.

Mick and I went to some of the exclusive clubs in London with Pattie and George, usually The Scotch of St. James or The Ad Lib. They were exciting places to be at that time, filled with pop stars, actors, fashion designers, old aristocracy, models; everyone that was part of this young, hip, Swinging London scene. Now we were all smoking dope, it seemed to create a bond between everyone, a sense of camaraderie and mutual respect and a breaking down of social barriers. How you looked, how you dressed, and the music you liked, spoke volumes.

The music was loud and lights were low, listening to the soulful heart-rendering sound of Otis Redding singing *Dock of the Bay*, or dancing to Stevie Wonder, whatever they played, which was mostly Motown or R&B, was an integral part of the atmosphere created in the clubs. I would grab Mick's hand every time I was moved to dance, lead him onto the dance floor and get lost in the music. Mick was a wonderful dancer and I loved dancing with him. How history repeats itself, it was everything my mother had said about my father; she thought him very handsome, but most of all she loved the way he danced.

The Flamingo was another nightclub which Mick and I would often go to, but this one was situated in Soho: renowned for its many strip joints, sex shops, seedy massage parlors, great music, and clubs. There was a strong smell of disinfectant mingled with wafts of weed as soon as we walked down the stairs into the basement. Groups usually started playing late in the evening and on weekends would continue throughout the night until 6am. Georgie Fame and the Blue Flames was the house band. John Mayall and his Bluesbreakers were regulars (with a young Eric Clapton on guitar) as well as all the up-and-coming groups from the UK and America. A large proportion of the audience was made up of American serviceman from the airbases and west Indians. Musicians were part of the audience as well as fans, gangsters, pimps and prostitutes.

Mick wanted me to come down with him when he played the all-nighters at the Flamingo. This time, his group had Pete Bardens back on keyboards, a base player, and a blues guitarist from the East End, with mutton-chop sideburns and short hair, called Peter Green. A few months later, Rod Stewart and Beryl Marsden joined them as lead vocalists. Beryl was a British R&B and pop singer from Liverpool; she had performed and toured with The Beatles and played at the Star Club in Germany. She was a powerful vocalist and when she sang with Rod, together the energy generated between them was electrifying. They called themselves The Shotgun Express and sang mostly rhythm and blues.

There were about five or six rows of cinema seats in front of the small stage, so most of the space behind was set aside for dancing. As I sat in the audience one night, watching Mick on stage, a young woman came up to me.

"Is your name Jenny Boyd?" she said in between songs, speaking in an American accent.

I nodded.

"I saw your picture in the paper this evening. I thought I recognized you."

She pulled down a seat and sat next to me, leaning closer to my ear once the band started playing.

"It was an article about what you liked to wear. It was cute." She had also seen me in 16 Magazine, an American magazine that ran an article alongside my picture, about me being Pattie Boyd's sister, who was girlfriend of Beatle George Harrison. I knew about this article they had also printed my address for American teenagers to write to me. Because of this, I received a sack full of mail, asking all kinds of questions about George and Pattie. Although it was exciting to see all these letters with their American stamps arriving on the mat, and though many of them were complimentary towards me, I knew their main objective was to make contact with a Beatle.

The band stopped for a break and the lights went on, lighting up the shabby seats and rubbish littered around the black dance floor. Judy carried on talking. She had just arrived in England a few weeks earlier from Sacramento, California. It was her first trip to England, and she had been told about the Flamingo as a good place to listen to blues. I wasn't used to strangers coming up to me and chatting at length so I didn't know what to make of Judy until she told me she had met Pete Bardens at the Flamingo manager's office earlier that week and was now going out with him. We didn't know then, but this chance meeting with Judy was the beginning of a friendship that was to last for fifty years. I saw more of Judy over the next couple of weeks. She suggested one day that we share a flat together and told me she'd seen one in Notting Hill. And so I left home; my first step into the big wide world.

This flat became a place where Mick and members of the band would come over after playing a local gig to smoke pot, listen to music, or have a beer. Rod brought with him a record by Sam Cooke one evening, singing, 'A Change is Gonna Come.' He put it on the record player and while Mick listened to the drums Rod memorized the words.

I was now modeling full time, dragging my heavy portfolio around London filled with photographs to show photographers, going on shoots, or interviews for magazines, catalogues and television commercials. I usually did my own make-up once I got to the studio, black liquid eyeliner and false eyelashes when I remembered to bring them, with mascara. I didn't wear red lipstick as my mother had always worn, it seemed to me to represent her generation, not mine, and so I put pan stick on my lips, a pale matte foundation by Max Factor.

Modeling took me everywhere - I had photographs taken at The Cavern where the Prime Minister, Harold Wilson, had been invited to officially open the club. The walls were painted black, lights beamed on stage while they took the photographs, and people bustled around the hall, getting ready for the opening scheduled for later that evening. I danced in Amsterdam, Brussels, Rome, and different parts of England showing the latest 60s fashion in unusual settings, train platforms and streets, all to live music or records blasting out of speakers. In these moments I felt carefree, like a child, feeling part of the vibrancy, excitement, and aliveness of what it felt like to be in my generation. It was a time of wonder, innocence and creativity.

I felt very comfortable when I was asked to be part of any film that encompassed this same youthful spirit. It started with our visit to New York for Youthquake which was followed up by a promotional film a couple of months later. Mick and his friend, John Dominic, the lead singer from the Bo Street Runners, appeared in the film with us. Three other models and I were dressed in Foale and Tuffin, and Mary Quant clothes, and together, along with the boys, we ran around London in front of trendy shops, jumping in and out of red phone booths, driving in a Mini Moke, dancing at The Ad Lib, having our hair brushed by Vidal Sassoon, and doing anything else that represented a 'Young London', interspersed with footage of 'Beatlemania'. I also starred in a short film about the 60s that was shown in Cannes, called, *The Reflections of Love*. It was filmed against a backdrop of Swinging London and was directed by Joe Massot who two years later directed *Wonderwall*, a film featuring a soundtrack by George Harrison. I was asked to appear in one of the *I Love Lucy* television episodes called, *Lucy Goes to London*. We ran around all the 60s London landmarks along with three other models and the 60s group, The Dave Clark Five.

Although I looked confident on the outside, there was still a part of me unsure of how to be in a relationship and would occasionally misread the cues from Mick. One morning, having spent the night together, I got up early to catch a plane to Rome for a one-week modeling job. Mick was very casual, hardly saying goodbye as I walked down the stairs and out into the street. I took this to mean he didn't love me anymore, and because deep down I was emotionally unsure of myself, I easily felt rejected. Consequently, to hide my hurt, I cast him out of my mind. Little did I know his face was at the window, watching me as I made my way towards changing our destiny, knowing I was hurt and wishing he had been more affectionate. It was to be the first of many separations that needn't have happened, that was always just a hairs breadth away from staying together.

I stayed in a beautiful palazzo in Rome that belonged to a wealthy family. The inside of the house was cool, with marble floors and walls and ceilings covered with murals. I danced along a railway platform for the fashion show. I loved Rome. It felt so romantic.

On my return, having been together for a year, I told Mick I'd met someone else and that it was over between us. I had felt rejected by Mick and didn't know at that age how to cope with my feelings. I thought I'd opened the door to independence but really, I was afraid of getting hurt. Even so, I was shocked to see Mick's reaction. Having not been sure of the depth of his feelings left me unaware of how much I'd hurt him and it wasn't until later that he told me he had spent many evenings parked outside the house I now shared with Beryl Marsden, silently watching the upstairs bedroom window, but never letting me know. Mick had always seemed so nonchalant and aloof, a quality that would rear its ugly head continuously throughout our relationship, always fooling me into believing he didn't care when he did, and always the reason why we would separate.

Lots of visitors congregated at our house, either Beryl's musician friends, or my pot-smoking buddies. Friends appeared at our front door at all times of the night. I would think nothing of opening the door to someone at 2am or 3am, sitting up with them in my pajamas and smoking a joint while listening to Bob Dylan's latest record and having far-reaching discussions about life.

It was here that I was first introduced to a young Eric Clapton, a man who would one day become my brother-in-law, and to John McVie who was soon to become the bass player for Fleetwood Mac.

Judy Wong was staying with us before returning to California and was going out with a singer from a band called the Chevelles. On this particular evening we'd arranged that her boyfriend, Mike, would meet Judy at our house after his gig. She and I had gone to The Cromwellian that evening, a nightclub on Cromwell Road in Kensington where we'd often meet friends, and where I had in the past watched Mick playing.

We arrived back at the house just in time to answer the door to Mike. As John Mayall's Bluesbreakers had been the accompanying band on the same bill as the Chevelles, Eric Clapton and John McVie had given Mike a lift to our house. We invited them all in. Beryl arrived at the same time with her friends and a party began. The house was full of people, wandering from room to room, drinking, smoking and listening to music. I went downstairs to the kitchen at one point, and found a drunken Eric and John McVie lying on the floor, arm-wrestling, laughing, sobbing and hugging each other as they lamented Eric's last gig with John Mayall that evening.

Although there were times when the house was filled with people, there were other times when, apart from modeling, I would spend days and evenings there alone. After the break-up with Mick, I could feel a deeper part of myself emerging, questioning my place in the world. I had started to feel disengaged from the life I was leading, a feeling of restlessness and lack of purpose.

I was sitting alone in the house one day, cross-legged on the carpet; leaning against an armchair and wondering what direction my life was going. It was then that something extraordinary happened, a feeling as though I'd suddenly awoken from a long sleep. Everything around me took on a warm fuzzy glow and at the same time my mind snapped to attention. I drew a circle on the carpet with my finger, "Everything's a circle," I mused. It wasn't linear as I'd been bought up to believe, it was cyclical – life, death and re-birth. I sat in this timeless zone for I don't know how long, with one existential ah ha moment after another. When I finally stood up, my life had changed. This awakening was profound and left me feeling inspired and in need of talking to others about my experience. It was the first time I had something that really felt like mine; a depth within me I'd not known before. I felt strong and inspired by my new awareness. It set me on a path that I would stick to throughout my life and although, there were times I wavered dangerously close to the edge, I never abandoned the path.

I began to spend a lot of time in Watkins, a bookshop off the Charing Cross Road selling esoteric and religious books. Old Mr. Watkins stood behind the counter, surveying his shop filled with books on astrology, UFOs, and, to my joy, books on Eastern philosophy that validated what I now believed. I would sit on a chair beside a bookcase for hours, leafing through the different books before choosing one to buy. Although I was on a search, a journey, I was still unsure in which direction it was headed in or what it was I was seeking. I needed to know more and find people who felt the same.

Mick and I saw each other occasionally during this time, but our worlds were now drifting further apart. I was inspired to search for people and books that could enlighten me and nourish my spiritual awakening. I longed to tell Pattie and

George who at that time, the spring of '66, were staying with George's mentor, Indian musician, Ravi Shankar.

When they finally arrived back from India, to my surprise they both spoke of a similar experience. Pattie and I spent a lot of time at their house in the country, with the smell of incense permeating their home and the sound of Indian music, Ravi Shankar or Ali Akbar Khan, drifting out of two large speakers sitting either side of the fireplace. Although comfortable sofas and armchairs were scattered around the room, most of the time we sat cross-legged on the floor discussing feelings and thoughts about our new awareness. She told me stories about India in a way that only Pattie could, her eyes wide open as she brought to life her descriptions of Kashmir and the houseboats where they stayed with Ravi. She captured my imagination and I longed to go to India. I often felt as though I was in an altered state during our conversations, as if we were connecting to something new and exciting; an energy that, although we were not aware of at the time, was being felt by many people of our generation. People who were at the heart of what the 60s represented, those who rode the wave could feel the temperature changing. The zeitgeist was starting to move, and we were transitioning into a different phase. The innocent, light-hearted, and carefree movement was now seeking depth.

As I became more involved in what I saw as my spiritual journey, the modeling took second place. I had worked hard up until this point and had moved to a one-bedroom apartment in Knightsbridge. My room was usually filled with friends who slept on the floor, when they had nowhere to go or were too stoned to move. When Pattie and George came to tea one winter's afternoon, laden with biscuits and cakes, George took me aside, and whispered, "It's not very cool to have all these friends crashing on the floor when you're paying the rent." I knew he was right, but I didn't have the heart to send anyone away.

A friend introduced me to Mark Warman whose house, just off the Kings Road, had become the place where friends congregated to smoke dope and drink endless cups of tea. We sat on the floor around a low circular table and every few minutes a joint would come around, but nobody spoke. Just listening to music and browsing through one of his books was enough to tell me that Mark was also interested in spirituality.

It was while sitting around his table that I picked up a book called *Karma and Rebirth* by Christmas Humphries. I began reading it until I came across a passage that said, "Life goes on within you and without you". I read it again and then again, marveling at the double meaning. It was so clever and so true. My first inclination was to call Pattie and George. George answered the phone. "Listen to this," I said, and then repeated the sentence. It inspired him to write *Within You Without You*, which he later recorded for the Beatles album *Sgt Pepper's Lonely Hearts Club Band*.

One day, as I was about to leave, Mark told me he was taking some acid the following day with a friend. His eyes stared at me, bright and piercing.

"Would you like to join us?" he asked.

I felt scared, realizing that even though I'd spent almost every day for the last few weeks with Mark, I didn't really know him that well. No more than a nod or a smile had ever passed between us. I hesitated.

"It will be very Zen-like," he said. "You've nothing to fear."

The round table had disappeared when I walked into his sitting room the following day. Against the left-hand wall sat Mark's American friend, looking like a Buddha. I was handed a little tab of LSD and sat on the floor next to Mark, leaning against the wall, and opposite his friend while I waited for something to happen.

As soon as the air began to swirl, I felt scared, dreading what would come next on this roller coaster with no way off for the next nine hours. The Buddha look-alike melted into the wall. I was desperate for contact, to get out of the frightening world that I could feel myself slipping into.

"Let's talk," I said as I reached out my hand to touch Mark's arm. He smiled, looking like a Cheshire cat, nodding, but saying nothing.

I got up, found my way to the bathroom and threw up; then, looking into the mirror, I saw hundreds of faces merging with my own, faces I knew but had forgotten. "Where am I?" I whispered. "Who am I?" I looked down at my hands, suddenly old and wrinkled, just like my grandmother's.

After what seemed like an age, I was brought back to consciousness by the sound of a doorbell. A man walked up to the wall that I was leaning against and handed me a pipe. I inhaled automatically and then on looking around saw a swirl of vibrant, rainbow colored smoke wafting out of the speakers, weaving its way towards me in time to the music. Gradually, the acid wore off and the sun came up. It was a new day and I felt relieved to feel normal again.

Although I had a group of friends who were on a spiritual path, I felt it was time to move on. I had enough money for either three months' rent on my apartment, or a one-way ticket to visit Judy Wong, who was now living in San Francisco. She was about to open her own boutique and asked me to stay with her for the price of working in her store. I told everyone it was time to leave. I needed to strike out on my own.

That night, sitting alone in my flat, my mind drifted back to myself as a small child walking through all the changes, disruptions and uncertainties and how that may have affected my life, giving me an inner strength and resilience to keep walking into the unknown.

EARLY DAYS

His friends knew him as 'Wild Jock Boyd', a fearless pilot who loved to drink, to dance, to ride, but above all, my father loved to fly. My mother thought him very handsome with his blond hair and piercing blue eyes. He was six years older than her and preparing to leave for war.

My mother was born in India and came from a family that was part of the British Raj. Her parents and grandparents had lived in India. She and her brother, John, were sent to boarding school in England starting at age seven and during the holidays they were looked after by two aged aunts in Somerset. Their mother would visit them every couple of years taking the long journey to England by boat, but she remained a distant figure watching the children from the upstairs bedroom window as they played in the garden. Rural English life was tedious to her compared with the social whirl of India and its bubble of lavish dinners and cocktail parties. But in 1940, following the outbreak of the Second World War she came back to England for good.

Once settled in England, my grandmother focused her attention and social ambition on her daughter, my mother Diana, now a beautiful, extremely eligible young woman of sixteen who was showered with expensive jewels and clothes and sent to a finishing school in Lyme Regis. She was inundated with social events during the holidays, a program devised by my grandmother in order to get her daughter married and off her hands as quickly as possible. It was at one of these dances she met my father who was preparing to leave for war and had just been seconded into the air force as a bomber pilot.

Diana and Jock had seen each other only a few times before he was stationed in Tel Aviv for the bombing of Benghazi. Letters were exchanged and in due course he sent a proposal of marriage, which, with the encouragement of her mother, she accepted. The wait for him was not as long as expected, nor the reunion as happy.

In March 1942, while taking off from Malta in his Wellington Bomber fully loaded with bombs, her husband-to-be was in a head-on collision with another plane. He and the other pilot involved had been given the green light simultaneously at opposite ends of the same runway, a horrendous accident in which several men died. Jock was lucky to escape, but it left him with severe burns on his face and body. In time, his burns healed; but no one foresaw the damage to his psyche.

Gone was the gaiety they had shared, gone the romantic dream. Nothing prepared my mother for the first sight of the man she was about to marry: his head wrapped in bandages as he lay on his hospital bed, a silent creature with only his eyes visible, staring at her. She was pledged to marry him and believed she had no option, his mother having made clear her view that only his love for Diana was keeping Jock alive, and that if she backed out of the wedding, he would die. Long silences now filled the air as my mother sat in the corner of his hospital room, a girl of just seventeen.

By September 1942, following plastic surgery, Jock was physically strong enough for their wedding to take place in a little church in Somerset. Before their marriage my mother had only known him superficially; a dashing young man, handsome in his RAF uniform, who had taken her in his arms and whirled her around the dance floor. Her romantic dreams of being whisked away by the man she'd fallen in love with were now replaced by a disfigured and traumatized husband in need of a much more mature woman to look after him. Diana told me many years later, (once she'd allowed herself to talk about our father), that she knew as she was getting married that it was a mistake.

The couple continued to spend most of their time apart once they were married. Diana served in the women's army, the ATS, as Jock went in and out of Victoria hospital in East Grinstead for more plastic surgery. The tendons in his right hand had been burnt through and his fourth and fifth fingers were crooked and immovable so on this hand he wore a sinister-looking black glove. Eventually he was sent up to do desk work in the Nottingham war office, while my mother, now pregnant with her first born, left the ATS and joined her mother at their family home in Somerset. Her father, having only seen his own children a couple of times on his occasional visits to England, had just returned from his many years in India, but was there in time for the birth of his first granddaughter, my sister Pattie.

Jock, the reluctant young father, could rarely bring himself to visit his wife and daughter, just the occasional weekend every now and then. Day-to-day support came from my mother's own parents who, when the war ended a year later, moved north to West Lothian in Scotland. Once she realized Jock was showing barely any interest in seeing her or securing a home for their family, a problem made more urgent by the discovery that she was pregnant again, she went up to join her parents in Scotland. She saw little of my father during the pregnancy, but finally my brother Colin was born in the spring of 1946.

Fortunately, Jock was persuaded to leave Nottingham when the war office offered him a job in London. He rented a small cottage in Surrey, from which he was able to commute. At last my mother had a home for her little family, something she had always wanted, but she was unhappy. The dream had turned very sour. Not only was the Boyd family money non-existent - its promise a complete fabrication - but Jock had become a terrible shadow of his former self, locked inside his own world. When at home he spent his days sitting in silence staring at the wall. Even so, my mother fell pregnant again, and nine months later she and I both survived the hemorrhage caused by my birth on November 1st, 1947.

When I was nine months old my Mother and Father decided to move to East Africa. Not only did this mean my father could take advantage of the British government grants to build homesteads and to farm the land in Kenya, but more importantly to him was the thought of playing polo, a sport too expensive for his pocketbook in England. My mother, too, was in favor of the change, hoping it would inject new life into their marriage, but she also wanted to see her parents who had retired to Kenya the previous year on finding the climate in Scotland too cold after their many years in India.

We left for Kenya in August 1948, my mother, father, Pattie (aged four) Colin (aged two) and me. We went straight to my grandparent's house in Langarta, near Nairobi. Before leaving England my father had prepared himself by taking a short course in chicken farming, but he had a setback almost immediately on arrival with the discovery that in Kenya, of all the domesticated animals, chickens were the most susceptible to disease and the venture failed dismally. After some time, it became clear to my grandmother that her son-in-law was doing nothing to get a job for himself or a home for his family. Fiercely protective of her daughter's welfare, she told my father to leave, insisting that he and my mother have an official six-month separation. It was not what Diana wanted but she had the three children now and was still very influenced by her mother. By the time we finally joined him, at the end of their separation, their already fraught relationship had become even more strained. It turned out that the new place Jock had found for us was an empty building near Nairobi that had previously been used as an arms dump for old rifles. Jock had managed to get a bathroom put in, but there was no furniture apart from some pieces he had scrounged and a few bits he'd made.

The family spent a short time in these sparse surroundings before my father found himself a job as secretary of the nearby Nakuru Racecourse and we moved to a house close to Nakuru Lake where pink flamingos covered most of the lake, and hippos often made their way into our garden at night. The house itself consisted of five circular thatched huts linked together by doorways joining one curved room to another. The floors were made of compacted mud covered by rugs and the rooms were sparse with very little furniture and exposed mud brick walls.

Not long after we moved in there was a fire that ravaged most of our house. It started in the outside kitchen, which was linked to the house by a long narrow walkway covered by a thin strip of thatched roof that helped to spread the fire. I remember being woken up and carried outside where I saw people huddled together, shadows flickering across their faces. The night was black, and the fire made a huge orange glow ballooning up into the sky. As the fire roared and sparks flew people ran around shouting words I didn't understand, carting endless buckets of water. I watched all this from the safety of warm arms, high above the ground. I like to think it was my father's arms that held me that night.

The wilderness was never far away in Kenya. Moments, flashes or memories of this wild, beautiful natural world have stayed with me, and have kindled a life-long love of wide, open countryside. By day the skies were vast and blue, with horizons that seemed to go on forever. And at night, to the sound of crickets chirping, I would look through my bedroom window in awe at the millions of silver stars twinkling in the blackened sky.

Occasionally while having a bath, the face of a hyena would suddenly appear pressed up against the windowpane, its eyes glistening and its mouth open. I would scream and jump out of the bath as it disappeared into the night. One night, so I was told, a lion sloped up onto the veranda of our grandparent's house in Langata, and in through the open door to their bedroom. Their trusty Alsatian, Lobo, woke up and attacked the lion, giving my grandfather enough time to reach under his pillow and grab his revolver, saving everyone from a dreadful end.

Our younger sister, Paula, was born almost three years after our arrival in Kenya and so our grandmother employed a nanny called Salome to look after us older children. She lived in one of the outbuildings adjacent to the main house, next door to the cook and houseboy. I don't remember much about my mother during our time in Africa, but I do remember Salome. Every day she lit a small fire outside the house and squatted on her haunches to prepare our food. Chapatti and burnt mealies (corn on the cob) are my mealtime memories - warm earth beneath me, and Jacaranda trees above.

Although Salome is a distant memory, there is one particular day I will never forget. After cooking our chapattis on an open fire Salome told us of vivid stories about her people, and about the Kikuyu and Mau Mau tribes. Stories that kept us spellbound with horror and fascination. I listened, tucked up in the safety of her warm enveloping arms, smelling the wood smoke while she whispered to her little audience in front of her. Even so, that was the day I lost the trust and feeling of safety I'd invested in our new nanny.

But on that particular day, I could feel the sun resting gently on my body as Salome, sitting on her stone, rocked me back and forth while talking and laughing. It was hard to believe she came from one of these tribes herself; she seemed so much to belong to us.

Although I loved Salome and she looked after us well, I knew, even as a small child, that there was a part of her that didn't belong to me. This was proved later that day when she took Pattie, Colin and me on one of her walks through the fields of corn and long grass. Once the sun went down, I was told it was time to start our journey home and I remember shaking my head defiantly; I didn't want to go home.

"I'll call the Mau Mau to come and take you away tonight," she threatened. I laughed at her; and then watched as she clasped her hands together and with her mouth pressed against her thumbs emitted a low sinister wail that travelled across the open fields. Seconds later the identical sound echoed from far away. "Do you hear that?" she said. "They will come and take you away tonight." I laughed again but allowed her to take my hand for home.

I thought no more about the incident until later that evening when Salome was saying her usual goodnight and settling me into bed. We both heard the knock. I watched her as she jerked her head up and looked through my window at the row of small houses where she lived. There were two men standing outside her door.

"The Mau Mau have come to take you away," she said in a scary, singsong voice. I went cold.

"No, they haven't," I insisted, trying hard to hold on to my flimsy bravado. She pointed to the two men and I panicked. Wailing and clinging to Salome, I begged her not to let them take me away. I promised to be good forever. She hugged me, tight and soothing; but from that evening on I never saw her through the same eyes and my attachment to Pattie and Colin deepened.

I learned many years later that my father had begun spending more and more time on his early morning rides, and evidence of his philandering behavior was becoming all too visible to my mother on the occasions his woman friend joined us for breakfast. Finally, my mother could stand it no longer, and the relative stability of our lives broke apart. She came into our bedroom one night, a year after Paula's birth, bundled us into my father's car and drove through the night back to her parent's house. With this dramatically assertive act, she effectively put an end to the marriage.

Further disruptions were to follow as a consequence. The most significant for me was the removal not long after of Pattie, one of the two main supports on whom I most depended. This happened when my mother took a job as a receptionist in Nairobi. As a single mother she was no longer able to look after us all. My sister was sent to boarding school, Colin and I to a children's home, and Paula she kept with her.

I must have been about four years old at this time, but I remember the journey Colin and I took to the children's home. I was huddled up in the back of the van, my arms wrapped around a box of Colin's Dinky cars and staring out of the back window at the dust swirling around in our wake. I remember feeling a sense of urgency from my mother as she deposited us at the home. Our banishment was brief, so when sometime later a house was offered to my mother with her new job, she brought me and Colin back, while Pattie continued at her boarding school, coming home for holidays. Life must have been difficult for my mother at that time - a single woman with little money and four young children.

Soon after her divorce in December 1952, my mother met a new man at one of the countless rounds of ex-pat Christmas parties. It was attraction at first sight for both of them. Bobby was twenty-seven and worked as a chief representative for a rubber company. He lived in Dar es Salaam but travelled throughout East Africa and had a chauffeur-driven car at his disposal. Bobby was in complete contrast to Jock: charming, outgoing and generous. To our astonishment and delight he showered presents on us all, something we had not known of previously, not having celebrated birthdays or Christmas with gifts. They married the following Spring and we children, apart from Pattie, went to their wedding under the care of a new nanny my grandmother had employed, one of the consequences of the marriage, ironically, was that we were sent back to live with Jock at his house in Molo, near Nairobi, while my mother and Bobby settled into their new life together.

All I remember of the wedding, as a little girl of five, was being plied with endless glasses of champagne at the reception. I stood at the back of the hall, surrounded by strangers, with the occasional glimpse of my mother and her new husband far across the room, never looking my way. Two of the drunken guests thought it funny to watch as I became quietly inebriated, doubling over with laughter with every sip they gave me. I was very ill that night, the new nanny and I getting acquainted on many trips to the bathroom.

Not long after their wedding Bobby and my mother left for England on board the SS Kenya, taking two-year-old Paula with them. It was arranged that we older children would join them one by one later that year. We never questioned the reason for this, but now as an adult, I presume it would have been too disruptive to the new marriage to include four children. By this time Pattie felt almost like a mother to me although she was only nine years old. She and my brother were sent to boarding school in Nakuru while I went to kindergarten, suddenly an only child, looked after by my nanny and occasionally getting a glimpse of my father.

Of the six months I lived with my father, I have absolutely no memory of him. He was either at the jockey club, out riding with his girlfriend or, as I've always imagined, sitting in a darkened room staring at the wall. But I do believe it was during this time that I, a sensitive child, felt his pain and my heart went out to him. It created a connection that has stayed with me always.

When the time came for me to leave my father, and Kenya, I didn't realize it would be the last time I'd see him for almost forty years. What I did know was that at this tender age there was no way I was going to get on a boat, as my mother had, to go to England. My fear of drowning gave me the courage to stand up to the nanny who, for some reason, insisted I should go by sea. Her words have stayed with me throughout my life.

"Do you want to go by ship or airplane?" she asked.

"Airplane," I answered without a second's hesitation. I had been terrified of the sea ever since my mother took Pattie, Colin and me to the beautiful Mombasa beach where I would sit on the white sand as far away from the water as possible while my brother and sister, looking like dots on the horizon, played in the waves.

"It'll crash and you'll die," the nanny said.

I didn't care. Somehow at that young age I found the ability to stand up for myself.

I flew to England and was greeted by a ready-made family; my pregnant mother, a new father and two-year-old Paula, all nestled together in a little flat in East Putney. It felt strange having not seen my mother or sister for months. My longing for Pattie and Colin deepened; they were still in Kenya at their boarding school and I longed for them to be by my side. I felt estranged from my mother. My last memory of her in Africa had left me clinging to my sister for comfort, frightened by her behavior.

It happened like this: Pattie, Colin and I had been sitting in an old tin bath one evening, in the care of our new nanny, while, as we understood it, our mother and Bobby were on their honeymoon. Happily swishing the water with my hands, all of us in our own little worlds, I looked up at one point and there in the corner of this cold empty room, dimly lit by a naked light bulb, stood my mother. I was shocked and bewildered at the sight of her, having settled down to a routine with a nanny in her absence. As she walked towards us, the nanny barred her way.

The atmosphere in the room changed. I felt confused, my stomach in a knot as the two women began shouting at each other, fierce, furious words echoing around the desolate room. My mother wanted to bathe her children, but the nanny refused to relinquish the authority bestowed upon her by my grandmother. She'd been told to look after we three older children, especially as my mother was soon to be leaving for England. And then to my horror a fight broke out as each one tried to push the other towards the door. I held onto Pattie and we both began to cry.

After my mother proved to be the stronger of the two, she bathed us and put us to bed. The next day we woke to find her gone, as mysteriously as she'd arrived. Now we had to face the retributions of the woman we henceforth named 'the wicked nanny' as she forced the three of us to write to our grandmother, apologizing for our mother's behavior. I invested my letter with all the gravity of the situation by drawing line after line of loops, having not yet learned to write.

By the time Pattie and Colin did arrive back in England we'd moved to a large house in Wimbledon. Bobby, our new stepfather, tall, dark and handsome was beginning to show less attractive sides of his personality. The generous, gregarious benefactor was turning into a loud, booming man who bellowed out orders, deaf in one ear and blind in his self-righteousness. He always kept us on our toes.

Instinctively I turned towards Pattie for a feeling of security, but my brother, a much more vulnerable child, was often bullied by Bobby. I would flinch whenever I heard him shouting at Colin or even kicking him if he was caught chatting to Paula and me in our bedroom.

Colin was the sibling I played with the most. I became a tomboy and loved running in the garden, playing cricket and in the winter making sledges, taking it in turns to pull each other through the snow. While riding our bikes and exploring the neighborhood, we once found a bomb crater in a wood, a hole in the ground full of water and tadpoles. We stayed there for hours, making a fishing rod and collecting bits of what must have been shrapnel. I loved the sense of freedom as we roamed around throughout the day, only going home when hungry. Very little was imposed in the way of restrictions on time keeping, and no one asked us where we were going or where we'd been. Our mother was completely preoccupied by our one-year-old half-brother, David, and another baby on the way.

My bond with Pattie and Colin was strong; we were there for each other within this uncertain world we inhabited, and I trusted them implicitly. Colin didn't need to say a word: often just a look in my direction would send me into helpless fits of giggles. Pattie was very different. She always seemed so grown up, and was a wonderful storyteller, captivating me with vivid descriptions of her life at school. Her hypnotic blue eyes sparkled and held me in rapt attention until the story ended, and then I would plead with her to tell me again. I missed them both when they were once again sent to boarding school.

Pattie shocked me with her rebellious spirit. She would quite happily cut up a skirt if it didn't look the way she wanted, but this always delighted me and filled me with awe. Pattie never asked permission, she believed in her right to do as she pleased. I loved and admired her for this strength and freedom and looked to her for my own direction, so that increasingly both parents remarked on how I was influenced by her. She was the first person I gave my trust to. If I'd had a pot of glue I would happily have stuck us together. Even so, I took these remarks to mean that my mother and stepfather couldn't see the real me, seeing me only as a pale impersonation of Pattie. I was quite happy to be standing in her shadow and content not to be seen. It was a safer place to be when I'd hear Bobby shouting, "Who shall I beat today?"

Although this deep need to merge and be content to stand under another's shadow suited me well as a child, partly to do with survival, as I got older it became my life's journey to emerge from under someone else's shadow and to stand up tall in my own light.

It didn't take long once we'd all settled in for the pattern of our family relationships to establish itself. Pattie was ten and old enough to be a threat to Bobby, the thorn in his side, someone who was not going to accept him as easily as we younger ones. By contrast, in his and my mother's eyes I was a good girl. Even so I remember inadvertently slipping up on a couple of occasions and paying the price, as he demanded I bend over and take my punishment. Otherwise, I normally did everything I was told and worked hard at school. One evening he summoned me to his study where he sat with my mother as we watched the ballet on television, and again, before telling me to go to bed, said I was a good girl but that Pattie was naughty. He warned me not to take any notice of her and to stay away from her as much as possible.

Little did Bobby suspect what a fierce loyalty to Pattie his words would ignite in me. When I told her what he'd said, she astounded me by sharing all her hostile feelings towards Bobby, how cruel he was, so loud and such a bully. We talked about our mother, feelings I'd hardly dared to admit to myself, but hearing Pattie voicing them comforted me and I no longer felt alone with these thoughts. We had formed an enduring allegiance.

My mother represented an unknown quantity to me as a child. I felt shy and uncertain in her presence, and a little frightened. I couldn't tell what her response would be to any given situation, which was often not helped by the tense atmosphere created by Bobby. I thought my mother was beautiful, elegant and composed, but I often sensed an undercurrent of silent fury bubbling just under the surface, which would lash out unexpectedly through a flash of her eyes. Her eyes were her way of communicating, her weapon that could stop you dead mid-sentence. Things weren't said, but they were felt. I became adept at tuning in to atmospheres and learned in turn to keep my own voice hidden, never speaking up for myself, expecting people to read my mind. I longed to have ballet lessons and would stand in what I imagined was balletic position with both feet on the floor and my toes turned out, hoping someone would notice.

But at other times, and especially at night, when she wasn't either fuming or distracted, she would speak with an intimacy that I treasured. She would tuck me into bed so tightly that both sides of the mattress almost met. As I lay in this nest, safe and warm, she would sing the most beautiful lullabies in a voice that seemed to belong to another world. I loved these moments, though they were sporadic and inconsistent with how she was by day. As the months passed and she gave birth to another child, her nerves were ever more on edge and her temper unsettlingly short.

The house reeked of tension when Bobby was around, especially on the few occasions we all sat together at meal times. There was always an underlying threat of being punished, usually with a stick or a cuff on the head for some minor misdemeanor. He seemed to delight in doling out punishments. Often, I would feel his dark hooded eyes boring a hole into my very being, willing me to slip up in some way; anything, no matter how small, that would give him an excuse to assert his authority and use his cane.

While sitting in the drawing room one afternoon what had, until then, been a peaceful setting suddenly exploded. The quiet of Bobby, Pattie and Colin reading - me sprawled on the carpet doing a jigsaw – was violently interrupted.

"Jenny," Bobby said sharply, "did you hear what I said?"

I looked up to see him staring at me. I turned to where Pattie was sitting, trying to find a clue in her expression. She smiled at me.

"Jenny!" He shouted. I turned back to face him. "I'm going to ask you again."

He mumbled something. I smiled at him, thinking that maybe this was some kind of joke. He pulled his newspaper down towards his stomach, his red, angry face, and dark eyes glaring at me. He turned to Pattie,

"Did you hear what I said?"

"Yes," she replied.

He asked Colin the same question. Colin nodded. Now his attention was back on me.

"I'm going to ask you one more time," he said slowly and deliberately, "and if you don't do what I say, I am going to beat you. Go ... and ..."

I stared at him blankly, not realizing at the time that I was deaf. My mother had plugged my ears with cotton wool a few weeks previously, ready for the night in Bobby's army tent in the garden but had forgotten to take it out. I hadn't heard what he'd told me to do; but I heard what came next, shouted in absolute fury as he threw his paper down and marched out of the room.

"Right! Go and get a cane from the shed and meet me in my study. I'm going to beat you."

Afterwards, while still sobbing from the pain and humiliation, Pattie and Colin followed me upstairs, impressed with my daring to challenge the all-powerful Bobby.

"So, what did he say?" I whispered, once we got upstairs.

Pattie looked at Colin and then at me, smiled and replied, "He said shut the door!"

"Is that all?" I said as the three of us began giggling uncontrollably.

Each day continued with us never knowing when and where the next eruption would come from. My mother never intervened. I think she was fearful of antagonizing her husband, and was desperate to keep the family together, even if it meant turning a blind eye to whatever was going on.

There was one adult in our lives of whom I was neither wary nor scared. She had come to live with us after working for Bobby's aged parents. Lily was a cook and house cleaner, but to me she was a special grown-up, always ready to hear my thoughts. I loved Lily dearly. She was always in the kitchen baking something or sitting at the table, telling me stories of her life in service or of how she'd had half her stomach removed by this 'wonderful surgeon'. Thin and frail, clothed in either a pale yellow or blue nylon housecoat with a clean crisp apron over the top, she took her office seriously and with great pride. I used to sit with her for hours in the kitchen, helping to stir a bowl or clean the silver.

Lily had seen me listening and dancing to rock and roll music with Pattie, and one day surprised me by handing me an acoustic guitar. I was thrilled. It was everything I had dreamed of, the shape, the smell and the strings that tied so neatly around little wooden pegs. I felt very special – a feeling that attracted swift retribution from my older brother and sister. As we were washing our hands in the basin together that day, before having lunch, they stared at me.

"Why did she give it to you?" they asked. "Why you?"

Despite our closeness it was obvious they were very upset by my being singled out and I immediately downplayed any sense of favoritism. I would love to have had lessons, but that was now unthinkable.

Paula, even when still very young, seemed to be quite different from the three of us; much more out-going. We were thin, shy and introverted, whereas Paula was quite the opposite. Where we stifled our emotions and held ourselves close, she was gregarious, chubby and made friends easily, the apple of our mother's eye.

The only time I was sure to be seen and acknowledged by my mother was when I brought home a gold star from school. I remember vividly how the gold star shone out on the brilliant white slip of paper, with the headmaster's signature written in black ink at the bottom. I had to wait for the ink to dry before I was handed this award, given with all the seriousness it deserved. I could tell, the instant I gave it to my mother that she felt proud of me. I became a clever girl in her eyes, and it made me want to get more.

But when I tried to express myself by doing something creative, I didn't get the same reaction. I became aware of this after I'd drawn and colored in a picture of which I felt particularly proud. I took it into the kitchen to show my mother but on seeing our neighbor standing by the door, I showed it to her. The neighbor was delighted, affirming my joy and pride in my achievement, but that was quickly and silently squashed by one glance from my mother, and I was later told not to blow my own trumpet.

This next-door neighbor was a very smart and glamorous woman, with well-groomed and perfect children. My mother probably felt quite inadequate in comparison, as she struggled to bring up six children, with little or no time to see if we brushed our hair or what we wore, even at one point all sharing the same toothbrush. Unfortunately for our mother, even we older children could see the flirtatious behavior between this near perfect neighbor and our stepfather.

Not long after this, the whole family, including Lily, moved to a large house in Hertfordshire at my mother's insistence, she was feeling the pressure of looking after six children as well as a husband who was rapidly falling in love with the neighbour. It was also at this time that an attempt was made to send Pattie, Colin and me back to Kenya to live with our father. Our hair was washed and combed, photographs taken, but because he had re-married and was in the middle of starting another family, he refused. In my mind I no longer had a father, the only contact I'd had was a card one Christmas with 'Love Daddy' scrawled at the bottom.

No one mentioned Jock once we'd moved to England. It was as if he'd never existed. The only time I remember my mother uttering his name was when I was about ten years old. Pattie, Colin and I were lolling around, standing at the bottom of the stairs arguing about something when she suddenly appeared from nowhere, her eyes flashing as she shouted,

"You are so B...O...Y...D!"

She spelled out the unspoken word in her fury, glaring at my brother, sister and me, not daring to say the name. I believed that to be the worst swear word she could ever have uttered.

While we lived in Hertfordshire, Pattie and I went to the all-girls convent. It was a large converted house with beautiful grounds and inspirational teachers, most of them nuns. Every day at break or after lunch I would run down to the gym, where one of the fourth-year girls played her guitar and sang Buddy Holly songs. I was enraptured by her voice, and the words of the songs made my twelve-year-old heart ache.

But we only lived here for a couple of years before my family moved back to London. Bobby had decided that the upkeep of this large house was too expensive, which meant Pattie and I became boarders at the convent. I liked being a boarder, away from the turbulent atmosphere of home life. Even though we were not Roman Catholic, as boarders we were required to go to chapel for mass and benediction where I found the singing of benediction combined with the smell of incense stirring and otherworldly, even though at times it felt overpowering. On one occasion, after dipping my finger in the wet sponge, and kneeling at the pew, I felt strangely giddy. As more and more clouds of smoke filled the room and pungent smells of incense took over, my head began to spin. My body tingled as if a hundred pins were piercing my skin and I could feel myself slipping away. The girl next to me grabbed my arm as I fell towards her, then a firm grip held onto my other arm and I was marched out of chapel, made to sit in the hall with my head between my legs, and told never to come to mass again.

Pattie left school after the first term while I continued on until the end of that school year. I didn't hear anything from my mother, and it was only when I came home for the holidays that I noticed Bobby was not around. To this day I don't know the actual date he left home because his departure was never mentioned. It was as if he'd miraculously disappeared without trace. The only hint of what my mother must have been feeling was when she came back one evening after going out to dinner, the smell of gin was overpowering as she wrapped her arms around my neck, giggling uncontrollably as her knees began to give way. It was the only time I'd ever seen her drunk and the smell of gin even to this day conjures up that night and the depth of her sadness.

I joined Colin at Holland Park School, one of London's first comprehensive schools that became a showpiece of progressive post war education. At age fourteen I became one of a mass of 2,000 children of all ages in this huge modern school in Notting Hill Gate. To begin with I was continually getting lost; walking up and down the seemingly endless corridors looking for whatever class I was meant to attend. My interest in learning lessened as I witnessed teachers struggling to keep control of the class.

Because I found it difficult making new friends at my school, I was encouraged by my mother one evening to go to the Valentine's Day school dance. The thought of dancing and listening to music gave me the courage I needed to walk in alone. I wore a straight shift dress, a pair of cream Louis-heeled shoes and a suspender belt to hold up my stockings. I felt very self-conscious before I even arrived, a trussed-up chicken, the elastic of my suspender belt stretching with every step.

I don't remember whether I danced that night, but I do recall being horribly embarrassed when, towards the end of the evening, all the girls were invited to go on stage and stand in a line to be judged. A panel of school prefects and teachers sat in the wings with note pads on their laps, jotting down information. As girl after girl was asked to step down from the stage, I was left standing, with two others, looking down on a blurred sea of faces, feeling very exposed and wondering how an innocent idea of going to the school dance had lead to this. Suddenly my name was called out and I cringed. People clapped and a teacher walked up the steps to my left, with a bright blue sash in his hands. He put the sash over my head and across my skinny body, as I stood feeling silly and uncomfortable. I saw the words 'Miss Valentine' embroidered down the side of the blue sash in silver lettering. I didn't know how I was ever going to live this down. I didn't like being singled out and I knew it would have repercussions.

The following Monday I paid the price while walking past a group of girls on my way to a class. They were huddled in the school corridor with their short haircuts, twin sets and black leather coats. Their white faces looked distorted, chewing gum as they spat out their cruel words.

"How did they choose her of all people?" I ignored them and kept on walking. "God, here she comes, Miss Valentine herself!"

While I was licking my 'Valentine' wounds, my mother was licking her own wounds. She had been given a small, three-bedroom, modern, terraced house in Wimbledon Park, which had previously served as her ex-husband's love-nest. It was a tight squeeze getting her children comfortably installed, but the lack of tension that now prevailed made it all worthwhile.

3

SAN FRANCISCO

I arrived in San Francisco on March 7th, 1967, a few months ahead of the Summer of Love. I had no idea that this particular time and place would become so auspicious in years to come. Somehow, I seemed to find myself in these remarkable places at pivotal times that would one day come to epitomize an era. As the zeitgeist shifted, so did I, internally changing with these shifts.

I had never heard the name Haight-Ashbury before, or of the hippies, and yet it had already become a rebellion against the establishment by the time I came to San Francisco and was gaining momentum. I didn't know that just a few weeks before I arrived, a man called Timothy Leary had stood up and told the crowd of thousands at the 'Human Be-In' to "Turn on, tune in and drop out."

All the San Francisco bands, poets and philosophers had spoken and played for free on this momentous occasion in Golden Gate Park. Although this gathering was based on a reaction to the new law banning the use of LSD in California, it marked the beginnings of what turned into the "Summer of Love." The Haight Ashbury district became a symbol of American counterculture.

I was nineteen when I arrived, having no idea what to expect, but willing to take a leap into the unknown. Amongst the crowds of people and their luggage pouring out of the terminal, I spotted Judy sitting in her sporty black '57 Thunderbird parked alongside the curb. She jumped out and together we heaved my large suitcase into the trunk.

"What have you got in here?" she asked, "Weighs a ton."

"Books," I said, and then jumped into the car.

We drove to her one-bedroom apartment on 1645 Filbert Street. What was to be my bedroom had been her walk-in closet, but having taken her clothes out and replaced them with a put-up bed it was now given over as mine for the

next few months. I hadn't seen Judy for some time and there was a lot to catch up on. We sat cross-legged that evening, facing each other on the floor beside a large glass ashtray, talking non-stop, drinking endless cups of Constant Comment tea and eating soft round biscuits. As the evening progressed, Judy began filling me in on all the difficulties she was having with builders and bank managers, and the trouble she'd had trying to get the shop open by the time I arrived. As she spoke, she would nervously tap her lit cigarette on the side of the ashtray, hardly inhale as she put it to her lips, and then back it would go tapping on the glass. There were so many things that I wanted to ask her about San Francisco, but as the evening wore on and tiredness took over, I sat patiently in front of her until I finally made my way to my new bed in the cupboard.

The following morning, Judy drove me to North Beach, which had been up until that time one of the famous bohemian districts in San Francisco, similar to Greenwich Village in NY and Venice Beach in LA. This area was now on the verge of morphing into a hippie commune, the beginnings of a larger counterculture. Apart from being instrumental in the literary movement, by the time I arrived the Beats were almost interchangeable with the hippies; they both held similar beliefs and values of non-conformity, creative expression, sexual liberation, and spiritual awareness.

My vision of American teenage boys up until that time had been clean cut, fresh faced, all smiling with crew cuts and sneakers, but as we walked along the street I saw young, interesting looking men with long hair and beards wearing faded jeans, boots, cowboy hats, and leather fringe vests or jackets. They appeared to have just stepped out of a Western movie. Both the men and women looked cool, self-assured, with long hair, walking around barefoot or wearing sandals or moccasins.

As I looked into the eyes of some of these people, I experienced a sense of recognition, a nod or a smile, as if they'd also experienced this same spiritual awakening. Judy chatted to friends along the way, introduced me, and then carried on walking until we stopped outside one of the many, 'head shops', as the hippies called them.

A line of small copper bells tinkled as she opened the glass door. We were greeted by the familiar smell of incense. A striped cat lay sleeping in the window. Hookah pipes, necklaces, beads and other hippie paraphernalia were displayed on long tables covered with Indian fabric and little circular mirrors that glinted in the sun. Psychedelic posters hung on the wall in all the colors of the rainbow with names of different groups written in big fat swirling letters. From behind a makeshift curtain at the back of the shop, a tall swarthy-looking man wearing loose-fitting jeans and biblical sandals appeared. I stared at him. Apart from the jeans, he looked like an

Old Testament prophet. His long, black, curly hair was thick and oily. He brushed it off his forehead with slender fingers as he glanced at me and then looked at Judy.

"Hello, Judy," he said in a loud voice as he walked towards us. Judy introduced me to her friend, Arab, and told him I'd just arrived from England. I felt very polite and English as he bombarded me with questions about England and The Beatles. His dark brown eyes twinkled and while laughing, he told me not to take myself so seriously. He took a quick look outside, and then beckoned us towards the drawn curtain.

"Come and meet my dad," he said in a half-laughing, half-singing voice.

I saw a pale, white haired older man in deep conversation with a hippie, they both looked up. "Welcome," he said, his wrinkly face breaking into a smile. "Who's this? Who's this?" His arms opened wide, as if to embrace us.

"Thanks, man," the hippie got up, putting a small bag in his pocket, "I'll see you later." He nodded to us and walked off. I noticed this but said nothing.

We were offered a chair around a low wooden table covered with books, pencils, cigarette papers, and ashtrays. Leaning against the walls were a number of large canvas paintings and drawings.

"This is Berkley, my dad," Arab said, his arm gesturing towards the white-haired man. They looked so different; I couldn't see any resemblance and wondered if he was speaking literally or whether he meant a soul connection. Berkley began rolling a joint while Arab picked up one of the drawing pads from the table and continued with his questions. Judy talked to them about her shop and the problems with the carpenter. They talked about people they knew.

After a few hits of the joint, both Arab and Berkley began talking excitedly about the mysteries of the Egyptian pyramids, about the symbolic meaning of each room being a certain size, and how it corresponded with certain dates throughout our history. I listened carefully, feeling as though I'd landed not only in a different world but also a different universe. Along with this thought was my newly found belief that anything was possible, but by the end of our visit I guessed that Arab and his father had taken a lot of LSD, which I later found to be true, not only had they, but also their striped cat.

That was to be the first of many visits to this shop with its cozy den behind the makeshift curtain. It was where I was to spend endless happy hours drawing, chatting, writing poetry, and meeting interesting people. As well as Judy, Arab and Berkley were to play a crucial part in introducing me to some of the key players who were part of the San Francisco counterculture in the city. The more time I spent with them in their little den the more I noticed that their interest in metaphysics knew no bounds. The deeper they went into their mystical stories gleaned from around the world, the faster they talked and the more excited they became until such time when Arab would jump up, compelled to paint his vision for them both on a large canvas. Many hippies saw smoking pot or taking psychedelics as the key to opening one's mind, to getting in touch with and sharing far out experiences or ideas about mysticism. I was soon to find out that Arab and Berkley were no exception!

Judy pointed to her shop a little further down the street, on the corner of Grant Avenue and Vallejo. It was now an empty shell with sawdust and building materials scattered on the floor. She gave a sigh.

"He was meant to be here," she said, waving her arms at the surrounding mess on the floor, "but this happens every time."

Judy was close to tears. After telling me that she would stay there and wait for the carpenter, she gave me directions to City Lights bookstore. I later found out that City Lights was a literary landmark known for championing the Beat movement with authors such as Jack Kerouac, William Burroughs, and Allen Ginsberg. As I made my way to Columbus Avenue, returning looks and smiles along the way, a warm breeze on my face and a feeling of lightness in my step, a wave of excitement flooded through me. I was on an adventure in a world that was completely different to anything I could have imagined, and yet I felt at home.

I stepped into City Lights and immediately the warm, musky smell of books transported me back to Watkins bookshop in London. I trawled through the bookshelves, hungry to find more information about Eastern religions, looking for words to ignite my imagination and spiritual thirst. As I stood in the shop, absorbed in what I was reading, I heard someone say hi. I lifted my head and my eyes settled on a young man sitting on a bench by the window.

"Hi," he said again as our eyes met. "Are you from around here?"

I smiled. I must have looked quite different from the locals in my very stylish linen Foale and Tuffin minidress. "I just arrived from England," I said.

"Did you go to a convent?"

"How did you know?" I asked, breaking into a smile.

"The way you're standing," he said, a cheeky grin on his face.

I looked down at my feet and noticed my legs looking as though they were stuck together with glue. It was not the free-flowing stance of a San Francisco 'Flower Child'.

Judy had briefly told me about the hippies as we drove over to Haight-Ashbury, but what I was about to witness that day was very different to what it turned into four months later. Rents were relatively cheap here and so many of them shared multi-story Victorian houses. Communal living had become part of the hippie philosophy and so it was a perfect place to set up home.

My first response as I walked along the street was how different the men looked compared to my friends in London. Most of them were larger, more heavily built, but not only that, many of them looked like Native Americans with their long hair and headbands or scarves across their forehead. Young men and women dressed in loose fitting colorful tops or pants, jean jackets with ban the bomb symbols emblazoned on the back, flowers in their hair, beads, bells or wearing anything else that was colorful and creative. The smell of incense, patchouli oil and pot wafted out of the doorways of shops that were filled with handmade crafts such as jewelry, hash pipes, rainbow colored clothes, tie-tied tops, bells and beads. Psychedelic posters advertizing different bands playing at the Fillmore or Avalon lined the walls, or slogans such as 'Make Love, Not War'. People sat in clusters against trees or lampposts playing guitars, singing, drawing, painting, or making Native American dreamcatchers. Complete strangers would greet one another with knowing nods or stop and chat, give flowers or sweets, or make the peace sign with their fingers and smile.

These were kindred spirits who had found a place where they belonged and where they could set up a community that housed their own set of beliefs and values. The San Francisco bands were a major part of this movement, many of the musicians lived in the Haight-Ashbury area and through their music and lyrics they represented the hippies, giving free concerts for them all in the Pan Handle of Golden Gate Park.

Another major player of this psychedelic era were The Diggers. Their main objective was not only to give free distribution of food, clothes, temporary shelter, and medical care, but to share with others their fundamental belief they shared in communal living and a political conscience. Their aim was to create a society free of capitalism.

Having recently arrived in this distant land from England, but then finding myself in the middle of a separate culture, another world, it took me a while to realize it wasn't something just happening here in San Francisco. I had no idea it was a growing, pulsating energy that would within a very short time spread around the western world and affect a whole generation and beyond. And yet, I had sensed the underlying transformation in myself while in London before I knew anything about the hippie movement. Somehow, even though I thought I was heading to San Francisco just to help Judy with her shop, the energy of kindred spirits coming together in a common belief was unconsciously drawing people to its center. I had become part of the spirit that was to define our generation.

San Francisco felt new and exciting to me, and I could not think of anywhere I would rather be. The early mornings were beautiful, a freshness in the air that felt exhilarating. I loved the mild weather, gentle sun and warm breezes. Everyone was so friendly. There was a tremendous feeling of unity amongst the young, and although there was a part of me that was always on 'observer mode', due to my English reserve, most of the time I felt part of the scene. Smoking pot had connected us to each other, broken down barriers, and 'Love' was the password.

Apart from seeing the anti-war slogans on badges pinned, or embroidered on jackets, or on psychedelic posters, in the words of songs or any other creative expression, the closest I came to rubbing shoulders with anyone who had actually fought in Vietnam was one evening at Judy's apartment. Two childhood friends of hers from Sacramento had just returned from there. They were a year or two older than me, in uniform, with young fresh faces and closely cropped hair. After being introduced, the boys followed me into the kitchen and leaning against a cupboard began asking questions about my life in England while I made tea for us all. One of them, in a clumsy sort of way began teasing me, trying to chat me up, egged on by the other. I didn't laugh or flirt back, I remained serious, and instead asked what it was like fighting in Vietnam. Their whole persona completely changed, the atmosphere in the room became thick and still, and as I looked into the eyes of the one who only a minute ago had been flirting, I saw tears hovering. Together, they talked about their feelings of helplessness, hopelessness and as they opened up and released the horrors of war, these two young guys who only a short while ago looked so tough and cocky had now transformed into two frightened little boys.

It was my first experience of hearing directly about the war, and the first time I had met people who had fought in it. I felt moved and shocked by what I heard, but what I couldn't bear was for the boys to gloss it over by flirting. I wanted to hear them talk, the sad, the serious, I wanted us to be truthful with each other and not pretend everything was normal.

A routine began to emerge as the days went by. Judy would drop me off in different parts of the city on the way to her shop and I would spend the day walking around Fisherman's Wharf, buying chocolate in Ghiradelli Square, jumping on a cable car, or taking the Greyhound bus across the Golden Gate Bridge to the little town of Sausalito or further on to Marin County. Often on these trips, I would feel a deep longing for a friend to accompany me so we could listen to the sound of the ocean together or look at the pinks and purples of a sunset. I wanted to show Pattie the pretty town of Sausalito with its houseboats moored, bobbing up and down alongside the water's edge, and the quaint, old fashioned shops lining the streets, hippie shops filled with candles, hand-made jewellery and pottery. I would often give one or two dollars to the longhaired earth mothers sitting on the quayside crocheting or making third-eye symbols from brightly colored wool and wooden twigs. Every day brought new ventures, new sights and sounds, but only with pen and paper was I able to share them.

I wrote letters to Pattie and George, telling them about this feeling of utopia I had experienced walking along Haight-Ashbury, the creative people, the wonderful music, the feelings of love from everyone, and the free style of living. I frequently wrote letters to my mother, to each of my brothers and my sister Paula, letters that were written on swirling multi-colored paper, describing the weather, the hippie movement, and how a woman I had recently met could, just by shaking a bell around my neck, tell what my astrological sign was. There was a lot of reference to astrological signs and I began to take an interest in astrology. It was a common occurrence for people on first meeting to ask or guess one's star sign.

As I became more enchanted with my days, Judy was becoming more stressed as the deadline of her shop opening was moved further and further back. One day as we were walking down Haight-Ashbury, I saw a young man with bare feet standing beside a small basket playing his guitar. He looked at me and smiled.

"Oh, Judy," I said, "let's put a couple of dollars in his basket."

Judy stopped walking and turned to face me. "I don't think you realize how hard it is for me trying to open this shop," she said. I could see tears starting to form in her eyes. "Bank managers, builders, it's too much and I can't keep giving away a dollar here, a dollar there, each time you see the hippies."

We carried on walking in silence. I understood. She was right. I had little regard for money and was filled with a naive belief that it would always work out. I was often bailed out of situations: George unexpectedly sent me a $100 bill one day and Judy would sometimes pay for meals. I had a lot of angels on my shoulder, I realized, and one of them was Judy.

Although I didn't see much of her during the day, and often Judy was too frazzled to hear about my travels, we made up for it in the evenings by listening to live music. One of these places was the Fillmore Auditorium.

The Fillmore had recently become the focal point for psychedelic music. Judy and I would become one with the crowd in the hall either sitting cross-legged on the floor, dancing or just standing shaking our bodies in time to the music. We would listen to the distinctive sounds of San Francisco bands such as The Grateful Dead, Country Joe and the Fish, Quicksilver Messenger Service, and my favorite, Big Brother and the Holding Company with their dynamic singer, Janis Joplin. Everyone in the hall was riveted when she sang, moving their body, or shaking their head as the colored lights swept across the audience. Grabbing the microphone and stamping her feet, she would belt out at the top of her voice, her body shaking as if possessed with raw emotion, the lyrics of *Ball and Chain*. The audience was with her every step of the way; she transported every person in that hall, and we all felt it. The sense of unity at these times was palpable; the feeling that permeated everything and everyone was that through music, life would change. Musicians were the messengers, the spokespeople of our time. Music was an integral part of this counterculture.

One evening, while I was sitting at the back of Arab's shop, a place I now visited frequently, smoking, chatting, and listening to music, a young, blond haired guy wearing glasses and a Russian-style embroidered shirt appeared. He told me his name was Paul Kantner and he was a musician in one of the local bands. Later in the evening, after taking Arab aside, he offered to drive me back to Judy's flat. Once we arrived, and just before I got out of the car, he asked if he could see me again. I felt flattered, but also suddenly self-conscious. "I don't know, yes," I mumbled, and then leapt out of the car. When I told Judy, she was thrilled. "He's the guitarist from Jefferson Airplane," she said. "They're one of the biggest bands in San Francisco. You should have said yes, he's very nice." Two minutes later, Judy put their latest album, *Surrealistic Pillow*, onto the record player. I recognized one of the songs instantly, having heard it full volume in many of the shops along Haight-Ashbury, a song that was to become one of the all-time greats of the hippie era: *White Rabbit*.

There was a sprinkling of little bars on Grant Avenue, where performers would sing and play their guitars. One night while Judy and I were sitting at a table, drinking our tea and listening to the powerful voice of a young, dark curly-haired, acoustic guitarist, I looked round to the back of the room, and saw Paul Kantner. He smiled at me. Standing next to him was a man with a fringed, buck-skinned jacket, and a black cowboy hat on top of his round, jovial, face. I wandered over to say hello, and was introduced to Paul's friend, David Crosby from the LA band,

The Byrds. He'd met Pattie and knew George, and with a glint in his eyes and a wicked smile, told me how alike Pattie and I looked. It felt comforting to meet someone who knew Pattie and George, a little thread of connection amongst all these people I'd never met before. Once he'd finished his set, the guitarist walked up to us and with big smiles of greeting to his fellow musicians, introduced himself to me as Dino Valenti.

Searching for a higher consciousness while I was in San Francisco didn't preclude the growing attraction I was feeling towards Paul Kantner. We drove to the ocean in silence one evening, smoking pot along the way, which, because I felt he was attracted to me too, made me feel horribly self-conscious. I was screaming, scrambling to say something cool but hardly spoke a word throughout the whole evening and felt miserable when he dropped me off at Judy's apartment. I felt as though I'd failed on my first date and couldn't quite believe my ears when he said, just before I got out of his car, that he was off on a short tour the following day but would write to me.

Although Judy consoled me by saying that meant he liked me, I moped around the apartment, my enthusiasm deflated, my search for enlightenment and enjoyment now over-shadowed by a longing for someone to love, projected onto a man I knew nothing about and too stoned to speak to when we did meet. Every time the phone rang my heart jumped.

"What are you going to call your shop?" I asked Judy one day as we were driving to North Beach.

She stole a glance at me, a sheepish smile on her face. "I wondered when you were going to ask," she said. "I'm calling it Passion Flower."

We both smiled. It was the name Peter Bardens, the keyboard player in Notting Hill Gate, had always called Judy since the day she and I met in the Flamingo Club. She had brought not only her memories of the clothes she liked in London, but also her reminiscences of an early love affair during that time.

Judy's shop finally opened after three months and my days were spent selling the clothes she'd copied from designs in London, as well as antique beaded dresses and shawls she'd bought from Portobello Market. Together, we painted the shop windows with black Aubrey Beardsley swirling designs and inside we hung glass chandeliers from the ceiling. While waiting for customers, I would stand at the entrance looking out onto the street, seeing now familiar faces, smiling, chatting, and listening to music that came drifting in from surrounding shops. It was while standing there one day, feeling the warmth of the sun on my face that I first heard

The Beatles record, *All You Need is Love*. Although I knew Paul, John and Ringo, and George was now my brother-in-law, when they sang together as The Beatles, it was different; they somehow became something larger-than-life. Their music seemed to tap into and speak for the very spirit of this youth movement. Even though it became an anthem for a generation, I felt as though the song was speaking directly to me. It was so simple, all the deep questions I'd asked myself over the last year suddenly evaporated. The timing was perfect. They were right on target and completely in-tune with this whole ever-growing movement. The zeitgeist was connecting to everyone, both sides of the Atlantic, and it was transported by the music through The Beatles, Bob Dylan, and other like-minded bands.

Arab and Berkley's little den was where I spent most days when taking a break from the shop. I'd sit on the shabby little sofa or curled up in an armchair behind the curtain. Other people came and went, as they rolled joints or drank tea.

"You're a pretty good artist," I said to Arab one day, looking around this little den at the drawings and paintings hanging on the wall or leaning against a cupboard, paintings of biblical figures and esoteric images.

"Thanks." Arab smiled at me. "Dad and I are kinda hooked into the mysteries of the pyramids." He gave a hearty laugh.

I looked over at Berkley, sitting at the table smiling at me and nodding while he rolled another joint. "That's right," he said. "They were so far out, those cats, every event that happened was aligned with the stars." He inhaled then passed the joint to a large bearded man who was standing by the curtain.

"Hi man, come on in," Berkley said, holding his breath, beckoning him towards the sofa, and then looking back at me, "Yeah," he said as he exhaled smoke, "they were pretty hip, those guys. Pretty cool cats." He began laughing again, looking at Arab and nodding.

"Meet Chocolate," Arab said, pointing to the new arrival who was now sitting next to me on the sofa. I turned to face him and saw two large brown eyes in a round weather-beaten face, surrounded by a mass of disheveled hair and a raggedy beard. I looked at the colored tattoos emblazoned along his tanned, muscular arms as he reached forward to stub out the joint. A Hells Angels biker jacket lay on the sofa beside him with 'Chocolate George' embroidered on the back.

"What's your name, little lady?" he asked as he picked up a carton of chocolate milk from the table and after glugging back the contents, tucked into one of several chocolate cupcakes.

"That's Jenny from jolly ol' England," Berkley said, mimicking a bad English accent. They all laughed.

Suddenly Arab jumped up. "I'm painting a portrait of you, Jenny, I'll show you." He scrabbled around amongst his canvases and pulled out a large painting of a girl with long blond hair looking out into the distance. She was standing in front of a bookcase wearing a short, purple spotted dress and with one leg forward as if striding out into her future. He leaned it up against the wall in front of his canvases.

On looking closer, I could see the painting was filled with all the signs of the zodiac subtly blended in with one of my limbs, my dress or a chair. On top of the bookshelf, a scorpion fought with Leo the lion, and across my heart was Cancer the crab. "Interesting," I thought, "Mick's star sign is Cancer."

"You have to look at her hair with this," Arab said, handing me a magnifying glass. What looked like hair from a distance, when I looked through the glass became more animals and signs from the zodiac. As I moved the magnifying glass onto the dress, I noticed that in some of the purple spots I could see the faces of George, Paul, John, and Ringo.

Chocolate George heaved his large body off the sofa and reached his hand out for the magnifying glass. His knees creaked as he bent down to study the painting.

"That's cool, man," he said, turning to look at Arab. "You're a genius."

Arab laughed. "It's called, *The Colors of Jenny*."

I was flattered, but at the same time I was beginning to feel a little self-conscious. I had a feeling that Arab was getting a crush on me, and yet I felt comfortable spending time in their cozy little back room.

"It's getting late," I said, standing up. "Think I better go."

Chocolate George stood up. "I'll give you a lift, pretty lady. You can hop on my Harley."

I glanced at Arab. He nodded in response.

"Chocolate will take care of you, Jenny. We'll see you tomorrow."

The Hells Angels had been one of the most feared motorcycle gangs in California before the Sixties but had now become friends with and taken on the philosophy of the hippies. Once Chocolate delivered me safely to Judy's flat that evening, he gave me a signed card that read, 'You have been assisted by a member of Hells Angels Frisco'. From then on, as he told me that night, if ever I needed help, he would be there

The following Saturday, we were invited to the Hells Angels party in Marin County. Judy drove Arab, Berkley, and me because none of us knew how to drive. I don't know how she found it, but a couple of hours later we came across a log cabin in the middle of the woods. We knew we'd found the right place because of the Harley Davidsons scattered on the ground. Before we walked in, Arab gave us what he called mild acid, which made everything sparkle and slightly surreal.

The cabin was full of smoke, and as we walked inside I saw a swarm of big, muscular Hells Angels standing around, talking and laughing, smoking joints and swigging beer. Their faces were made all the more extraordinary by the onset of the drug. Emerald eyes sparkled, diamond rings glittered from their fingers, and they stomped around like bears in the wood. I felt so fragile amongst them. I remember looking around the room for Chocolate George, but I need not have worried, he'd already seen me.

We left at dawn. I looked up to marvel at the lacy tendrils on the branches, making webbed patterns against the pale blue sky, and contemplated the extraordinary evening. The four of us made our way to the nearest House of Pancakes, where I was introduced to my first American pancake breakfast.

Now when I think of that evening with the Hells Angels, a shudder runs down my spine. The very thought of two young women, high on acid and in the middle of nowhere, in a cabin full of biker boys – fills me with dread and I thank my lucky stars we came out unharmed. But in many ways, it is an example of that time, of the trust and innocence, the feeling of unity we all shared.

On June 16th of that year, Judy and I drove to Monterey in her '57 Thunderbird. We were off to the largest pop festival ever put together, with an estimated 35,000 people, that was to last three days. Chocolate George rode his Harley alongside us, sometimes behind, and then in front. We drove up the coast road like this for miles, in the brilliant sunshine and under a cloudless sky. Occasionally, he would come across other Hells Angels swooping down the freeway on their shiny motorbikes, hair blowing in the wind and bands made of beads or fur fastened around their head. Chocolate George would join them, adding to their number and looking impressive as they roared away into the distance, the sun glinting against their chrome handlebars, before re-joining Judy and me, and continuing as our chaperone.

That was the last I ever saw of the wonderful Chocolate George. It wasn't until recently I found out that only two months after this memorable drive, he was killed in a motorcycle crash on Haight Street. Over 200 Hells Angels and other bikers took part in his funeral procession through the streets of San Francisco to the Cypress Lawn Cemetery. They had stashed two quarts of chocolate milk inside his coffin so he wouldn't get thirsty on his journey into the afterlife. Afterwards, along with 300 hippies, a wake was held in Golden State Park where The Grateful Dead and Big Brother and the Holding Company played in his honor. I felt honored to have met him.

The site for the Monterey Pop Festival was crammed with colorful hippies, many of them with small children in their arms. Alongside the chairs lined up in front of the stage were booths and stalls covered with velvet clothes and silk scarves, posters, pot smoking paraphernalia, beads and bells, just about everything we'd seen on Haight-Ashbury. It was not so different to the 'Human Be-In' event in San Francisco but on a much larger scale. Bands from New York, San Francisco, Los Angeles and the UK came with the hippie communal mind-set and played for free at this first festival of its kind.

We watched Jimi Hendrix picking the strings of his guitar with his teeth, setting his guitar on fire and smashing it on stage The audience clapped and cheered, knowing this theatrical performance was in response to the Who's guitarist, Pete Townsend, who had smashed his guitar on stage, which now looked pretty meager in comparison

Jefferson Airplane were one of the major attractions at the festival, having by now built up a large following on the West Coast. People wandered around the Country Fairground with badges pinned to their jackets saying, 'Jefferson Airplane Loves You'. The applause was almost deafening when they walked on stage, especially when the band's beautiful dark-haired singer, Grace Slick, began singing their iconic song, *White Rabbit*, that along with The Doors, *Light my Fire*, and Scott McKenzie's, *Be sure to wear flowers in your hair*, had now defined the hippie movement.

The list of the most popular singers and bands was endless, bands such as Big Brother with Janis Joplin, the Mamas and Papas, Simon and Garfunkel, the Grateful Dead, Otis Redding, and many more. I waited patiently for Sunday afternoon when I knew Ravi Shankar would be playing. It rained beforehand, a little drizzle, but as soon as Ravi and his tabla player Alla Rakha, sat down, both dressed in their white traditional Indian attire, the rain stopped. The silence was breathtaking; everyone listened with complete dedication. When I met Ravi a few months later with Pattie and George, he told us how nervous he'd been about playing at a festival that consisted only of rock and pop artists and to an audience that were perhaps mostly unfamiliar with classical Indian music. He need not have worried. The hippies revered music from India; it had become part of their culture and due to George's affiliation with Ravi, he was the most well-known and respected.

The Monterey Pop Festival was considered a huge success all round and became the inspiration behind other festivals, but none would ever live up to this first one. It was in many ways the calm before the storm, the feelings of love and peace and all the ideals of the hippies came to the forefront that weekend and made it what it was, but it wasn't long after this peaceful festival that the hippies around Haight-Ashbury were replaced by thousands of dropouts, calling themselves hippies, and begging for money. The shadow side of the original ideals was beginning to show its face.

Jefferson Airplane were recording in Los Angeles, and Paul Kantner had invited Judy and me to visit him during our few days in the city. We walked into the recording studio a couple of days later and were told Paul was expecting us and to go straight inside. Through the glass partition we could see Grace Slick sitting on a stool with headphones on and singing into a microphone. Paul came into the room, his sleepy eyes looked directly at me, and he smiled. "Good to see you both," he said in his West Coast, stoned, drawl. He gave my hand a squeeze. Jack Cassidy, their bass player followed Paul, and with a surprised look on his face, gave Judy a big grin. She'd met him before.

I was offered a joint that circulated around the room. After no more than a few seconds my head was whirling, I wondered why we were there, and wanted to hide behind one of the tape machines. I sat on the sofa, silently watching the proceedings as each band member walked in and out of the smoky little room and sang or played their instruments in the studio next door. After what felt like an interminably long time, Judy leaned over and suggested we went off to find our motel and get a bite to eat. I nodded.

"Why don't you both come over to my motel later this evening," Paul said, as we got up to leave. "We won't be here much longer, and it would be great to see you." His eyes rested on mine, and I mustered up a smile.

Later that night, in Paul's motel room, after smoking and talking to each other for a while, Judy fell asleep in the armchair. I wasn't sure if she was really asleep or if she was pretending. I knew she didn't inhale when she smoked dope, so she couldn't have passed out.

Paul led me into the bedroom next door. I lay down, fully clothed, while he undressed and got into bed. The more dope anyone I knew smoked, the more uninhibited they became. Except for me. I was stiff as a board as I lay on his bed. I felt like a freak. We were into Flower Power, and Free Love, I told myself, it wasn't meant to be that big of a deal, not any different than giving someone a flower or a smile. But it didn't work for me. I had spent the last couple of months fantasizing about Paul, getting letters from him, and now, here we were, and I couldn't let go. Although I was unable to put it into words, and wasn't fully aware of it at the time, what lay tangled up inside was a strong feeling of uncertainty about Paul. I hadn't been with anyone since leaving Mick, and the thought of casual sex without the inevitability of a committed relationship didn't sit well within my being.

I looked at Paul and could see confusion in his eyes, knowing we had both felt attracted to each other, but instead of anger he showed respect and was cool, which made me like him even more. We fell asleep.

Judy and I spent a few more days in Los Angeles, going to the Farmers Market with Jack Cassidy, and driving up to Laurel Canyon one night, with most of the band stuffed in the car. Paul was very sweet, which made me feel worse. I continued to spend the whole time struggling to get outside of myself, while smoking pot with them all. I still wonder to this day why it took me so long to realize that smoking pot, in the quantities I smoked with Paul, didn't suit me, it sent me deep down inside myself and there was no way I could emerge until the effect wore off.

Not long after we returned from L.A., Judy and I moved into an apartment on 415 Vallejo, a couple of blocks up from Grant Avenue and in short walking distance to Judy's shop on the corner. I was no longer dependent on her driving me everywhere, and I felt more like one of the locals. Wandering down to the shop every morning gave me a stunning view of the city, but the steep climb at the end of a long day or evening was a schlep. Even so, I was happy to be living in North Beach.

I was surprised to get a call from Pattie one evening. She and George had just arrived in Los Angeles that afternoon and she wanted to see me. It was August 1st and I'd been working at the shop for a couple of months and was quite ensconced in my day-to-day life, but the following morning I took the flight to LA and a car up into the Hollywood Hills to Blue Jay Way; the name of a street that was to gain prominence as the title of George's song on The Beatles album, *Magical Mystery Tour*.

I was thrilled to see Pattie. We had spent the last six months writing letters, but it wasn't enough, and I had missed not having her close by. She had changed. We had both changed since we last saw each other. Taking LSD had altered our perception on life, and I wanted to share with her how we'd been affected by our experiences. But there was no time to explain in a few days what we'd experienced in six months with all the new sights and sounds around us, and no time to talk in depth to each other with the continual presence of their travelling companions.

George greeted me with a warm hug and together they introduced me to Alex, a blond-haired man from Greece who they referred to as 'Magic Alex'. He was an electronics engineer who had become friends with the Beatles, and because he'd conjured up what John Lennon thought was a magical electronic device, had been given the name, Magic Alex. Another young man who had flown over with them was Neil Aspinall, the quietly spoken Beatles friend and road manager.

Another Beatles long-time friend and press officer, Derek Taylor, had recently moved to California. It was Derek who became the inspiration behind George's song, *Blue Jay Way*. Having given Derek instructions on how to find the house and while waiting for his friend to arrive, he wrote the song. I was later to find out that Derek, who was also the publicist for a lot of the California bands, had been a major player in helping to set up the Monterey Pop Festival.

I spent almost a week in LA with Pattie; either swimming in their pool, going to the Farmers Market in Hollywood, or to Disneyland along with Alex and Neil. George spent most of his time seeing Ravi Shankar, buying a sitar, or taking us all down to Ravi's music school where we watched about fifty of his students playing the sitar. Even so, we did spend an afternoon downtown together in Olvera Street where we had our first Mexican meal and where George and Pattie bought for a few dollars, two brightly colored Mexican pictures painted on black velvet. But the height of my visit was going to the Hollywood Bowl to listen to an evening of Indian music played by Ravi, some of his finest students, and a number of well-known musicians from India.

After four or five days in LA, it was decided that we would all, including Derek, go to San Francisco for the day by Learjet. My visa was about to expire, and together Pattie and George thought it was time for me to come home. Once the jet landed in San Francisco, we climbed into a limo and drove to Judy's apartment so I could pick up my passport and pack a small bag. And so, the day I had longed for, the day when Pattie and George would arrive in San Francisco, proved to be completely different to how I imagined. I had wanted to share with them my impressions of the hippie utopia which I had witnessed earlier in the year. But by now, after all the media coverage and as endless kids flocked across America to 'Turn on, Tune in, and Drop out', the original spirit of the hippie movement had moved on and been replaced by what was to become homelessness and drug addiction.

Even so, they and their entourage, Alex, Derek and Neil, all arrived hungry to soak up everything I'd previously told Pattie and George; the flower children, the creativity, spiritual awareness, and Haight-Ashbury.

We each took the inevitable tab of LSD, handed to us by a friend of Derek's from one of the radio stations, the necessary precursor, so they thought, needed to fully appreciate the Haight-Ashbury experience. We'd been driven in a limo up until this point, but now the driver refused to take the car down Haight-Ashbury and insisted on parking in a street nearby. It was too conspicuous.

"Well, let's walk," said George. We got out of the limo, all wearing our colorful clothes, smiles, bells or beads and feeling the psychedelic effects of the acid. The smile on my face felt hollow. I had an ominous feeling as our beautifully dressed entourage, a sight that would have stuck out in any crowd, wandered down the street, Pattie and George leading the way. I felt as though everything I'd held dear during my time in San Francisco was about to be put to the test. Would it be the same for Pattie, George, and their friends now as it had been for me when I came here in the spring? I didn't think so. I felt wholly responsible for their presence and lagged a few steps behind, observing the reaction from the surrounding hippies.

We had walked fairly anonymously amongst the crowd for all of a few seconds, and then as one person after another recognized George in his denim jacket, red, black and white swirling colored pants, beads and heart-shaped sunglasses, they began following us. My sense of dread was well founded as the word got around and crowds behind us grew. I could hear snippets of conversation spoken in wonder, "George Harrison!" "George Harrison's here, one of the Beatles!" At first, they kept a respectable distance, stopping as we walked into a few of the shops. I heard one girl say, as she looked at Pattie with her long blond hair, her calf-length purple suede sandals, mini-dress, and a long row of beads and dark glasses, "They're the best dressed hippies I've ever seen."

Someone gave George a crown of flowers that he put on his head at a slightly tilted angle, all smiles and obviously still enjoying the walk. "Where are we going?" he asked Neil at some point. Neil guided them towards the Panhandle, known as Hippie Hill. George sat down on a grassy slope, surrounded by masses of adoring fans who were obviously thrilled at having a Beatle in their midst. A guy with a guitar appeared and pleaded with George to play it.

"It's your guitar," George said with a smile. "You play it."

Although he looked reluctant to play in front of a Beatle, George persuaded him and so he did, which was probably the bravest thing he ever did!! Everyone seemed to be having a good time. I watched from a distance, slowly unwinding and relieved to see George laughing and answering questions. Then the guitar player stopped singing. "Please play us a few chords," he said, handing George the guitar again.

The crowd joined in, "Sing us a song; play us some chords."

I looked at George, knowing what state of mind we were all in and wondered how he was going to pull this one off. He placed his fingers on the frets and while strumming the strings with his other hand, he said, "This chord is G, this is C, and this is E." He gave back the guitar, stood up, and began walking towards the street. The crowds were stunned into silence!

We headed for the limo. The walk back seemed to take forever, as the crowd got thicker. One voice from the back kept repeating, "Hey George, let me lay some acid on you, let me lay some grass." The voice got louder and more insistent. I could feel waves of fear emanating from Pattie and George. "I'm cool, man," George replied, and quickened his pace. "You're our leader," someone else yelled. "You have to lead yourself," George shouted back.

The last few steps, once the limo was in sight, seemed like an eternity. Neil and Derek snapped into protective mode, something they were not unused to, while they urgently ushered us along like mother hens. The atmosphere in the crowd had quickly changed from adulation to anger and I could see and feel the fear mounting in our little troop as the crowds pressed against us and we walked faster towards the car. Their 'hero' hadn't delivered sufficiently as a fellow member of 'Love, Peace, and Good Vibes', and he hadn't accepted the grass that they so willingly wanted to 'lay' on him. This was not what I had envisioned all those months ago; I had wanted their walk along Haight-Ashbury to be peaceful and inspiring, but here we were, virtually running away from a situation that looked as though it could easily get out of control.

With the engine running and the door open we dived into the cool back seats of the limo. As fists banged on the roof and smiling, tearful or angry faces pushed up against the darkened windows, the driver moved slowly through the crowd and on towards the airport.

I looked at everyone leaning back in their seats, staring ahead as if in a trance or eyes temporarily closed with a sigh of relief. I wanted to tell them, "It didn't used to be like this." I wanted to say, "it was different before and they wouldn't have done what they did today." But instead I just closed my eyes, thankful for the blast of air-conditioning against my body, leaned back, and joined the silence.

The Learjet was waiting for us at the airport. It was only then I noticed George was carrying what looked like a spear, bound in different colored wool, but on closer inspection saw it was a peace pipe that one of the hippies must have given him. Once we were airborne, I stared, mesmerized by the lights in the cockpit as my mind drifted off, mourning the abrupt loss of what had been my home for the last six months. There had been no chance to say goodbye to friends, or to pack my suitcase, never to be seen again all my precious books or my Foale and Tuffin clothes. I half-listened to the pilot as he mumbled into his headphone speakers, wondering how different my life would be back in London, when suddenly, I felt a wave of panic spread through the small jet. The lights in the cockpit went out. The pilot's body tensed, and I heard the sound of urgency in his voice. Pattie, who was sitting next to me, put her hand on mine. No one moved or said a word. The engines cut out. We sat there in silence, all praying in our own way until, just as suddenly, they started up again, and, still not daring to speak, we continued our journey towards Los Angeles.

The following day, apart from Derek, we all left for England.

I stayed with Pattie and George at their bungalow in Surrey; at times feeling as though I'd lost my way. My experience of living in San Francisco during such a pivotal time was appreciated more with the passing of time. I was an idealist by nature and believed in this new way of being and what the original hippies were trying to achieve; spiritual awareness, creative expression, appreciation of nature, peace, being kind to one another, a sense of community and anti-racism. It was a world I felt part of, unconsciously drawn to; I identified with the spirit of our time. Although I was filled with idealism and naiveté, and although part of the hippie culture included smoking pot and taking psychedelics, what I didn't know but was soon to find out was that I could find spiritual awareness without the use of mind-altering substances.

INDIA

JENNIFER JUNIPER

Transcendental Meditation was founded by Maharishi Mahesh Yogi who over the years, had managed to attract Westerners interested in a meditation technique that was both simple and allowed them to carry on with their lives as normal. They were told that meditating twenty minutes in the morning and evening was all that was needed to obtain an alert and peaceful mind.

Pattie happened to see an advertisement in The Times offering Transcendental Meditation courses in London and so while George was on tour in August of '66 Pattie and a friend attended weekly meditation classes where they were initiated by one of Maharishi's followers, given their own mantra's and taught how to meditate.

Paul McCartney was the first to hear that Maharishi would be coming to London in August '67 and told the rest of The Beatles. I accompanied Pattie and George, the rest of the Beatles and their wives (except for Ringo and Maureen who were just about to have a baby), Mick Jagger and his girlfriend, Marianne Faithfull, to a lecture he was giving at The Hilton Hotel in Park Lane. Having only been back from San Francisco for a couple of weeks and still feeling rather lost and shaky in myself, I was a little daunted and not quite so enthusiastic as the others about meeting the Yogi.

Maharishi sat cross-legged on the platform surrounded by an abundance of freshly cut flowers. He was a slightly built man with long, brown wavy hair that appeared freshly washed and oiled. As he surveyed the audience, the lights above caught silver streaks in his hair, his moustache and his completely white pointed beard. He wore clean white robes and he clasped the stem of a vibrant flower in full bloom in his hand. With his eyes darting from one person to the next, he would hit the flower against the palm of his hand, or on the floor, while stressing a certain point about the meditation. Petals flew in all directions, which he seemed unaware of until the flower became bald, when he'd reach for another from a vase in front of him and the cycle would begin again. The lecture on meditation was often interrupted by his sudden outbursts of high-pitched laughter, and then, just as suddenly he'd pull himself together and carry on talking. I found his description about the benefits of meditation interesting, but the message was more compelling to me than the messenger. My idea of a yogi was Parmahansa Yogananda whose book, *Autobiography of a yogi*, George had given to me before I left for San Francisco. Reading about him and his life affected me deeply; his face looked familiar, long dark hair and gentle brown eyes. I didn't know at the time, that Yogananda's teachings were to play a significant role in my life. And that still to this day I would keep a photograph of him with me at all times.

After his lecture Maharishi invited our little party to join him at his 10-day retreat in Bangor, Wales. Two days later I boarded the train with Pattie, George, the rest of the Beatles and their wives, (except for Cynthia Lennon who had missed the train), plus Mick Jagger and Marianne Faithful.

Our compartment was filled with earnest talking and laughter; each one of us was excited by this new adventure. At some point during the journey some of our party decided to visit Maharishi who we found sitting cross-legged on a seat in his first-class compartment. I was still not convinced by this Indian yogi; made worse by my first interaction with him on the train. Pattie sat down next to him and I sat next to her while the others sat on the seats opposite. During a lull in the conversation Maharishi turned his head towards Pattie and in a high-pitched voice said,

"What do you do?"

"Oh, I'm designing clothes for The Beatles new boutique," she said, sounding worthwhile and interesting. Even though it was the first I'd heard of it, I was impressed how she'd circumnavigated the question.

"Very good," came the reply, as he looked at her, nodding his head approvingly. I tried to look invisible, knowing what was coming next.

"And what do you do?" he said, smiling in my direction.

"Nothing," I said. My face feeling as though it was on fire, knowing I'd failed the test of sounding like a worthwhile person.

His smile vanished as I sank lower into my seat.

My mind drifted back to San Francisco and how I'd witnessed what I thought was my own little flame become part of a mass movement. While using psychedelics and smoking pot, I had searched for self-awareness and for others who spoke the same language. Even so, my quest had somehow left me feeling disillusioned. I'd tied myself in knots looking for answers to my never-ending questions, desperate to find a sense of meaning, but the more pot I smoked the further away I felt from the truth and the more confused I became. Thankfully, all this was to change as soon as I received my mantra and became initiated into Transcendental Meditation.

We arrived in North Wales to be greeted by hundreds of fans and flashbulbs as we were all bundled into cars and taken to Bangor College. The simple and basic bedrooms were a far cry from the expensive hotels and luxurious homes the Beatles were used to staying in; and yet these austere surroundings were in many ways more in keeping with the search for spiritual awareness. My bedroom was near Marianne's and so the next morning, not knowing quite what to do next, I made my way to the lecture hall where Maharishi was due to give an introductory seminar about Transcendental Meditation. I noticed as I walked along the corridor that Marianne's door was ajar. She was sitting on her bed, looking down as if deep in thought and then lifted her head on hearing my footsteps and smiled. "Come in," she said, patting the bed. "Come and sit." I'd felt a little disconnected up until this point, shy and lacking confidence, and so it was a relief to see she was alone.

Marianne was very pretty, with long blond hair, blue eyes and a lovely smile that curled up at the corners of her mouth. I sat on the bed next to her and we began talking of our feelings about Maharishi. I told her that although I felt ready to learn how to meditate, I could sense a dark residue of doubt about him, and maybe the darkness was inside me. I feared I wasn't a true believer and felt like an imposter. To my surprise she described similar feelings, a sense of darkness that wouldn't allow her to be as open and trusting as the others. Talking to Marianne that day, sharing our innermost thoughts, making a connection for those few moments, released me from feeling quite so locked inside. It helped to know I was not the only 'black sheep' in our party. We made our way to the main hall that was already filled with about three hundred people and where we found our little group, sitting like good children with open hearts and minds ready to listen to their new master.

This time, as Maharishi delivered his message, he looked as though he was the goose that had laid the golden egg. Sitting on stage with him, for the entire world to see, were The Beatles. Having witnessed the hundreds of fans mixed with press, reporters, police and passengers as we departed from Euston Station and then seeing the same reaction as we got off the train in Bangor, it was clear that Maharishi knew he had a means of expanding his following.

After the lecture and before we all got initiated into Transcendental Meditation, a press conference was held outside the college with Maharishi and The Beatles. It was here that The Beatles declared to the world that they had given up taking drugs and were now following Maharishi and learning to meditate.

Although I didn't hold the same belief and trust in Maharishi, or feel the need for a guru, I became initiated by one of his helpers that day and given my own secret mantra, a Sanskrit word we were told to silently repeat, but not tell anyone. I was never quite sure if I'd heard mine correctly which added to my doubts around Maharishi and his meditation, but I kept these thoughts and feelings hidden. I wanted to believe just like everyone else in our party seemed to be doing. I watched George with his endearing innocence, echoing every word of Maharishi's with such devotion. How much easier, I thought; to believe and trust. I hoped I could get closer to it in time.

After our little gathering had been initiated, we sat in one of the rooms at the college, surrounding Maharishi as he talked about The Beatles being involved in a Transcendental Meditation Centre in London. They all agreed that the publicity would be enormous, and people would become meditators on the strength of The Beatles involvement. Maharishi invited them to join him at his ashram in India, a training center where they would learn to become initiators. I listened to this discussion with a sense of longing. I would love to have gone to an ashram in India to meditate, it would have restored a part of me so in need of being wrapped up in the arms of the Great Mother. I kept quiet, hoping I could, at least, be part of the meditation center in London once they returned.

It was decided that The Beatles would leave the following February for three months, after which they would be involved in setting up the Transcendental Meditation Center. I remember how excited everyone in the room felt, The Beatles, Pattie, Cynthia, Jane Asher, and me as we sat cross-legged around Maharishi. The thought of being involved in helping people raise their consciousness grabbed us all and the hope of bringing peace to the world gave a higher sense of purpose; something I'd spent the last few months looking for.

Brian Epstein was due to arrive the following day, ready to learn how to meditate, but on that very day, instead of greeting their manager, they were given the shattering news of his death. Everyone's emotions hurtled from one extreme to the other – from the feelings of euphoria about Maharishi to a deep sadness over the death of such a beloved friend and mentor. I'm sure it was horribly poignant for The Beatles, as they had never done anything of such significance without Brian; now he would never be part of this giant step they were embarking on or anything they were to do in the future. It marked the end of an era. Brian had guided them so expertly towards establishing themselves as The Beatles. Now what they were about to do was to disassociate themselves from their collective 'Beatle persona' and dig deeper into themselves as individuals. And so it was a time of rebirth in many ways, of new beginnings. Maharishi consoled everyone and encouraged The Beatles not to hold on to Brian in their mourning but to release him with feelings of love and happiness. It was heartbreaking listening to them reciting these words in front of the press. Maharishi was their leader now, and he was the one they were about to follow and spend time with in India.

Ever since experiencing what I called my 'Spiritual Awakening', I knew I would go to India one day. Apart from knowing my family had lived there for three generations as part of the British expat community, I found myself drawn towards everything to do with the culture, including the gods and goddesses, the smell of incense, belief in reincarnation and the deeply resonating sound of the sitar. I was fascinated to see how the hippies had embraced India, especially those I'd encountered in San Francisco. When George and Pattie invited me to accompany them to Maharishi's ashram, I was overjoyed.

The invitation came when the three of us were in a taxi on our way home from Bangor. It was a sad journey; both Pattie and George were deeply in shock after hearing the news of Brian's death. When we reached London, I got out of the car and looked at the two of them still sitting quietly. I held my hand up to wave goodbye, when George suddenly jumped out, walked up to me and said, "How would you like to come to India with us next year?"

I was stunned, taken by surprise. In my wildest dreams, I did not imagine that I would be included in this trip. I was delighted at the thought of going there with Pattie and George and felt that they, more than anyone I knew, understood this spiritual path that I was so earnestly seeking.

"How can I ever repay you?" I asked.

"Just be yourself," George replied.

And that's it, I realized many years later, that's all we ever have to do, but at that time I'd felt out of touch with myself and maybe Pattie and George had sensed that and because we were all on this spiritual path together wanted to include me on the journey.

It was while I waited patiently for our trip to India that I was offered a job in the Beatle's new Apple Boutique, which opened on December 7th, 1967. The Beatles asked four friends of theirs, known as The Fool, to design a mural for the outside of the building. The Fool consisted of two young couples from Amsterdam: Marijke and her husband Simon, plus Joskje, and her husband Barry. A few months previously they had painted the surrounding white brickwork of

Pattie and George's fireplace at their bungalow in Surrey with silver stars, crescent moons and planets. After they'd finished, they were asked to do the same on the outside of their house. I'm sure the Surrey neighbors must have been shocked!

The Apple shop stood on a corner on Baker Street, and a month before it opened, The Fool and some students painted an enormous mural on the outside wall. A swathe of every color from the rainbow, plus planets and stars, swept across the front and side of the building from the ground all the way up to the fourth floor, including the chimney. Nothing like this had ever been seen before! It was shocking and wonderful and attracted all kinds of people to stop and peer through the window. Baker Street, up until this point, was basically 19th century conservative and the only thing it was famous for was the Sherlock Holmes Museum.

The publicity and curiosity brought crowds of people into the shop once it opened. Occasionally the Fool would arrive, their arms full of clothes and knick-knacks. Mariike usually lead the way looking tall, proud, and strong, with her piercing eyes, pale skin, and flaming red hair. One behind the other they would stride across the shop floor as the crowds parted and every head turned. Together they looked like wandering medieval tradesmen carrying exotic clothes from the East; cloth from India, beads from Greece, jewelry and shoes from Morocco, and embroideries from secondhand stalls. They were the beautiful gypsies in striking colored clothes, made from velvets, silks and satin. The girls wore silken scarves in their hair, or tassels of rainbow ribbons tied around their neck, or wrist, bands across their forehead, and sandals held on by ribbons to their knees. They ignited the imagination of those who had taken LSD, people who could identify with the swirling colors and mystical meanings that surrounded everything they created.

There was a lot of interest in the Apple Boutique. Because I managed the shop along with John Lennon's friend, Pete Shotten, journalists often asked me to describe this new way of thinking the boutique represented. I finally felt in sync with myself and in my environment. This shop symbolized everything I believed in and I was happy to talk to people about our philosophy. Expensive clothes that The Beatles' wives and girlfriends wore were now made available to the masses. It allowed people's imagination to soar. The upstairs of Apple was filled with Indian posters of gods and goddesses, incense, bells, and anything else that was affordable and from the East. Down the creaky wooden stairs, customers were greeted by a splash of color, every kind of garment on hanging rails, in rows across the floor.

I rented a room in a large Victorian flat a few minutes' walk from Baker Street, with Mick Fleetwood, John Dominic, and two other boys. Mick and I had seen each other periodically after our break-up. He would sometimes take me out for a drive in his old Alvis and we'd spend the day chatting about our different lives. It always left me wondering whether we should get back together. He seemed so sweet and gentle, so safe after navigating my way through such unsettled waters. The guys teased him unmercifully once I moved in, knowing he still held a flame for me.

I had my own little room, just big enough to hold the top of a bunk bed, which was reached by climbing a ladder. Underneath the bed, I pinned a map of the stars against the wall, and there I would meditate, twenty minutes in the morning and early evening, with incense lit and the door closed. This room was just off the long narrow corridor, leading towards the kitchen, and right opposite Mick's room.

Although our paths didn't cross that much while I lived at the flat, as Mick worked at night and I worked during the day, when we did see each other we were like an old married couple. He never tried to persuade me to rekindle our relationship, but I would hear from the boys in the flat how sad he'd get sometimes. I felt bad when I heard these things, but at the same time I knew I'd changed in the last two years. And maybe I was fearful. He felt so familiar and comfortable to be with that if I went back to him I might fall asleep and never wake up to my purpose in life. There was a part of me that unconsciously believed Mick would always be there, waiting.

I was standing behind the shop counter in the basement one day, cup of tea in hand and chatting with a friend, when I heard the clumping and creaking sound of footsteps traipsing down the stairs. An impish face with dark curly hair popped out from around the corner. As his foot touched the bottom step, his face lit up.

"Jenny!" he exclaimed, his eyes wide open. "I didn't know you worked here."

It was Donovan, England's answer to Bob Dylan. I had met him and his girlfriend a few months previously at Pattie and George's house. He had some friends with him, one of whom I recognized as Gypsy Dave. They spread around the shop with cries of joy, touching all the bright and wonderfully colored clothes as they walked around the rails. Donovan carried on talking, his eyes darting about the shop and then back to me.

"Let's sit in there." He pointed towards one of the dressing rooms with a curtain hanging on one side. He drew the curtain once we'd both sat down and began asking me questions about Maharishi, meditation, and San Francisco. Time and the shop disappeared while we sat there engrossed in our own little world. He wanted to learn how to meditate and was hungry to know more.

"I'm taking the train down to Cornwall," he said, "to be photographed for my new album." He smiled at me, his eyes sparkling. "I would love you to be in the photos. Can you come?"

I told him I would, and we arranged to meet at the station.

The photograph session, taken by Karl Ferris, was for Donovan's album, *A Gift From a Flower to a Garden*. Donovan was a poet. The way he spoke, his beautiful lyrics about folklore and fairytales, everything he did conjured up another world; a world of child-like innocence that as the days went by we recognized in each other. He stood in front of the sea, wearing a black embroidered kaftan with beads around his neck, and flowers in his hand, while I sat on a rock, my long blond hair blowing in the wind, playing a wooden flute. Karl videoed us while we played like children in the sand; dressed in our velvet clothes and colored chiffon scarves as we skipped along the dunes, looking into caves along with a young boy in green who looked like a pixie. I had no idea who he was or where he came from, he just skipped along with us, a silk scarf tied around his head and green make-up on his eyelids. We had, just for that day, all escaped into another world, a world of fairytales.

I saw Donovan in the shop a few days later but this time he didn't stay long. He'd come to ask me if I'd like to spend the following Saturday with him at his manager's house in the country. When I arrived, there were a few people chatting and milling around, including his manager, and after being introduced we were herded into the dining room.

After lunch, Donovan took me aside saying he'd written a song and wanted to play it to me. I followed him into one of the bedrooms where he sat on a double bed, and as he leaned his back against the wooden headboard, he picked up his guitar. I took my shoes off; jumped on the bed and sat cross-legged opposite him, trying to ignore the sudden feeling of intimacy sitting on the bed together had created. He began singing, *Jennifer Juniper*. He looked at me as he sang, and I could feel my eyes welling up as I realized it was a song about me. I thought it was the prettiest song I'd ever heard; I loved the sound of his acoustic guitar and his gentle voice. He reminded me of a troubadour or minstrel from days of old, of courtly love and chivalry. As I listened closely to the words, "Is she breathing, yes very low," I knew it was about me meditating. But as it got closer to the end, "I'm thinking what it would be like if she loved me," I realized it was a declaration of his love. Luckily, as the lyrics changed from English to French, I had a chance, not understanding a word, to look up and smile at him, but inside I knew this song could take our friendship onto another level and was I ready?

Jennifer Juniper has stayed with me always, having been a huge hit and loved by many, I continue to hear it on the radio or even, once, coming out of speakers in a supermarket. I've known mothers who have called their daughters Juniper and are delighted when they hear it is my namesake. Hearing it always has the same effect. Having a song written about you is very flattering, but also, as the years go by and having taken it with me into my life, I am aware how it instantly transports me back to not only that first time I heard it, but also, and probably more prominently, it personifies for me that particular era of innocence, idealism, and hope. It was the meeting of two dreamers.

Donovan and I saw more of each other over the next few weeks, but the romantic side of our relationship, even though I'd been given the most beautiful and precious song, was a slow progression due to my uncertainty. I couldn't help but feel we were like two innocent children, and together we could very easily have hidden away from the harsh reality of daily life and dreamed poet's dreams. I loved listening to Donovan sing, and the words of his songs were filled with everything that ignited my imagination, my love of fairytales and far-off lands, but I wonder to this day if at the back of my mind, even though we weren't together, I was internally married to Mick.

Before I went to India, I rented a room at Magic Alex's house in Pimlico and the more Donovan and I saw each other, especially when he'd come to the house, the more competitive Alex became, vying for my affection. I didn't feel he was attracted to me; he was playing a game and it felt more like jealousy. The night before I left for India, John and Cynthia Lennon came to visit us. John held Alex in high regard, especially after making what he called a 'Nothing Box' with blinking lights that stimulated John's LSD trips. From their conversation that night, I could tell that Alex was also jealous of John's trust and loyalty to Maharishi, he wanted John to go to his guru rather than going to Rishikesh and study Transcendental Meditation. Alex, as it turned out, was to play quite a significant role in our relationship to Maharishi and our time in Rishikesh.

In February 1968, I took the long flight to Delhi with Pattie, George, John Lennon, Cynthia and their assistant Mal Evans. Paul, Jane, Maureen, and Ringo had decided to come a couple of days later. Actress Mia Farrow greeted us at the airport. She had come to India with Maharishi a few weeks before we arrived and was now on her way to Goa before heading back to Maharishi's ashram. The eight-hour drive to the village of Rishikesh, nestled in the foothills of the Himalayas, was bumpy, emphasized even more by the old Austin Ambassador cars we travelled in with their lack of suspension. The sights and smells were intoxicating, a mixture of the early morning pink sky, tropical flowers, pyramids of red, yellow and brown colored spices and the overall smell of incense. We drove through small villages with the sun beating down, and the sound of car horns incessantly hooting. Big old-fashioned trucks were everywhere, decorated with garlands that glittered in the sunlight, and paintings of Vishnu and a multitude of other gods and goddesses.

As we drove further out of Delhi the buildings gave way to rows of makeshift tents. I wound down my window, breathing in the warm, dusty air as I stared at the women hunkered down by the side of the road, stirring a pot over their little fires with the smoke and pungent smells making their way into the car. I glanced at a man shaving as he stood in front of a fragment of mirror attached to the wooden pole of his tent. I could feel the dust in my eyes and between my teeth.

There were magnificent sights of rickety old carts pulled by oxen, loaded high with sugarcane and drivers sitting cross-legged on top with sticks in hand, hitting the beasts as they trundled on to the next village. Women walked gracefully in their colorful saris, with baskets balancing on their head. We drove along miles of deserted road, which led to the foothills of the Himalayas as the morning sun turned the countryside yellow. We passed tall eucalyptus trees and banana groves with flocks of large white herons gliding from field to field. Then miles of deserted road between villages, except for the occasional figure of a man wearing a loincloth or saffron robe, holding a staff as he walked along a stony path, old and weather-beaten but with vibrant colored eyes. Periodically we'd see young children in the distance herding cattle along the side of the road.

The car stopped halfway there and pulled over by the side of the road. Pattie, George, and I got out to stretch our legs. As we stood looking around, taking in the sounds and smells, I had an overwhelming feeling that I'd been here before, a sense of recognition. It was everything I had longed for since the day I began this inner journey.

After a long and fascinating eight-hour drive we came to a turning off the main road and as the taxi drove slowly up the sandy path a banner greeted us strung between two bamboo poles with the single word 'Welcome.' We passed the guard standing in front of a wooden gate behind which lay the fifteen-acre estate. I picked out the jacaranda trees along a stony footpath, the sight of which immediately transported me back to Kenya, the heat, the smells, but most of all the brilliant purple blossoms standing tall against a blue sky. But here in India, between the lush green trees and bushes stood the snow-clad Himalayas towering high in the distance. So this is my view, I thought, in a euphoric, dreamy, jetlagged state, as the car trundled on into the compound, this is my home for the next three months.

The car stopped outside one of the many flat-roofed stone bungalows set in groups along the path, with its own courtyard. I followed the driver, laden with suitcases, as he deposited mine outside one of the doors. The room was very basic and sparse with a concrete floor, just a bed, a chest of drawers and a bathroom, which I later found out, I shared with the occasional scorpion. It looked like heaven to me, and I couldn't wait to look around the ashram.

A narrow stony path opposite our bungalow led to the eating area and towards the Ganges where we met the two boys from Australia who did the cooking for everyone in the Ashram. The smell from the makeshift kitchen was exceedingly welcoming. A long, narrow table stood out in the open, shaded by trees with a wooden lattice fence running alongside the edge of the compound and overlooking the Ganges. This is where we were to spend many hours, eating our porridge and toast in the morning, drinking cups of tea made with Carnation milk, eating rice and dahl and vegetables and getting to know our fellow meditators. Often, as we'd get up to leave the table, I'd see monkeys sitting in the over-hanging branches waiting to jump down and gather any leftover food.

On that first evening of our arrival, along with a cup of tea and biscuits we were given directions to the auditorium, and told we were just in time for the evening lecture. It had never occurred to me to think about what the other meditators must have thought as we walked down the middle of the aisle that evening. I assumed, as they were all meditators, we would naturally blend in and there would be very little reaction. Our fellow-meditator and friend at that time, Richard Blakely, has described in his book, 'The Secret of the Mantras', a completely different picture:

"I was aware of other people coming in and sitting down around me and then there was some brouhaha and laughter at the back of the hall and Terry, keeping his voice low, said, "Holy shit!" Get a load of this!" Since Terry was a man of few words and all those words carried weight I figured it was worth coming back up (out of meditation) to take a look for myself and when I did what I saw at first glance looked like half a dozen gypsies traipsing down the aisle. They reached the front of the hall and nodded and smiled at Maharishi who was already sitting on his bench up on the stage, and then while two bramacharies fell all over themselves removing the rope from the reserved seats, George and John turned to the rest of us and smiled and nodded and waved and there was, (what Maharishi called) 'a spontaneous expression of joy, as everyone applauded."

The lecture hall was where Maharishi would give his talks, two or three times a day to begin with, as well as giving the participants an opportunity to ask questions about their meditation or to air grievances about anything to do with their rooms or with the ashram. Some of the people living in the last row of bungalows would often complain their water had been cut off.

When we first arrived, there were at least sixty meditators at the ashram, but as time went by many of them had disappeared into their rooms as they began their long meditations lasting for days and for some, weeks.

Much to the annoyance of the older dye-hard meditators, our little group was given the VIP treatment, with full access to Maharishi most days. We'd sit in a semi-circle around him, overlooking the Ganges and feeling the warmth of the sun as he talked to us about meditation and how to conduct our lives. Each time his eyes caught mine, I always sensed he knew I was not as doting as the others. Although I had been meditating in England, twenty minutes in the morning and evening, and had felt the benefit of feeling more centred and calm, I was still not convinced Maharishi was such a holy man. I questioned his motives, especially when he talked about the gold aeroplane he wanted.

Mia Farrow joined us for lunch, a week or so after our arrival. She looked very much the same, with her short blonde hair and her gamine, boyish elegance, as she did on the soap opera that was so popular at that time, *Peyton Place*. Having recently separated from her husband, Frank Sinatra, she seemed at times quite on edge. Her brother Johnny and her sister Prudence had accompanied her to the ashram and were both meditators. There were many interesting people around the dining table; Mike Love from the Beach Boys and Paul Horn, the flautist who'd made a recording of himself playing his flute in the Taj Mahal. I enjoyed his company and met up with him in Los Angeles many years later while writing my book on musicians and creativity. One woman was a faith healer. She met me every day in my room, and by using the palm of her hand held a few inches from my leg, she eventually got rid of my eczema. There was the now-legendary "Bungalow Bill," whom the Beatles wrote about and were later to record on *The White Album*, an eccentric man who went out hunting every day, looking for tigers, and then came back with tales of what he'd shot.

To begin with, we were meditating for two or three hours at a time. Occasionally Pattie and I would wander down to the Ganges where a man with a boat would row us across the river to the village. People stared at us, especially children, their hands covering their mouths as they giggled and looked at each other. We were probably the only Westerners they'd ever seen. To get further into the village, we had to walk past a row of lepers, sitting against the wall with limbs missing or misshapen with grey sack clothes around them. It was a sight I had previously been afraid of, and yet, as disturbing as it was, somehow it all seemed part of an accepted way of life here. It was in context with everything around us. As we wandered around the village, we came across an Indian woman in a plain colored sari standing beside an open door. We could hear the excited sound of children's voices. With a big smile and her head nodding from side to side, she beckoned us into her schoolroom. We wandered inside and stood in front of the children, smiling at them as they laughed and giggled and squirmed in their seat. We could have come from the moon and they would not have been more surprised. All we could do to connect with them was to smile and laugh and put our hands together in the gesture of Namaste.

One day while a group of us were playing in the Ganges, jumping around in the freezing water and sitting on the rocks, we saw two slim, white figures walking towards us. They had long brown hair and wore loincloths.

"Hi man," one of the young men shouted. "Where you all from?"

"We're from the ashram," one of our party replied.

"Far out, brother," said the boy. "We're here to find enlightenment too. We're living up in that cave on the other side of the river." He pointed to a clump of rocks in the distance, and then looked at us.

We stood and stared at them, not saying a word.

"We've been here for a few weeks now, and wondered if you guys would like to take some acid with us? We've got some good shit."

We smiled at them and shook our heads. "No, thanks," one of us said, "we're fine." Once they were out of sight, we laughed at the thought of them coming all this way to sit in a cave and take acid. It was now the furthest thing from my mind.

When Maharishi found out that a lot of us younger ones were going down to the Ganges not only to sunbathe but also to swim, he forbade anyone going in the water, which we all ignored. As Richard Blakely mentions in his book, it inspired a little song from John while we were sitting round the dining room table – "Maha don't allow no swamis swimmin' in here. I don't care what Maha don't allow, swamis gonna' swim here anyhow." We'd been told by Maharishi in the lecture hall that we were all swamis.

Once I'd started to meditate, especially during the longer sessions, I experienced moments when my thoughts completely stopped. Where everything became still, like a clear, motionless lake. Occasionally a thought would arise and create a few gentle ripples and then become still again. It was in complete contrast to daily life, especially my life in San Francisco where my thoughts and questioning almost bore a hole in my head!

As the days got warmer, our little party would spend more time sitting on the roof of our bungalow; John, Paul, and George playing their guitars and singing their latest songs to each other, songs that were later to be heard on their next album. It always amazed me how the inspiration for their songs came from daily life, nothing extraordinary, just people, places, and situations were used to inspire yet another song to reveal itself.

One of the songs George played on the roof, which never made it to the *White Album*, was called *Beggars in a Goldmine*. It was about seeing people leaving the ashram for a day's visit to the Taj Mahal or a town near Rishikesh called Dehra Dun. He couldn't understand having come all this way to be in meditation why anyone would want to go "shopping for eggs" as he saw it, in Dehra Dun. Part of his lyrics to this song were, "See them move along the road in search of life divine, unaware it's all around them, beggars in a goldmine."

The warm rays of the sun, the soothing sound of guitars, and the exotic smells felt blissfully peaceful. Pattie, Cynthia, and I, and Jane when she was there, would chat quietly, listen to the songs and sometimes have our hands painted with henna by one of the Indian women, or be shown the correct way to wear our saris.

Even though we spent a lot of time with one another, there were times I felt shy when the Beatles were together. I got used to sitting quietly and not saying much, just listening. I'd learned to be unobtrusive as a child, to take in what people said, receptive to their thoughts and ideas. When they were together, there was such a feeling of unity, which I later witnessed with the members of Fleetwood Mac. It was as if they had an invisible membrane around them, their own creative world. They all spoke so eloquently, and all had the same quick-witted humor.

One day while we were on the roof, John told us how difficult it was for him to sleep at nights, and I listened while he sang and played the beginnings of *I'm So Tired*, a song that later was recorded for the *White Album*. We believed he was hitting what Maharishi called an 'iceberg'. As our meditations lasted longer each day, we all began to experience different degrees of these so-called 'icebergs'. They were described as a knot or block in the psyche from tension, anger, or any negative feelings from the past. The only way to release them, we were told, was to keep meditating. The idea being that the longer one meditated, the deeper one reached, and finally the iceberg would be released. But it was possible to come out of meditation still attached to whatever negative emotion the iceberg represented.

I experienced what I thought was an "Iceberg" one night after meditating for a few hours. I'd been listening to the hypnotic sounds of George's sitar, drifting in from his room opposite, while I floated in and out of meditation. I had meditated throughout the day successfully, but halfway through the night I felt as though my head was about to explode. My body was on fire one minute and then freezing the next. Finally, when I couldn't stand it any longer, I went out in search of Maharishi.

I passed the young guards outside our block; their faces lit by the fire as they sat huddled around in a circle. Maharishi's house was near the dining area, in an isolated grove of trees, with a wide view of the Ganges. I was told to wait in one of the rooms, while Maharishi was sent for. Standing alone, hot and sweaty, I looked up at the painting of Maharishi's great swami, Guru Dev, surrounded by Christmas tinsel. When Maharishi arrived, I described to him how I felt. "Go back and keep meditating," he said calmly without any concern. "You're going through an iceberg."

I meditated until morning, sitting on the floor; slumped against my bed until I heard a knock at the door. I thought it was probably the mango man. Every morning he would knock on the door, and call out, "Mango." Usually a glass of mango was welcomed but now I had no strength to get up. The door opened and it was Pattie, seeing if I wanted to come for breakfast with her. She took one look at me, helped me into bed, and sent for the doctor. Much to my surprise, he told me I had tonsillitis even though I'd had my tonsils out years ago. Later, a second doctor, who happened to be in the Ashram that day, told me I had dysentery.

As I was sitting up in bed the following morning, leaning against my pillow and still feeling weak, John and Cynthia walked into my room. John handed me a picture he'd drawn of a man sitting cross-legged with a turban on his head. He was playing a flute and in front of him was a snake, coiled up in a basket with his hooded head peeking out. The inscription underneath read:

"By the power that's in and the power that's out, I cast your tonsil-light-house out. Love John and Cyn."

Very soon meditation became a way of life. The heat of the day began to creep closer to the chilly early mornings, while the sight and color of the Himalayas was constantly changing and always breathtaking. At night, I'd look up at the blackened sky littered with millions of stars and follow the moon lying on its back like a silver boat as it gradually became a golden ball floating above the Himalayas.

Some mornings, I would take a chair from the kitchen and meditate in front of these awe-inspiring mountains. As the gentle sun made the snow sparkle while the Ganges gurgled below, never had I felt happier or more at peace. I would sit there with the notepad I'd bought in the village and write poems, trying to find the words to describe these beautiful surroundings and the feeling of such utter contentment.

As well as peace, there were also times of joy and celebration. George, Pattie, and musicians, Paul Horn and Beach Boy Mike Love, all celebrated their birthdays within a few days of each other. On Pattie and Paul Horn's birthday we all watched Paul playing the horn with an Indian musician called Shah Jahan. Donovan, who had recently arrived, played and sang a Beach Boys-inspired song, along with Paul and George, for Mike Love's birthday celebration. Whether it was a special occasion, I can't remember, but there was one day when we all traipsed down to the Ganges in our colorful Indian kurta shirts and loose fitting cotton pajamas, made by the tailor who sat cross-legged in a tent at the ashram, ready for our special outing. We sat with Maharishi beside the Holy River; George, John, and Paul playing their guitars with Donovan while everyone else sang some of the better-known songs.

George set up a little organ on the roof of the lecture hall, which soon became a popular hangout before or after lectures or in between long meditations. Some of the younger meditators would join us there to socialize and listen to George playing the organ or strumming his guitar. We sang songs together and talked excitedly about the Beatles involvement in Transcendental Meditation and how it would get more young people meditating. We all felt inspired and talked about the future of our world and how we could make a difference. This was in complete contrast to the older generation, the old-time meditators, who felt since our arrival the rules had been broken, they had less time with Maharishi and a carnival-like atmosphere had descended upon the ashram. Even though we younger ones were all there to meditate, our arrival had brought a breath of fresh air to the ashram.

Although Donovan had come to meditate and stay with us at the ashram, he asked me one day if he could take me to the Taj Mahal. By the time he arrived, I was well ensconced in the ashram way of life and didn't want to be anywhere else. Together, we took walks to the Ganges where he sat on the riverbank and played his guitar and sang to me. I loved listening to him sing and enjoyed having him as a friend, but he had other things in mind. He was a romantic and mentioned the idea of marriage. But since I was not ready for any kind of relationship, he left after a few weeks, though we continued to see each other once I was back in England.

Mia's sister, Prudence, had a room in our block, opposite my room. One evening, after George and our young meditator friend, Richard, had been chatting with her they noticed something was wrong. They walked her to her room but the following morning nobody could rouse her out of a trance. We knew she'd been doing extensive meditations, non-stop, and wondered if she'd gone too far.

One by one, we walked into Prudence's room, trying to bring her back to normal. But she continued to sit bolt upright, cross-legged on top of her bed, and staring into oblivion. John went in with his guitar and played for her. *Dear Prudence*, another song that later appeared on the Beatles *White Album*. I went in with the flute I'd bought in San Francisco and made some sounds, but it was all to no avail. Prudence looked as though she was locked inside herself. Her condition got worse and the following night she completely flipped out, shouting, throwing things around and screaming. She was taken to Maharishi's bungalow and from there was moved to block 1 in the last row of the bungalows. A private nurse stayed with her around the clock and in the doorway stood one of the guards. We heard later that her condition was possibly more to do with the psychedelic drugs she'd taken before becoming a meditator, but even so, after this incident Maharishi advised us to take breaks in between long meditations. I heard many years later that Prudence completely recovered not long afterwards and still meditates.

'Magic' Alex arrived a short while after Donovan left for England. I was surprised to see him knowing how he'd tried to convince John not to go to the ashram. Every now and then, I would see him walking hand in hand around the compound with one of the meditators, a young woman from America, and wondered what he was up to.

On the morning of what turned out to be our departure day, George knocked on my door and told me to pack my bag, that we were leaving for South India to join Ravi Shankar on his tour. I jumped out of bed in complete shock. I had no idea what was going on. I found out later that there had been accusations made against Maharishi and that things had rapidly escalated. It was all very sudden. Alex's friend had told him Maharishi had made a somewhat inappropriate advance towards her and Mia Farrow. Alex was delighted with these stories and of course brought them straight back to John. When George heard, he and John went to Maharishi's bungalow with a couple of other people that evening and told him we were leaving the following morning. They stayed up most of the night, talking about him and trying to work out if the accusations were actually true, but when Pattie told George she'd had a dream that night depicting Maharishi in the same light, it confirmed their decision.

The next morning, while our taxis waited, we walked along the stony path past Maharishi, a small figure in white, sitting on a chair under the shade of a large black umbrella.

"Why are you leaving?" His thin shrill voice cried out.

"You should know if you're so cosmic," John had told him the night before when Maharishi had asked the same question. But now nobody said a word.

As we walked past him, I remember feeling more like a traitor than I had throughout the whole time I'd known Maharishi. I'm sure everyone had a bad taste in their mouth, bearing the weight of mixed emotions; anger, betrayal, fear and sadness tinged with guilt at the niggling uncertainty of having made the right decision. But that day, we all just kept walking, past Maharishi, out of the gate, and away from our joyful life at the ashram.

We were driven back to Delhi where we stayed while everyone made plans. I felt disappointed about our departure. With time, my feelings about Maharishi had not weighed so heavily on me as the meditation and environment took over and calmed my previously restless spirit. Being in Rishikesh was a time of recuperation and it had now come to an abrupt halt.

The Beatles were concerned as to what they should say to the press. Would they be ridiculed after all the publicity prior to their departure from England? Were they to tell all, and disappoint the kids that had followed their lead by meditating instead of taking drugs? Such was the weight of being heroes. They decided in the end to say nothing. *The White Album*, though, said a lot.

Maybe none of us will ever know what really happened at the premature end of our two-month stay in Rishikesh. Everyone probably has their own story of what caused a change in attitude, but I think that after being in such a totally remote and secluded place, so different in every way from our other world, and to be meditating in such an intensive manner, something inside us rebelled. Looking back on it, I think it was a number of incidents, all occurring at the same time, in addition to the culture gap. I do believe that Alex came to cause trouble, to prove to John that Maharishi was not as good as his own guru.

George's reaction to the sudden departure was a paranoid belief, goaded on by Alex, that Maharishi was capable of putting a bad spell on him. This fear only grew when he contracted dysentery as soon as we got to South India.

As the plane landed in Madras, Pattie, George and I were greeted with the heat of an oven, hotels with mosquito nets in every bedroom and the mildest curries that burnt the roof of my mouth! I met Ravi, who was always laughing and very gentle, especially towards George whom he loved as a son. He took his fear of Maharishi seriously and organized a Puja (a religious ceremony) to protect George and his home from any negative forces. Pattie and I watched as George sat within a circle of flowers and incense, listening to the sound of people chanting as we all breathed in the exotic smells.

We travelled with Ravi and his troupe from city to city watching his concerts. There was a fresh sort of energy in his company, which was very loving and warm, and listening to his music was soothing and meditative. We spent a week travelling with Ravi, his tabla player, Alla Rakah, and his beautiful tambora player, Kamala Chakravaty. They were all such good company, always vibrant and laughing which made the transition from the ashram to England easier to bear.

During our time at the ashram, I had many deep conversations with Cynthia Lennon about meditation and her life at home. She confided in me about her concerns for John as she watched him changing before her eyes, the distance between them growing each day and becoming more obvious. When we returned to England, she asked me if she could come to Greece with Donovan, Magic Alex, and me.

Greece was a good distraction for Cynthia, but her homecoming was desperate. Alex and I were with her when she opened the door to their house and found John with Yoko. Following Cynthia as she walked into their den, John then lay on the chaise lounge, looking completely unrepentant. With his bare feet resting on the arm while Cynthia stood staring at the floor, speechless, John wiggled his toes next to where I was standing, and said in a squeaky voice, "Hello, Jenny." I couldn't help but smile. He was like a naughty child, caught misbehaving by his mother.

I spent a lot of time thinking about our experience in India and our spiritual searching before that and wondered what it all meant. The expedition to India helped me become aware that the answer to my own quest lay within. I learned through meditation that that there were other ways of connecting to spiritual awareness rather than experimenting with LSD.

The trip affected other members of our troupe in different ways. There had been such hope that we could all be instrumental in changing people's lives by setting up a Transcendental Meditation Center in London, endorsed by The Beatles. And now, that dream had turned to ashes.

George and John were the most affected by what they saw as a betrayal of trust by Maharishi. George had instigated the whole trek to the ashram and both he and John had become totally committed in their devotion to Maharishi and T.M. I wondered if the abrupt ending and our sudden departure from the ashram was because they were still reeling from Brian's death. They'd always had a leader and Maharishi had been quick to assume that role. When he didn't turn out to be who they thought he was, they were left with not only a sense of betrayal but also a feeling of unresolved grief for Brian and the void that his passing had left? Brian had guided them, looked after them and protected them. The Beatles had looked for that, and more, in Maharishi, only to come up empty.

Now for the first time as The Beatles, they were truly on their own. We were all about to go in a new direction.

A journey beyond the muse

CHELSEA

Mother, Paula, Colin, Pattie and me, Kenya, 1953

Me, Paula, Pattie, Colin, Boo, Mother and our uncle, Hurlingham Court, 1962

Colin and me, Kenya, 1953

READY, STEADY, GO!

Rediffusion London invites you to come along and dance in Studio 9, Television House, Kingsway, London, W.C.2. Friday, 26th June, 1964, 6.10—7.00 p.m. Doors will be open from 5.30—5.50 p.m. Age limit 16-24 years. No chewing gum, smoking or autographs in the Studio please.

For conditions see back

R!S!GO

...ket is for dancing only and should be returned if you are not prepared to dance ...out the programme

Above: Ticket for Ready, Steady, Go!, 1964
Left: Modeling a Foale and Tuffin suit, 1964 (photo by John Cole)

STRICTLY FOR THE BOYDS

FUNNY how careers run in the family, isn't it? One girl becomes a hairdresser and before you know it, the whole family is in the business. These three girls are models. Take a closer look at the pic. Recognize the girl on the right? 'Course you do . . . it's top model Pattie Boyd. But do you know the other two? They're Pattie's sisters, Jenny (left) and Paula (middle). And who do you think started modelling first? No, not Pattie. Young Paula, who's fifteen now, began when she was eleven—doing TV commercials. That gave twenty-one year old Pattie (then eighteen) the idea to try her luck and naturally, eighteen year old Jenny followed suit. And who do you think retired first from modelling? That's right, the girl who started it all—Paula. Her final word on modelling: "I haven't got enough clothes for a model's wardrobe— Pattie and Jenny keep theirs padlocked—so I'm dropping out." The other Boyd girls will, we're sure, be busy with the cameras for a long time— unless art school calls them, too!

Above: Sisters, 1965
Right: Modeling, 1966 (photo Roderick Delroy)

Being goofy, 1966

Me, Pattie, Cynthia Lennon, Maureen Starkey modeling for Apple Boutique, with clothes made by The Fool (photo by Ron Traeger)

Photo shoot with Donovan in Cornwall, 1968 (photo by Karl Ferris)

Above: On the banks of the Ganges at the Maharishi Ashram with Richard Blakely

Right: At the Maharishi Ashram, Rishikesh, 1968 (photo by Paul Saltzman)

Below: A letter I sent to my mother while I was in India

With George Harrison, Haight Ashbury, 1967

In Greece with Donovan, Alex, Cynthia, Gypsy Dave, 1968

Me, Mick, and Amelia at Bridge House, 1971 (photo by Sally Fleetwood)

Biddy and Mike on the way to the South of France

Communal living at Benifolds, 1970

Christmas Day at Benifolds, 1972

The sub-culture I'd left behind in San Francisco had taken root in London by the time I returned from India. Young people had grabbed the freedom of this movement; drawn together by the search for meaning. The fundamental ethos was harmony with nature, and the use of recreational drugs. On a collective level taking drugs wasn't just about getting high, drug use at the time was primarily used as a means of expanding one's consciousness and enhancing the search for spiritual awareness. There was a child-like innocence that permeated much of this movement including some of the songs from bands like Traffic, The Who, The Beatles and Donovan.

Many of us were like children; children who didn't want to grow up or had missed out on their own childhood. It was a silent rebellion against conventional life. The class distinction between the traditionally wealthy and ordinary young people had become blurred; in a way, almost unimaginable today. We created our own world.

It was the summer of 1968 when Pattie and I set up a stall selling Art Nouveau and Art Deco. It was a little booth in the ally of the Chelsea Antique Market on the Kings Road and was run by a very glamorous and exotic woman called Ulla Larsen. We called our stall 'Juniper'. Most of our stock came from either Bermondsey market near Tower Bridge, or from 'little old ladies' who had read about our stall in the newspaper. As I was the one who lived in London it was my job to man the stall.

I moved into a house in Blantyre Street just off the Kings Road and walked to work each morning, greeting people I knew along the way. When friends came to visit me at the stall, I pinned a notice on the door saying, 'Upstairs in the café back soon', and off I'd go up the rickety stairs to the Antique Market café. This was the place where all the young Chelsea people hung out and where I met Alice Ormsby Gore who was to become one of my best friends.

Our friend and author John Michell often sat at a small table drinking coffee and chatting to people about Ley lines, the alignments of landmarks and ancient sites, or about U.F.O.'s. He inspired us all with his discussions on mystic links and druid monuments and was in the process of writing a book called View over Atlantis which influenced many people in the hippie movement, having already written one about U.F.O.'s. He embraced the counter-cultural ideas in his gentle way and was a key figure in representing the philosophy of our generation.

Mick Jagger came to visit me a couple of times, having just come from 'Granny Takes a Trip', Nigel Waymouth's radical shop nearby or Michael Rainy's men's boutique, 'Hung On You'. Both shops were part of the 'Swinging' fashion scene and were filled with celebs and Rock 'n' Rollers.

I never knew quite what to say to Mick as he sat close to me in this tiny little booth, which was the sort of place you'd go to have your fortune told. His presence always made me feel nervous so I would point out one of our latest purchases, just to make conversation, but he would just laugh and tell me what he always told me, "I can see you're growing up," and then he'd leave. On another visit he told me he'd written a song about me. It was sort of about me but not, he said. I never asked what it was called and later wondered which of their many songs it could have been! Occasionally I still wonder...

Opposite our stall, and along the passageway was one of my favorite places to browse. A very sweet man called Robin, a collector of illustrated children's books, owned this stall. He had first and second editions of old fairy books, illustrated by Arthur Rackham. I spent hours in here, my love of fairy tales enhanced by these beautiful illustrations, wondering whether I would have children, someday and if so, imagining myself reading these books to them.

A letter from Mick Fleetwood, addressed to me care of the Antique Market arrived one day. Fleetwood Mac were on their first tour of the States after the great success of their single, Albatross, which went to number one in the British charts. The band was getting its deserved recognition, and they found, to their surprise, a much larger following than they'd expected. Doors were now beginning to open up for Mick. He loved playing with Peter Green who, he said, "just oozed with feeling," and although he felt he would never be a great drummer himself, he knew with absolute certainty that he had the ability to appreciate music. In this letter he asked me to marry him which took me by surprise. The thought of marriage had never occurred to me. I had not seen him since before I went to India and we lived in such different worlds. Although I felt moved and flattered by this proposal, I feared it had arrived too late. I was too immersed in my own world of friends and like-minded seekers.

"Have you read The Hobbit?"

I was sitting in the audience at The Royal Albert Hall, waiting for Eric Clapton's band, Cream, to come on stage. It was to be their final concert, a significant occasion and one that brought with it, as well as the excitement of hearing them play, a touch of sadness. The question came from Nigel Waymouth, a frizzy haired young man wearing wire-framed glasses who was sitting in the seat behind me. I'd bumped into him earlier in the week at the Baghdad House on Fulham Road. Friends had taken over the downstairs restaurant, and a hookah pipe with hashish in it was passed around the table, compliments of the manager. Nigel stayed at the Pheasantry, a large studio on the Kings Road where Eric Clapton and his girlfriend Charlotte had lived. This studio flat belonged to an Australian artist called Martin Sharp who worked on graphics for the monthly Oz magazine. There was always a buzz in the studio; it felt like the epicentre of creativity, these artists represented the voice of our time both visually and verbally.

Nigel was also a graphic artist, and along with Michael English, made psychedelic posters swirling with bright acid colors for clubs and albums. He had opened 'Granny Takes a Trip,' a couple of years previously, the first boutique to sell unisex clothes. Flowered jackets, richly embroidered shirts, velvet trousers, silk scarves and romantic apparel lined the rails of his shop. He was one of the many people along Kings Road we would often drop in on for a cup of tea.

On one of my visits to the Pheasantry, Pattie came with me and brought with her an acetate of The Beatles *White Album*. They had just finished recording and the album was about to be released. It was as if she were holding a golden nugget when she handed over the disc. We all listened intently while drinking tea and savoring every new track. Many of the songs took me back to Rishikesh, sitting on the roof of our bungalow under the warm sun, listening to John, George and Paul strumming their guitars.

I had become part of an ever-expanding group of kindred spirits, which now included kids of the aristocracy - they and the rock and roll world had merged, turning the class system upside down. Another person in the forefront of this new world was Mark Palmer, a British baronet who formed an exciting and different kind of modeling agency with my long-time friend Kelvin Webb. They called it English Boys.

The idea was born as they sat in the Picasso, a well-known coffee shop on the Kings Road, where we all hung out. It was different from the conventional modeling agencies. These models were all friends, part of this sub-culture and many of them in need of earning a living. Their office was above the Quorum shop owned by fashion designers Ossie Clark and Alice Pollack. It was also where Mark lived, and it became the center of all the hip and exciting things happening at the time.

Once the agency was up and running Mark adopted an alternative lifestyle and became the first of our group to leave London, buying a horse and an old gypsy caravan and roaming the English countryside. He was very much a pre-cursor to the modern-day New Age Traveller. It became quite common to ask who was visiting on a certain weekend, as more and more people bought a horse and joined him.

Being in the countryside became more fashionable and many of the people we knew began spending time in North Wales, though always with one toe in Chelsea. Often a whole crowd of us met up at Glyn, the Harlech's family seat in Wales. David Ormsby Gore, 5th Baron Harlech, had been the British Ambassador to the United States and was very welcoming to all his children's friends, turning a blind eye to the pot smoking that went on late in the evenings, while listening to music and talking with friends. I saw a lot of them while we were in London, Jane who was married to Michael Rainy, Victoria and her boyfriend Julian Lloyd and, especially Alice who was a couple of years younger than me.

Alice and I were inseparable. We saw each other in London, spent time in Wales at her father's home and at a house nearby called Plas Llandechwyn belonging to a friend of hers called Martin. He was tall with dark frizzy hair and knew everyone who was part of our 'scene'. He was clever, determined, and after a short while had decided he wanted to get closer to me. I was not so clever and couldn't see what was happening before it was too late. Lots of our close friends came to stay at his house in North Wales and as soon as I arrived at this old farmhouse it felt familiar, as if I'd been there before. There was no heating or running water, and meals of brown rice and vegetables were cooked over the open fire in the main room. Brightly colored rugs covered the stone floor and music was played at all times. Bob Dylan's new album, *Nashville Skyline* became our bible. It was a gentle place to be, a return to nature, and embracing the simple life. Gradually Martin and I became a couple, hanging out together in London for a while before he asked me to leave the city and live with him in Wales. I never felt a particular attraction towards Martin but because he was part of the group - and now we no longer had the stall to keep me in London - I went along with it.

At times it was as if we had created our own world with our own rules, as if we weren't part of the conventional way of life. I became aware of this on one of my visits, as I was driving back one night from one of the market towns in Martin's Land Rover (without a license or insurance). There were three or four stoned, slumped bodies in the back of the car, and Martin was sitting next to me on the front seat. It was past midnight, the streets were empty, and I'd been at the traffic light for what seemed like ages when I decided to simply drive on. No sooner had we passed the lights, than I was alerted to a flashing light in my rearview mirror. We blanched. The fear that ran through everyone's veins was the hash we had on us, and the possibility of getting busted. Everyone at the back instantly sat up and while I was waiting for the policeman to poke his head through the open window, I struggled to pull the gold ring off my right middle finger and swap it to the left. Quick as a flash, I had my story ready. When the policeman asked me to hand over my driving license, I gave my name as Pattie Harrison and her address in Surrey. He let us go, telling me to produce my driving license with identification at the local Police station in Esher within the next few days. It was a close, and lucky, escape. Of course, Pattie was not amused, but even so she gave me her license, and a photograph and because we both had long blond hair, I got away with it.

The day came for me to move out of Alice's house in London, where I'd been staying for the last few weeks, and embrace the rural life. We loaded up Martin's Land Rover with my few possessions, including the sitar George had given me. Nigel Waymouth and our friend Alexis de la Falaise were going to meet us there. Ever since I first met Alexis, I had a huge crush on him; he was beautiful, a gentle soul, and I felt as though the feeling was mutual. Unfortunately, we were both so horribly shy with each other that it never went any further, instead we stayed together within the comfort of the group but talked about it many years later and laughed at ourselves.

Just as we were about to leave, Mick Fleetwood's blue Alvis drew up alongside the curb. He knew I'd been staying with Alice in London since Pattie and I closed the stall and somehow found her house. I was so pleased to see his familiar face and would have jumped in beside him if he'd come ten minutes earlier, but now, much to my disappointment, I felt my fate was sealed. I had relented to Martin's insistence that I leave London and live with him. Mick had just come back from his tour of the States and told me he'd see us in Wales once he had some time off.

Snow was falling as we drove up the hill to Martin's home. There wasn't another house in sight, just sloping fields covered in snow, and woolly sheep huddled together. More friends arrived that evening, including Nigel and Alexis, so after supper we all went for a walk across the fields to what was known as the witch's pool. It was a clear night and the moon was full, lighting up the wintery landscape. After about forty minutes of clambering over ditches and hedgerows we gazed down into a dark and murky-looking pool with the moon shimmering on its surface.

"Why is it called the witch's pool?" I asked.

"A witch was rolled down in a barrel and drowned," Martin said.

"When?" someone else asked.

"The locals say it was about a hundred years ago."

I shivered, unable to get the picture of a barrel rolling down into the dark, dank pool out of my mind.

The following day I went for a walk with one of the dogs, compelled towards the direction of the pool, but I soon got frightened and turned away.

That night as I lay in bed before drifting off to sleep, I thought of the pool, deep and dark, lying silently nestled in the mountains. At some point during the night I woke up to the sound of someone calling my name.

"Jenny, Jenny," the voice whispered.

"Yes, who is it?" I asked, half asleep.

"It's Betty."

The night was black. I sat bolt upright, goose bumps all over my body, my heart pounding. I knew who it was.

The next day I walked to a cottage further down the hill where Mrs. Williams, who'd lived in Wales all her life, would be able to tell me about the folklore around these parts.

"What was the name of the witch who was rolled down the hill in a barrel?" I asked as I sat at her table, hands clasped around a mug of tea.

The old woman jerked her head up. I could feel goose bumps creeping down my arms again. I knew the answer and half dreaded hearing it.

"Her name was Betty," said Mrs. Williams. "You've heard her, have you?"

When I returned to the house the soulful voice of Bessie Smith singing the blues came through the speakers. A fire had been lit and someone was standing over a saucepan of brown rice, which was jammed up against the burning logs. This is basic living, I thought, as I was handed a large pan to fill with drinking water. I put on my boots, grabbed the torch and walked through the snow to the well. I looked up at the millions of stars shining in the clear night sky. Part of me loved being in Wales; it seemed so old and mysterious, but in my heart I didn't feel I belonged there. I filled the pan and stood out in the cold a few minutes longer, my mind drifting back to Mick and how by coincidence, he'd arrived just in time to see me off. Had he arrived ten minutes later I would have missed him, and he would never have known where I was living.

As the cold winter days drifted by it became harder to get out of bed in the mornings. I would lie there as long as I could, listening to everyone clattering around in the room downstairs, making porridge and getting ready for the day. I hated having to wash the dishes in the stream, my hands blue with cold, but this was nothing compared to my dislike of having to find a bush to hide behind every time I wanted to go to the loo, day or night. It was cold up in the mountains and the only warm place was in front of the fire.

Martin was always up at the crack of dawn and he could tell I was becoming despondent, not as involved in the communal living as he was. I knew my thoughts about Mick were beginning to get in the way.

I can't remember how long I stayed at that house in Wales, but one day while emptying the compost bucket I looked down into the valley and noticed a blue speck winding its way up the hill towards the house. I put the bucket down and followed the car with my eyes, my heart soaring. I waved when I saw Mick. He stopped in front of the house and opened the car door.

"Mick! You made it!"

He got out of the car, his long Afghan coat almost touching the ground as he walked towards me and gave me a hug. "I didn't think you'd come," I said, showing him to the door.

"Of course I would," he said, smiling. "Martin gave me directions when I last saw you."

Mick walked into the room and shook hands with Martin and was introduced to everyone. He looked very different from my hippie friends, very smart, as if he had walked straight out of Dr. Zhivago.

Mick's visit to this hippie environment made me wonder what I was doing there, and how I'd managed to get myself into this position. I'd felt rather bamboozled into the relationship with Martin and didn't feel I had the guts to stop it going further.

Once Mick had checked out the scene, he picked up a small knife and joined in with the wood carvers. I'd seen a beautiful angelic figure being carved earlier by one of my friends, and now watched as one of the boys whittled a flute. I walked over to Mick, curious to see what he was carving and flushed with embarrassment when I realized he was carving a dildo for the gearstick of his car. It seemed so base and sacrilegious; I tried not to laugh.

The following morning Mick and I drove to the nearest town for breakfast. I breathed in the smell of worn leather seats as I sat in the Alvis, happy to be driving away from the cottage and listened contentedly as he talked about Fleetwood Mac's American tour and his enormous respect for Peter Green, as a friend and musician. Once happily ensconced in a little café we started chatting.

"Are you happy?" he asked, looking into my eyes. "Is this what you want?"

Tears welled up. "I'm not sure what I'm doing really," I said. "I love Wales, but I don't love Martin. He takes the hippie thing a bit too far."

Mick smiled. He reached across the table and held my hand. "It's beautiful here, I get it, but it's fucking freezing." We both laughed. "Having to go outside to take a shit at night, what does that prove? To pump the well to get water?"

Once we'd stopped giggling, he asked if I'd received his letter. I nodded.

Although Mick and I had stayed in contact over the last couple of years, this time was different. He seemed more confident within himself and I believed America had been good for him. An underlying part of me had often played with the idea of us getting back together, he felt safe and familiar, but the adventurous side of me needed to step out and experience life alone, away from the safety net that he represented. Occasionally though, I would lose my way and the adventurous side would become deeply disillusioned by life or people, and at these times, when the world felt big and scary, I wanted to be with Mick.

When I got back to the cottage and Mick had left for London, I told Martin I no longer wanted to live at Plas or be with him. I don't remember much of a reaction, and so a few days later, with Nigel's help I took the train with my few possessions down to Devon to stay with my mother. I needed time to think. It was while I was there sitting in an armchair, reading in the room that overlooks the garden, that my mother opened the door and said, "Martin's here to see you," and then disappeared. I stood up, walked towards the door and there was Martin, with his frizzy hair and pale face. Our eyes met as we stood facing each other and then without saying a word, he slapped me hard across the face.

I stared at him in shock, my face burning, stinging like tiny pin pricks where his hand had been, making my eyes water. Only once had I ever been slapped across the face before and that was by my mother when I was a teenager. No boyfriend had ever slapped me, except for this man, this self-proclaimed hippie who was living the gentle life with a bubbling fury beyond words; only he had struck me. I didn't move. All I could think of saying was, "I hope you feel better now."

I arranged to meet Mick a few days later in a restaurant called Alristora, just opposite his brother-in-law's Art Nouveau shop in Kensington Church Street. As we sat facing each other in this noisy, buzzy restaurant, before we'd even ordered, I looked into his eyes and smiled.

"I accept your offer, Mick," I said, my stomach churning, my body shaking and my eyes watering. "I want to be with you." As I spoke these words I felt as though I'd finally come home. The relief was all encompassing, knowing that this was the man I wanted to spend my life with.

Mick held my hand, tears in his eyes, and nodded.

After lunch we took a taxi to Shepherd's Bush where he was meeting the other members in the band, ready to make their way to wherever they were playing over the next few nights. As we kissed each other goodbye we both knew our journey together had begun. Once he returned, we stayed with his sister and brother-in-law in Notting Hill Gate until we found our own flat on Kensington Church Street.

BENIFOLDS

Mick and I were still only twenty-one and after spending a few weeks with Sally and John, having seen each other sporadically during the last two years and never having lived together before, we were about to cement our relationship. We held onto our attraction for each other and with very little thought or time to prepare for the change, we jumped into the deep end!

After finding a two-bedroom flat Mick told me his musician friend would be sharing it with us. Andy was a bass player in the five-piece Blues band, Chicken Shack, which had Christine McVie as their singer and keyboard player. Having just left the communal way of life, I'd hoped that initially we would find our own place. But true to form, Mick knew if you split the rent you get more for your money.

Andy was from Manchester and had previously shared a flat with Mick in London. They'd developed a lot of similar mannerisms and sayings, and wore almost identical clothes; blue jeans, tee shirts from the Chelsea Antique Market, Converse sneakers, and woolen waistcoats from Norway. He was slim, with straight brown hair and a face that hadn't seen much daylight. Like Mick, he was gentle, but always seemed to appear self-conscious when we spoke.

The two of them often stayed up into the small hours, sitting together on the floor, a pair of headphones clamped to their ears listening to soul music. They would nod and smile at each other, as yet another drum break or riveting bass line sent them into raptures, arms flailing as they mimicked the instrument. The next morning, I would be greeted by a scattering of album covers across the carpet. Music was their world; it was how they connected with each other, easier for them than speaking. It reminded me of being in India with the Beatles, that same feeling of being on the outside, looking in. At times, I wondered what I was doing there.

Once we'd settled in, Mick immediately set to work on soundproofing the little attic room upstairs where he kept his drum kit. I would hear him practicing day after day on a part he was to play on Peter Green's song, *Oh Well* and there was one small bit, just five beats, he was having a lot of trouble with. He'd thought about it for too long, and because he was naturally an instinctive player, it threw him every time.

Our new home was sparsely furnished in the sitting room, apart from the stereo system, a deckchair, a mirror above the fireplace, and then later a long pine table, it was bare. The lack of money, plus the fact I was not a natural homemaker, resulted in a flat where when friends came over, they'd either sit on the carpet in the main room, or around the small table in the kitchen.

One of our visitors was a very different-looking Peter Green. Gone were his mutton chop sideburns, boyish mod haircut, and scruffy jeans. In their place was a wiser looking man with long, curly, black hair and wearing red velvet trousers. He carried himself with more confidence, with an air of dignity and refinement. I was pleased to see him, having not seen him for a couple of years.

One evening, Mick and I met up with Peter and his girlfriend for dinner. Sandra was a model, tall and slim with long, thick blond hair. I was to hear later that she'd harbored a grudge against me for years, ever since I'd walked off with the modeling job in Rome. She had spent a lot of money learning to be a professional catwalk model, and here I was, not even as tall as her, dancing my way through many jobs she felt should rightfully have been hers. That evening she was a little cool towards me, although later we were to become lifelong friends.

A few days later, I received a phone call from Peter, asking if I would meet him outside our flat. He was in a cab on his way to their manager's office and didn't have time to stop. I think he felt safer with me outside our apartment; there were a lot of unspoken rules about guys not getting too friendly with the girlfriends of their fellow band members. The taxi arrived and I ran downstairs. As soon as I jumped into the cab he asked,

"Can you tell me all about your spiritual beliefs? How did you get into it?"

I was stunned. I had from Notting Hill Gate to Marble Arch in which to describe the most important aspect in my life, and yet he spent most of that time telling me he could feel himself changing, that he'd become aware of a more spiritual side of himself, and needed to know what I'd experienced. I tried to put into a nutshell what I'd gone through over the last couple of years, including my trip to India, but unfortunately the cab ride wasn't long enough, and Peter never asked again. I knew he wouldn't mention it to the other members of the band.

Once Mick and I began living together it dawned on me how much we'd both changed over the last couple of years. Marit Allen had offered me a job as an assistant for *Vogue Magazine*, but Mick wouldn't hear of it. He wanted me at home and available to join him on tour at a moment's notice. I complied, it was a man's world at that time, even in the rock and roll community; but in doing so, I sacrificed a part of myself.

Occasionally in the evenings while Mick and Andy were on tour, I would listen to music, write poems and draw. At these times I felt peaceful and content, but at other times I felt frustrated and restless, with no direction in which to channel my energy. Sometimes, the overwhelming desire to get involved with something meaningful would haunt me. Had I sacrificed a core part of myself for the security of being with someone who felt familiar, whom I loved and believed loved me? I had known Mick and his family for so long, he represented a part of me that needed to feel emotionally safe and more grounded, but I wondered sometimes, still not able to gauge his feelings, whether the 'Jenny' he loved was the 'Jenny' he'd spent the last couple of years building a fantasy around. But the 'Jenny' he loved had changed and was now in the flux of transitioning from her world into his. That said, there were two people in my life now who were to have a huge impact on me, and those were Mick's parents.

I had met his mother, Biddy, a couple of years earlier, when Mick and I were first going out together. I had bumped into her standing next to Mick's then pregnant sister, Sally, as I jumped off a bus in Notting Hill Gate. She was tall and chic with blue eyes, sun- tanned complexion and her silver hair tied back in a ponytail with a black ribbon. I warmed to her immediately. When Mick and I resumed our relationship, we saw a lot of Biddy and Mick's father, Mike. They were a handsome couple, joyful, always laughing at the silliest things. They lived in Salisbury but made frequent visits to London visiting their children and their first grandson and so they became the parents I had longed for.

Fleetwood Mac were often touring around the UK or Europe and Mick would be away for a few days at a time or at most a couple of weeks. Now the call to America was getting louder and their tours longer and more frequent. Sometimes I would leave with Mick and other times I would meet him out on the road.

While Mick was away, I saw a lot of my sister Paula and her musician boyfriend. They looked like twins, both with the same short hairstyle and mischievous smiles. One evening Paula and I went with some friends to see Delaney and Bonnie play at the Albert Hall. They were a husband and wife duo from the States and were known to have a red-hot band. We sat for all of two seconds. The rest of the time we spent standing or dancing. It was riveting. Bonnie was slim, tall, with short blond hair, and a husky Southern voice that was pure dynamite. Delaney held a big acoustic guitar in front of his chunky body, and together, their harmonies were thrilling, heightened by the excitement generated by the band. Later that night, we all went to the Speakeasy, our favorite club at that time. It was a small, intimate club that always had good bands, but mostly, I went because the music they played was the best for dancing. Much to my delight Delaney and Bonnie were there, playing again, but this time with Eric Clapton on guitar. We sat at a table close to the small stage area, and just as before, they belted out their songs; the atmosphere in the club that night was electric!

One evening in December 1969, Mick called me from Michigan - something that took up to a couple of hours once the operator had connected the call - and asked if I would join him on the road. I had toured with the band a couple of months earlier in the States, but now we were in the dead of winter where the air in that part of the country was so cold it hurt to breathe. Fortunately, the band was scheduled to play on the West Coast early in the New Year where we could thaw out!

While we were on tour Mick and I took the opportunity of buying some Levi jeans, something you couldn't get at that time in England. And because they never had my size, I would buy the smallest pair, go back to the hotel, put them on and sit in a hot bath so they would shrink. It worked a treat. The only way I could get them on once they'd dried a couple of sizes smaller, was to lie flat on the bed which enabled me to do up the zip. Levi Jeans was my road uniform, Levi's, a sweater and my snakeskin cowboy boots. Mick had a different challenge to mine when buying jeans. Because he was so tall and skinny, and had such long legs, he had to buy the largest size available and once back in England I would alter them with my sewing machine. Because this was such a long and laborious task, when they were worn out at the knee or the bottom, which they inevitably did, I would sew on patches I'd embroidered, turning them into 'works of art'. I once knitted him a scarf for the winter tour and since I didn't know how to cast off, it wound around his neck a couple of times, before reaching the ground on both sides. The effect added to Mick's love of the absurd.

At the end of January, the band was scheduled to perform a couple of shows at The Warehouse, a huge old barn that had recently been converted into the first concert hall in New Orleans, with the Grateful Dead headlining. Both bands had met previously during Fleetwood Mac's first tour of the States, and they had also met their soundman, Owsley, known as the great LSD wizard.

The backstage hospitality room was up a flight of rickety wooden stairs, above the stage. On the second night, tables were laid with the usual unappetizing cold meat cuts and sticks of carrot and celery, bottles of coke and jugs of beer were shoved into a dustbin filled with ice. The road crew scurried around organizing the sound check, and I could hear Peter on the microphone downstairs singing to an empty barn. Eventually they all made their way upstairs, and we tucked into the food and drinks.

Just before the show started, I began to feel a little strange and decided to move around and watch the crowd as they milled into the hall. As I walked down the stairs Danny Kirwan, Fleetwood Mac's young guitarist, bumped into me.

"Oh my God! Owsley spiked all our drinks," he said, his boyish smile lighting up his eyes. "I don't think I can go on. I can't play my guitar."

He always looked like a schoolboy, nervous and jittery, but now he seemed worse than ever, looking at me and laughing nervously. As we gazed at the audience wandering into the hall and walking towards the stage, I noticed their eyes were glistening with bits of straw hanging from their mouths. I shook my head. The acid was getting stronger.

"You can do it," I said to Danny, as he grabbed the bannister and leapt up the stairs.

As soon as they started playing, I made my way to the side of the stage. Peter was hitting two sticks in time to the music as he sang into the microphone. I could tell he was having the same trouble as Danny but eventually he reached for his guitar and the show continued as close to normal as possible. The Grateful Dead were well known for playing all their gigs while high on acid, and Owsley always accompanied them, handing out the magic pills. I watched in horror as Mick turned into a skeleton while playing his drums and had to look away.

The next thing I knew the show had finished, the hall was bare, and Mick, John McVie, Danny and I were wandering around this empty space high as kites until Mick told me he'd found someone to drive us back to the motel. As we sat in the back of the car, I noticed our driver was steering the wheel with his knees, his head down while rolling a joint.

"This guy's out of it," I whispered, giving Mick a nudge.

"Good job we're not," he said with a grin, and then stretched both his arms either side of the driver's head, grabbed the wheel and steered the car through deserted streets and over disused railway tracks until we somehow found the motel.

Later, with the rest of the band in one of the bedrooms, the effects of the drug still lingering, we all sat around deep in conversation. This was a rare occasion as far as I could tell, since they were usually on their guard against Jeremy Spencer, their slide guitarist with a cutting wit. As I sat listening to all of them that night, I had the distinct impression that musicians were like modern day disciples. Everyone understood the language of music and it brought people together. I tried to explain this to them, but my words wandered around the room, and settled somewhere else. I wondered if Peter had sensed something of the same nature that night, because it wasn't long afterwards that he began wearing robes, growing a beard, and resembling a figure from The Bible.

The next day we heard the Grateful Dead had been busted at their hotel. The police were after Owsley, so they arrested them all. This bust turned into the inspiration for one of their biggest albums, Working Man's Dead.

Fleetwood Mac's two-and-a half-month tour continued, driving across America either in the equipment truck, or all together squashed in a car. One morning Mick and I were woken up to the sound of Peter knocking on our door. He was very excited, and while sitting on our bed, began telling us of his idea to give up our homes and tour around the world like gypsies. "We could give our money away to charities," he said. "We could dedicate our lives to a cause." He looked inspired, the intensity of his dark eyes shining as he delivered his message, trying to convince us that this was the way it should be. I loved Peter's enthusiasm and the idea sounded wonderful to my adventurous spirit, I wanted to be part of a greater cause, and for a split-second Mick was almost convinced. Peter's faith was strong; he believed we'd be taken care of and would want for nothing. We all walked into the manager's room, where we found him lying on his bed with an ice pack on his head. He'd already heard Peter's latest idea and was suffering from a pounding headache. He didn't know what to say.

Once we were back in London, I could see Peter was going through a profound change. The band was becoming successful with two hit singles in the last year, featuring his haunting and disturbing lyrics, but he was searching for something more meaningful than endlessly touring and singing the same songs over and over again. I had become friends with Sandra, his girlfriend, who, at Peter's request, made the long velvet robes he now wore on stage.

As Peter's dream got squashed, he seemed to retreat within himself. He was at the height of his creativity, but it was no longer enough for him to keep doing the circuit for fame, money and material possessions. He needed more. From here on he lost purpose and direction and no longer wanted to be in Fleetwood Mac.

'The Green Manalishi with the two-pronged horn', the lyrics to one of his songs, described to the world the turmoil that plagued him.

Although Mick had asked me to marry him a year earlier, it was never discussed again. I didn't mention it either as I waited for him to make the next move. But with their determined effort to conquer America came the old belief, encouraged by their manager, that band members who were single gave a much cooler, hipper image to the group than those who were married. Much to my horror, my mother began writing letters, asking me when the marriage was going to take place, believing we were living in sin. Mick saw these letters, which made me curl up with embarrassment.

Almost a year after Mick and I had started living together, my doctor told me I was expecting a baby. Suddenly things speeded up. With our excitement at the news, and plans to get married, came an overwhelming fear. One night, as Mick was painting the walls of our bathroom, I began crying, pleading with Mick, "Let's never get divorced." He held me in his arms and promised we'd always stay together.

When Peter had told them he was leaving the band, Fleetwood Mac almost fell apart. He'd been hanging out with some hippies in Germany and had taken more acid trips than he could handle. Mick was very upset since Peter had not only been his dearest friend, but also his mentor. Still, he was determined that Fleetwood Mac would continue, even, if necessary, without Peter.

At Mick's suggestion we all gave up our London homes and rented a house in Hampshire, called Kiln House. It was in the heart of the English countryside, and from there, Mick, John, Danny and Jeremy practiced for their up-coming tour and a new album called Kiln House. Without the strength of their previous leader they looked a sorry sight, and so Mick took over. This was the first time I was to witness Mick's tenacity and powers of persuasion. One night, after everyone had finally decided they wanted to leave the band, I watched Mick walk up and down the length of the dining room for four hours, listing countless reasons why they should stick together. With skill and steely determination, he managed to bring each of his flock back into line and by the end of the evening the band was committed to carrying on without Peter.

Kiln House consisted of a long narrow room upstairs, with a very basic kitchen down one end, a long thin table in the middle, and a couple of sofas down the other end. It had once been two oast houses that were now joined together, with bedrooms leading off either end of the sitting room and down the stairs. Three stairs up from the sitting room was a large converted barn, where the group practiced. Danny's voice could be heard singing along with the music, no words, just 'La la la'. Their main songwriter had gone, and so it was up to Danny to come up with new material. John's wife, Chris, and I sat down one day, I was four months pregnant by then, and wrote the words to a song we called *Jewel Eyed Judy*. It became one of the songs on the Kiln House album.

Mick and I got married on the 20th June 1970. On the morning of our wedding, the usual sight of people sitting round the table and rolling joints greeted me. Since being pregnant and feeling sick at times, I no longer indulged in any kind of mind-altering substances. I hadn't smoked since leaving Wales and was quite content to keep it that way. At mid-day we all piled into the local registry office, the band, a couple of roadies, and Mick's and my family. Once everyone was seated in one of the little rooms, I noticed that Mick had disappeared. I watched as the registrar began getting fidgety.

"I've got more people to marry after you," he said, looking rather hot and flustered. I peered through the window out into the garden, and there to my amusement was a stoned Mick slowly wandering around the grounds, his hands behind his back, looking as if he had not a care in the world. I watched him staring at the trees, and the sky, until he was shaken out of his reverie by a sharp tap on the window from the irritated registrar and signaled to come in immediately.

We had our reception at Kiln House. The day was sunny, and everyone sat on the grass, or on the steps leading from the house to the garden, drinking wine and eating sandwiches. Peter arrived, looking distant and strange. He was meant to have been best man but didn't show up and later told Mick he didn't believe in marriage anyway. It dawned on me then why Mick had been holding up the ceremony. He might not have been able to coax Peter back into the band, but he still wanted his old friend to be his best man. At the other end of the room, I saw my mother talking to Mick's parents, and a couple of his aged aunts.

As I walked past, I overheard her say, "I know who's going to win the election, I saw an image of his face as I was rolling out my pastry." I looked round to see bemused faces, waiting to hear her prediction.

"Ted Heath," she said, to roars of laughter. Mick's father, Mike, loved my mum even though they rarely met, but there was something about her giddiness he found charming ... and Ted Heath did win the election!

Just before the band left for America, Mick and I began looking for a house to buy. He came across a large secluded Victorian mansion in Hampshire, a few miles from Kiln house, called Benifolds. It had been used as a spiritual retreat for all denominations and belonged to the church. The grounds consisted of seven acres of forest and a dilapidated grass tennis court surrounded by trees. Foremost in Mick's mind was the importance of the rather fragile band staying together during this transitional time and so he proposed that John, Jeremy and he should all chip in and buy it.

And so, my dream of Mick and I buying our own little cottage in the country flew out the window. I wanted to start our family life in our own home, not as a commune. As it turned out, it did keep the band united, but not us as a couple. The band went off to the States, adding Christine McVie at the last minute, and because there was nowhere else for me to go, I went down to Devon to live with my mother for the next three months.

When I arrived, my sister Paula was staying with my mother, having just come back from Switzerland, where she'd spent three months working as an au pair. I was pleased to see her, having not heard a word from her since receiving a letter while I was on tour, saying she was going out and living with Eric Clapton. I was distressed to hear her news, and that at the tender age of nineteen, she felt as though her heart was broken. With sadness she told me about her tumultuous love affair with Eric, and how going to Switzerland had been her attempt at getting over him.

In the winter of 1970, when I was seven months pregnant, we all moved into Benifolds; Mick and I, John and Chris, Jeremy, his wife Fiona and their two small children. Danny and his girlfriend lived there during rehearsals and recording, while the road crew crashed out on any beds they could find on the third floor. We divided the house into three parts, Mick and I had one side of the sweeping staircase and the downstairs scullery which we turned into a kitchen, Chris and John had rooms on the other side of the house, separated by a swing door, and Jeremy and his family lived on part of the third floor and used the main kitchen downstairs. There was also a large music room on the ground floor, where the band rehearsed, plus a big room with windows on all sides that housed a full-size billiard table.

I felt rather self-conscious with John and Chris, who seemed very grown up as a couple. Chris would make delicious meals in her little kitchen, and John was always there with her, creating a warm and welcoming atmosphere. Chris was definitely like one of the boys. She had done her fair share of being driven up and down the motorways in a transit van, at all times of night, but she never complained. I don't think she felt she had much in common with me. I was very shy, very pregnant, and later spent most of my time looking after babies and young children on the other side of the house. John reminded me of a cowboy, there was always something rather 'West Coast' about him, in his faded jeans, shirt and leather waistcoat.

Jeremy Spencer was a little minx, always looking for trouble and someone to wind up. He had a lethal tongue, a cutting wit, and was a terrifying mimic. And yet at the same time, he looked like the most angelic little person, with his black curly hair, big brown eyes and round face. He played slide guitar and impersonated Elmore James and other blues singers. He and his wife were both small and had two little children. As for Danny, he was a bundle of nerves, much younger than everyone else, and seemed to be completely in his own anxiety-ridden world. He played his guitar beautifully, and came up with some sweet-sounding melodies, but he struggled with lyrics. I often heard him in the music room playing his guitar and still singing 'La, la, la la' desperate for some words. Since they needed lyrics for their songs, I volunteered some of my poems. Danny chose *The Purple Dancer* and recorded it on the 'B' side of one of their singles. I felt honored on one hand, but although I never mentioned it, disappointed that I hadn't been credited as the co-writer for that song or *Jewel Eyed Judy*. Their manager put them both under Mick's name.

In the second week of January 1971, the band was touring in Scotland when Mick got a call from the hospital to tell him I had gone into labor and things were not going well. He was told that both my life and the baby's were in danger and he should come down to Basingstoke immediately. I remember lying on a bed in an operating room after being in labor for what felt like days, holding the hands of two doctors either side of me, and feeling decidedly relaxed and misty. My mother appeared as if from nowhere, a worried, anxious look on her face. I felt so peaceful and couldn't understand what she was doing there.

"You'll be all right, don't worry," she said, her face full of fear.

I smiled at her, as if in a dream, while they ushered her out of the door. Out in the waiting room, she told Pattie and Paula to go home and forget the flowers. Soon afterwards, the doctors did an emergency caesarean, which was something quite rare in those days.

By the time Mick arrived, in the early hours of 17th January, our daughter was in intensive care. I woke to see him sitting beside my mother.

"We've got a little girl," he said. I smiled, a wave of relief sweeping over me, knowing the ordeal was over and he was nearby. When I woke up again the following day, I was in a different bed

"Time to try and walk," came the firm voice of one of the nurses. I slowly got out of bed and shuffled over to the intensive care room where my daughter, Amelia, lay in a see-through plastic cot. I took one look and felt at once that I knew her. I had to stop myself from saying "Oh it's you!"

A couple of weeks after Amelia and I came home, Mick went off to the States with the band for a three-month tour. He had painted our bedroom and placed the crib beside the wall, ready for its new occupant. I was very sad to see him leave we hadn't spent enough time together with our baby, but not long afterwards Mick's mother, Biddy, came to stay for a couple of weeks. I was very grateful for her support and companionship although I spent most of my time feeding and changing and hand-washing nappies for the baby.

Jeremy's wife, Fiona, and their children had also stayed behind, and together we lived in this huge, cold, draughty house, with heat and hot water supplied by an old boiler that was forever breaking down. Fiona was quietly spoken, and like Jeremy, came from the north of England. They were both religious, which always amazed me when I listened to Jeremy tell his crude phallic jokes. I'd heard she'd sewn a bible into the lining of his duffel coat before he went on tour. And so it was not too surprising when I got the phone call from an anxious Mick that Jeremy was missing. He'd gone off to browse round a bookstore in Hollywood before their show that night at The Whisky a Go Go and had never returned. After four days of searching with the club owner, people from Warner Brothers, employees from the British Consulate, the band manager, two roadies and the police they found him in a house run by a religious cult, the Children of God. He had left the band. Fortunately, Peter agreed to join them after a desperate call from Mick, and to take Jeremy's place, but only until the end of the tour.

Fiona's reaction was very cool. She was not at all surprised. Not for a second did she give the impression that she would be left behind, even though Jeremy, when asked about his wife and children, had said, "God will look after them." She continued as normal, looking after her children, chatting with me, while calmly waiting for her husband's call. He called, as she knew he would, a few days later and asked her to come over with the children and join him and the Children of God. Once she'd left Benifolds I continued for another eight weeks, rattling around in the draughty mansion, scared of every sound that emanated from the groaning pipes.

A pattern began to emerge. When Mick was on tour with the rest of the band, I felt lonely and frightened knowing there was only the baby and me in this big old house. Gradually it became a way of life, albeit a lonely one, and I carved out an existence of normality and routine. When Mick came home, usually after three months, and the house filled up with the band and road crew, my space, as large as it was, felt encroached upon. They had all returned from a different world, one that was. secluded and protected from reality, getting through the three months however best they could. Through one kind of trauma or another they would become even more tightly knit, having each other's shoulders to cry on or to rally round; just the kind of bond I longed for. If one strayed from the straight and narrow, the rest of the band would say nothing to the spouse or girlfriend at home. So, when they returned it was always a 'them against me' feeling, with no idea what world they'd inhabited for the past three months.

This feeling of being isolated from Mick was compounded by him spending most of his time, when he was home, in John and Chris's kitchen talking band-talk, while I quietly stayed on our side of the house with a baby that might cry and disturb their already shattered nerves. Over time, I became increasingly shy and withdrawn, and sometimes resentful towards Mick and his band. Neither of us said anything. It often took weeks before we fell back into a somewhat 'normal' family life and began to feel more connected to each other. But usually, around that time, the band would leave for another mammoth tour, and the cycle would begin again. By then, they had a new American guitarist called Bob Welch, who'd taken Jeremy's place. Bob was from California and had been introduced to the band by Judy Wong. When he stayed at Benifolds he would make endless cups of coffee in our kitchen downstairs. He was smart, funny and had a good sense of humor, but what was even more advantageous to the band, as well as being a guitarist they liked, he was also, along with Chris, a good songwriter.

There were times in between the tours, away from the band and Benifolds, when Mick and I felt close to each other and our routine together would resume. This usually happened when we stayed with his parents in Salisbury. It was then that we remembered our roots and became the family I longed for. Biddy and Mike lived in a long white house just outside Salisbury with a river at the bottom of the garden. Bridge House became just as much a home to me as it was to Mick. Biddy would produce delicious but simple meals and we would all sit around the dining room table enjoying each other's company. It wasn't the stiff atmosphere I'd grown up with; the Fleetwood table was filled with laughter, rude jokes as well as serious discussions. Mike was the most wonderful, gentle, sweet and wise man, often getting me to laugh at myself, which was much needed. Biddy became my role model in many ways as far as bringing up my own children. They were both very down to earth, and their family was everything to them, loved by everyone; all their children's friends as well as their own. I treasured them both.

In an attempt to alleviate my sense of loneliness I went on tour with our young daughter, but it only seemed to make it worse. Long car rides through the snow, from gig to gig, with all the band members, and with Amelia on my knee, were spent praying she wouldn't cry and disturb an already tired and tense group of people. In the early mornings I would spend hours pushing her pram along the streets of whatever city we were in, so Mick could get some undisturbed sleep after playing the previous night. I kept different hours from everyone else, felt immensely shy talking to anyone other than Mick and ended up feeling lonelier than when I was at home. I felt left out of the rock and roll world and much to Mick's dismay, I usually left the tours earlier than planned, exhausted and drained with no sense of identity other than that of Mick's wife.

While at Benifolds I often drove across the countryside to visit Pattie and George in their gothic-styled house in Oxfordshire. It was a large folly built at the turn of the century and underneath the house was a labyrinth of caves with stalagmites and water that came in from the lake. Little rowing boats were moored alongside the stone steps that were reached from inside the house. Winter evenings were spent in the big hall in front of a roaring fire or trying out the rowing boats down in the caves. There always seemed to be an air of excitement mingled with fear, like children playing in a big, perhaps haunted, deserted house. Sometimes Amelia and I spent the night in one of the rooms. One morning when I walked in to see if she'd woken from her nap, I saw George, kneeling down in front of her cot, stroking her little cheek.

My mother occasionally came to visit me from Devon for a couple of days. I didn't see much of her as money was tight, and she was working most nights at a hospital. I used to feel very uncomfortable when she came into the sitting room, hoping she wouldn't put on her glasses. Displayed in a corner cabinet was a collection of rubber dildos that Mick would sometimes take on stage attached to one of his drums. Tricks and jokes were a hangover from the schoolboy humour of the Jeremy Spencer days, and I knew she would never visit us again if she saw them.

There were some happy occasions at Benifolds, one of these was a Christmas party for family and friends. It was our first party after being there for two years, and I was six months pregnant with our second child. The billiard table was laden with food and drinks, decorations were put up around the room, and everyone was in good spirits. The room filled up quickly with friends and family. Pattie and George came, along with his sister. Paula arrived, seven months pregnant, in a Little Bo-Peep dress with rubber braces and a roll of rubber around the bottom, like a hula-hoop. It looked rather sweet when she was standing, but when she sat down, to her amusement, she found the rubber circle flipped up in front of her face, giving everyone a full view of her large stomach and more. All three of us sisters were now married to or involved with men in the music world. Paula's boyfriend, and later husband, was Andy Johns, a recording engineer who worked with bands such as the Rolling Stones.

George was heavily into his Hari Krishna phase and wore a cotton string across his chest attached to an orange bag filled with beads. With his hands placed firmly in the bag, he would chat to everyone, interspersed with mutterings of "Hari Krishna, Hari Krishna," while touching the beads. I came over to talk to him and his sister, at one point, while George, with glazed eyes, continued to stare into the distance, while mumbling, "Hari Krishna, Hari Krishna, who's that girl over there with the see-through dress? Hari Krishna, Hari Krishna." Trying not to laugh, I turned around to see Ronnie Wood's very pretty wife, Krissy in a thin white dress, talking to Judy Wong. It was an enjoyable evening and it was nice for me having some of my family there.

A guitar player called Bob Weston, from Long John Baldry's band, joined Fleetwood Mac in mid '72, a month before they were scheduled to do a six-week tour of Europe, and then the States. Danny Kirwan had flipped out and was finally asked to leave. I had met Bob when Fleetwood Mac were on tour in the States several months earlier, and both Chris and I thought he looked very like Stan Laurel. He was funny and everyone liked him immediately. Bob was different from the others - he would take time to talk to me as I was preparing food in the kitchen or looking after Amelia. Being able to talk with someone else was like a ray of sunshine. It made me feel young and alive.

In the spring of '73 I gave birth to our second daughter, Lucy, while Mick was on tour in the States. She was another caesarean birth, which in those days was unusual, but this time the doctors stayed with me throughout the night, monitoring every bit of the procedure. I remember crying as they wheeled me out of the delivery room, still woozy from the anesthetics, another major milestone and yet again without Mick by my side. I know it must have been hard for him too and having to wait for six weeks before he could see our newborn. As ever my mother and father-in-law came to the rescue and took me back to their house in Salisbury where I spent a few weeks with Amelia and the new baby until Mick returned from his tour in June.

It was an impossible situation for Fleetwood Mac, for each time they returned from their three-month American tours they felt they were that much closer to becoming a successful band and headlining their own shows. Mick's strategic mind never stopped for a moment, his head was filled with the Fleetwood Mac chess game, always trying to be one move ahead.

A mobile studio belonging to the Rolling Stones was now parked outside the house and the big room had been emptied out so the band could record their next album. Mikes and leads draped all over the two large rooms and the music from the amplifiers resounded around the house and grounds. Amelia and Lucy's lullabies, which came blasting full volume into their room upstairs, were songs from their new album, *Mystery to Me*. I came up with the title, because what I was beginning to feel for the band's guitarist, Bob Weston, was definitely a mystery to me. We would go on walks together through the woods and around the house, talking about all sorts of things. A new world opened up to me as we shared our ideas and beliefs, and I began to feel lighter and happier, without being aware of how vulnerable I was, how hungry and so in need for companionship.

Another US tour was set up at the end of September and Mick decided the children and I should go with him. I had discovered by this time that drinking alcohol helped with my shyness and a new me emerged that felt relaxed, funny, and, most importantly, it took away my feelings of loneliness. I became more sociable on tour, drinking with everyone else, staying up late, but still able to get up early for the children. The electricity between Bob and me became magnified on the flight to America when he would tease me and I would feel flattered, not realizing for a minute it was flirtatious.

While we were on tour Mick said something in our hotel room one day that I wished he'd said earlier in our relationship.

"I know it's hard for you, Jenny, me being on the road, and lots of people we know are breaking up. But let's try and stick together."

It was the first time he had talked about our relationship, but unfortunately it fell on deaf ears. I'd felt too lonely for too long. What I saw as Mick's aloofness had created a barrier I felt unable to penetrate, and now I had tasted what it felt like to feel noticed. I felt seen when Bob sat next to me in the hotel bar, or when he'd get up early and join me for breakfast with the children. The band spent a few days in Hermosa Beach during the tour and I remember sitting by the pool with the children, enjoying the sunshine and chatting to Bob. I looked up at one point, still laughing at something he'd said, when I saw Mick standing beside me, looking very stern.

Later that evening he asked me what was going on. I could sense myself shaking, a mixture of fear and excitement as I told him I was feeling an attraction towards Bob, and so I needed to go home. I couldn't quite believe what I was saying. I was stating my independence, standing on my own two feet, and yet I was terrified. I had been in a constant daze over the last few weeks, a mixture of infatuation, magnified by drinking too many brandies and not getting enough sleep. I was in a tailspin.

The following morning Mick packed the last of his things in silence, ready for their flight to Minneapolis. With eyes glazed over I sat on the chair watching him, my brain in a fog, unable to utter a word. I wanted him to talk to me, I didn't want this to happen, I cared for Mick deeply, but the wheel was turning. My hunger for connection had been too strong, and my heart sank as he picked up his case and without a word left the room. Five minutes later he reappeared with a bunch of flowers. "Be careful out there," he said, bending down and gently kissing my cheek. And then he was gone. I turned to look at the children sleeping peacefully as I sat on one of the beds and stared at the wall. Lucy was seven months old and Amelia almost three.

After staying with Bob Welch's girlfriend Nancy in Los Angeles for a few days, I took the long flight back to London. As I sat on the plane, Lucy lying in a cardboard cot attached to the wall in front of me, and Amelia asleep in the seat beside me, I felt a sense of relief. Flying through the night, after all the angst of the last few weeks, brought me back to myself. I believed I would now have almost a month to get away from Bob, enough time to contemplate the situation. Nothing physical had happened between us, not even a kiss, and maybe, I thought, it would all peter out when I got back to England. Even so, the excitement and intensity of a mutual attraction, even though it was pulling me apart, was too powerful.

I was offered a place to stay in Ronnie Wood's beautiful house in Richmond since Ronnie and his wife Krissy were spending a lot of time with Pattie and George, in Oxford. Cracks were showing in everyone's relationships at the time, and it was not long after this that Pattie and George separated. Ronnie and Krissy loved beautiful things and their house was filled with them; Tiffany lights, faded rugs from the Middle East, shawls draped on plump armchairs. We were given the full run of the house. Occasionally I would see Ronnie and his black, spiky hair and smiley face, which always made me smile. He didn't seem to mind too much when Amelia knocked down and broke one of his Tiffany lamps.

I decided to drive down to see Biddy and Mike. They had been very good to me and I felt I owed them an explanation.

Biddy greeted me sullenly, no smiles. I walked down the step and into the familiar kitchen where she leaned over the sink and continued washing the dishes. She squeezed the sponge and then began wiping the table. She looked at me as I stood, feeling miserable, leaning against the dresser.

"I'm shocked at your behavior," she finally said, "and I don't mind telling you." She stood up straight. "You've got no right to behave like this. It's appalling. And what about poor Mick? Do you care at all?"

"You don't know how hard it's been," I said, feeling the blood rushing to my cheeks. "He never talks to me. He just spends all his time in John and Chris's kitchen when we're at home, always talking band talk."

"You seemed perfectly happy when you were both here. What's the matter with you?"

I'd never heard Biddy talk like this. Naively, I hadn't bargained on this reaction. Of course she would take her son's side. Through good times or bad times, it didn't matter; this family stuck together.

She walked back to the sink, rinsed out her cloth and then placed it on the draining board and turning around to face me again, she said, "I've always treated you like one of my own daughters, Jenny. I just want you to know that I would say the same thing to them as I am to you."

I could feel my tears welling up. She was like a mother to me.

"Mike's in the sitting room and wants to talk to you."

As I passed the dining room table on my way to the sitting room, I noticed the cushion I'd embroidered for Biddy while waiting for Lucy to be born. Biddy and Mike were so much part of my life and I just wanted them to understand. I was desperate to justify my actions.

Mike was standing with his back to the fire.

"Hello Jenny, ol' girl," he said with a smile. "Come and sit down."

I sat in the green velvet armchair and looked up at him, at his checked shirt with a cravat peeking out from under a maroon V-necked jumper.

"Tell me what went wrong between you two. I thought you were both so happy together."

I could feel myself again on the brink of tears.

"I didn't realize how lonely I was," I said.

How gentle and understanding Mike was on that day. He was sad, but he understood.

He ended our talk by saying, "I hope Mick can now realize what a lucky man he was to have you as his wife. If I were thirty years younger, I would have fought for a girl like you." He looked at me and smiled his charming smile. I'm not sure if that was the talk Biddy had planned for him; he was, just like his son, forever the diplomat. He was a dear man, full of laughter and fun and very philosophical. He was the warm sun to Biddy's howling wind as they tried to get me to let go of this infatuation, and to step back into the family.

My own mother, on the other hand, dealt with the news rather differently. She was very angry and refused to speak to me.

Feeling unable to continue with Bob in the band, Mick cancelled the tour and headed for Zambia. Bob was given his marching orders and the others stayed in California for a couple of weeks. Much to my surprise Bob returned to England prematurely, taking away my hope for time alone with my children. That was when I realized he'd become like a drug to me.

Every night once the children were in bed, Bob and I would drink brandy and dance to the music on the record player or sometimes go to the Speakeasy. With Bob I got in touch with the free and easy childlike part of myself and believed I'd escaped the saturnine figure of Mick. I told myself I'd been abandoned by Mick, that the band was his mistress.

But deep down my nerves were raw. I was in a constant state of anxiety and confusion. One night while Bob and I were lying in bed, and before I went to sleep, Bob whispered, "Mick might have had the power to kick me out of the band, but I have his wife in my bed."

My heart missed a beat and my stomach tightened as I felt the impact of his words. In those days, I didn't know how to express anger or outrage; I just lay there fuming as he drifted off to sleep, knowing immediately and without doubt that, after two weeks of seeing each other every day, the bubble had burst. This was too much for me. However fragile I felt, my loyalty to Mick was deep and rose up in his defense. How dare he, I thought, he knows nothing of the years we've spent together.

The following day I went to Benifolds with the children to pick up some clothes and toys, and while I was there I arranged to see a psychic in the village. I was in need of guidance.

A few days later she did a reading for me at the house. As she rolled my wedding ring in between her fingers she closed her eyes and said,

"I can see your grandparents. They lived in Africa, didn't they?"

I nodded.

"They're not happy. Your grandmother has tears down her cheeks." She continued stroking my ring, exchanging it from one hand to the other.

"Your husband loves you and he's heart-broken." She paused. "Is he in Africa?"

I was flabbergasted. I had been to psychics before, but never to anyone as accurate as this woman. On the verge of tears, I waited for her to continue.

"This dark-haired man," she said as she opened her eyes and looked at me. "Watch out for him. He's like a Svengali and he knows how to mesmerize you."

I knew she was right. The woman reached over to me, put her hand on mine and then handed back my ring.

"You're being used as a pawn," she said. "There is something greater that will happen because of this situation, something that is not far off, but for now your place is with your husband."

I felt sad for Mick as I opened the door and watched the woman walk down the stairs and into her car, but at the same time I felt angry at the powers-that-be, I knew it was what I should do. Even so, the child in me stamped her foot and wanted to believe in free will rather than fate. Having always felt that Mick and I were meant to be together, I longed to have with him the connection I'd felt with Bob. But more than anything I wanted my children to have a happy and secure childhood, living with both their parents as a united family. Everything I hadn't had as a child, I wanted for them.

I called Bob to tell him our affair had come to an end. "You can't do this to me!" he shouted. "I lost my gig because of you!" "I'm sorry", was all I could think of saying, "I'm so sorry."

I sent a telegram to Mick in Zambia and told him I was willing to try again. I felt wretched that I'd been the cause of his pain and yet there was a part of me that wanted to break his aloofness, a characteristic trait I came to realize many years later was actually a mask he wore to cover his feelings of vulnerability. I wanted Mick to release me from my loneliness. My one previous attempt at daring to admit I felt lonely had fallen on deaf ears. "You have John and Chris to talk to," Mick had said. It was as if I'd been told to pull myself together.

I left Ronnie's house, moved back to Benifolds and waited for Mick to return. John and Chris arrived a few days after him and everything was as if nothing had happened, except that I walked around the house knowing I had been the cause of all this disruption and trying not to let it completely destroy me. I made an attempt to hold my head up, and yet, I felt guilt-ridden and resentful. I wanted someone to blame but had only myself.

I had fallen for someone who felt like a friend. When I was with Bob, I had a voice, I felt seen and heard, young and animated, but inside, my heart felt heavy. It wasn't right and I knew it. But truly, and in hindsight, the relationship with Bob was to be a catalyst. It marked a change that affected everyone in Benifolds as well as my relationship to Mick; it also showed me that being with someone else did not eradicate the deep loneliness I experienced. I was married to Mick and he was the one I wanted to feel connected to. Even so, the feelings of guilt, shame and betrayal were almost unbearable, knowing I would never be able to turn back the clock.

I watched as the repercussions of this affair unfolded, spreading wider than any of us could have imagined. The band's manager, Clifford Davis, had taken advantage of the situation by immediately putting together a bogus band, sending them on the tour that had been cancelled and calling them Fleetwood Mac. Of course, as soon as the group started playing, the audience noticed that not one member was from the original band and demanded their money back.

After countless long-distance phone calls and endless discussions Bob Welch and Mick filed a lawsuit against their manager, who then counter sued saying he owned the name. Gradually Bob convinced Mick that because the name was now frozen and they couldn't tour as Fleetwood Mac, we should all move to Los Angeles while the court case was going on. Their record company was in the US, so it made more sense to be there while rebuilding the band.

I heard Mick telling Chris and John, "We can go to LA for six months, reclaim the name, come back to Benifolds, make an album and then go out on the road again."

I continued to listen as they worked out the best plan of action, reminding myself and hanging on to what the psychic had said, "something big will come of this, you're being used as a pawn." But now we were abandoning our home and I felt responsible. I wandered around the house for weeks, struck dumb by laryngitis and knowing everyone would be packing their bags at some point, gearing up to leave. During the discussions in John and Chris's kitchen, I was thankful for all the talk and anger thrown at their manager, knowing it was he who was seen as the reason for leaving, rather than the real culprit standing silently in their midst.

As gentle as Mick appeared, at a young age he had forged a steely determination, knowing that all he wanted to do when he grew up was to play the drums. This fierceness of purpose had revealed itself once before when Peter left the band. He'd had a lot at stake: to find a home for his new wife, a baby on the way, and the need to earn a living, but underneath this driving force was an inner knowing, that he was part of something much bigger than himself. This tenacity had no bounds; he had scooped up everyone in the band and taken them with him. By taking his eye off the ball to lick his wounds, Mick had allowed the manager to take advantage, to creep in and steal their name. Never again would he allow anything to get in the way of achieving the success he distinctly knew was the destiny of Fleetwood Mac.

7

LOS ANGELES

It was spring, 1974, and we were embarking on the long flight to Los Angeles, and into the unknown - John and Christine McVie, our friend Sandra, Mick, me, and our two children. Although we retained our communal house in Hampshire, the do-or-die plan to reclaim the Fleetwood Mac name was now in operation.

I sat by the window, as if in a dream, watching the luggage van slowly making its way across the tarmac to our plane. The day had finally arrived, the day that would take me, take us, away from our memories and into a new life. I turned to look at Mick, his long legs stretched out in the aisle as he leaned forward to talk to John. Next to Chris sat Sandra and I could hear the odd animated word as she and Chris discussed life in LA.

Eleven hours later I allowed myself a moment of excitement as the plane flew over the myriad of twinkling lights. The green fields of England were now a thing of the past as everyone metaphorically opened their arms to embrace this entirely new world.

While looking for a house to rent, the children, Mick and I stayed in the Chateau Marmont Hotel on Sunset Boulevard. It was just like being on tour, familiar, everything slightly unreal and transient, but this time it suited me. I felt as though I was in an emotional vacuum. After locating a babysitter one evening Mick and I visited John, Chris and Sandra who were staying at their friend John Mayall's house in Laurel Canyon.

Chris and Sandra greeted us at the door, wineglass in hand and looking very Californian in flimsy skirts, bare feet, and brightly colored tube tops. Their smiles were heartwarming and I responded immediately to the air of fun and frivolity. It was just what I needed. The first thing I saw when I entered the house was a wooden semi-circular bar, filled with every kind of drink imaginable. This house and bar had gained quite a reputation over the years and was referred to as 'The Brain Damage Club'.

Swayed by the balmy nights and alcohol, we soon became very Californian. The release from our English upbringing was given full rein that night. Chris, Sandra and I, after raiding the bar, decided to have an evening swim together. I could see Mick watching from the balcony and hoped he would, just this once, let down his guard and join us. I so wanted him to play, to forget about the band just for the evening. "Come on Mick," Chris shouted up at him, "Come for a swim." But he shook his head, just smiled and watched from where he was.

Judy Wong decided it was her job to place glasses of wine or vodka and tonics on the side of the pool for us, and so with every sip we became more adventurous with our underwater tactics, and the release of our bikinis. The last bit of reserve Chris held on to was the cord of her bikini top, which she kept tied around her neck, floating above the pool as she swam under water. John, usually very cool and retiring, surprised us all by galloping down the stone steps stark naked, and leaping into the pool. An American man, called Kansas, a friend of John Mayalls, wandered around the edge of the pool advising us on swimming techniques wearing nothing but a cowboy hat! Welcome to Hollywood!!

We had very little money at the time, but, after buying an old, metallic gold convertible Cadillac for $1000, we managed to find a small two-bedroom house for rent in Laurel Canyon. At nearby garage sales, and for just a few dollars, we bought everything we needed, from chairs to cutlery. This was our first home together, something I had always wanted, but with it came unspoken feelings of betrayal, sadness and anger. We still never spoke about these feelings, but carried on a day at a time, Mick trying to keep the band together, and me looking after the children.

One day, while I was out in the garden filling up the children's paddling pool the phone rang. I ran inside and was delighted to hear a familiar voice. I hadn't heard from Pattie since we'd arrived and hoped the dream I'd had of her a few nights ago wasn't an indicator of what was going on in her life. In the past there'd been numerous occasions when each one of us would dream about the other, and more often than not the dreams were true.

After asking how we all were, and what it was like living in LA, she then came to the point.

"Can I come and stay with you for a few days?"

"When?" I asked, thrilled at the thought of seeing her.

"I've booked my ticket for the 4th July." It was only a few days away.

"Is everything alright?" I asked.

"I've left George," she said.

I knew things had been unsettled between her and George for some time, and in many ways, although I was sad to hear her news, it was not altogether a surprise. She and George were still living at Friar Park, but their lives were fraught with infidelities, friends becoming lovers, and the general upheaval of life in the fast lane.

"You can stay with us as long as you like," I said, thinking she was in need of some solace. "As long as you don't mind sleeping on the sofa."

She arrived a couple of days later, looking quite different with her red hair and wearing a turquoise dress and heels. After the children had gone to bed, I gave her a drink and we sat together on the sofa.

"What's been happening?" I asked. "I've had lots of disturbing dreams about you." She took a gulp of vodka and orange and then told me. "I'm on my way to meet up with Eric. He's on the road."

I knew Eric Clapton had been pursuing Pattie for some time and had written *Layla*, a tormented, love song for her. What I didn't realize until that moment was how far their love had grown. As she talked my mind drifted back to the last time I'd seen her and George at their home. We were sitting by the fire in the big hall, lots of friends had gathered there for the night, talking and drinking, and listening to music. Eric had suddenly appeared at the front door, looking wild and windswept. He'd stayed for a short while and then left. Pattie had grasped my arm tightly as she watched him walk away, her eyes glued to his retreating body. And then he was gone.

After staying with us for a few days in Laurel Canyon Pattie left to join Eric on the road, and to start her new life.

The music scene in LA was invigorating. There were nightclubs everywhere, a ten minute drive from where we lived; The Roxy, The Whisky a Go Go, The Rainbow and The Troupadour, places where musicians such as Linda Ronstadt, Neil Young, James Taylor, Bob Marley, Etta James and many more played to a small audience. I would sing along to every song on the radio, cruising down the Canyon in our convertible Cadillac, which, with its power steering, felt more like driving a motor launch. In the warm Californian sun, and the easy lifestyle, my anger and sadness subsided, and life began to take on a more positive feel. There seemed to be so many opportunities, and a young, hip attitude that infiltrated everything - so different from the old fashioned, stuffy atmosphere of Hampshire, and the isolation of Benifolds.

I immediately enrolled myself in an astrology class and then located the Self Realization Fellowship Lake Shrine on Sunset Boulevard, in Pacifica Palisades. It was a few blocks from the ocean and was founded by the Indian guru, Paramahansa Yogananda as a quiet oasis where one could sing chants and meditate. Once I found this little church it became my place of solace for many years to come, my special little sanctuary.

In the meantime, Mick had become even more business-like, not taking his eye off the ball for a second. Bob Welch would pick him up every morning and they'd drive off to visit studios, record companies or lawyers.

While waiting for Sandra to visit I'd often hear one particular song coming from the yard across the road, played at top volume over and over again. Looking out through the upstairs window I saw the couple who lived there and heard them shouting obscenities at each other or at their dog. The man was tall, and I watched him walk around their yard, dragging one leg behind him. Sometimes I found him waiting for me in our garage, trying to make conversation in a strange voice while I hurriedly unbuckled the children's seat belts. There was something about him that frightened me, and I dreaded hearing that shuffling sound if ever I returned home in the dark. I would park my car in the garage and then run up the stairs alongside our house to the front door. After a while I found out that he was Jan Berry from a well-known 1950's duo called Jan and Dean. They sang songs similar to the Beach Boys, California surfing songs, and had many hits before a car accident in 1966 left him with debilitating injuries. By the time we moved there he was back in the business and it was his own song that he was listening to so obsessively. It was all part of the crazy and colorful surroundings we now inhabited. Although I didn't know it then, the Canyon was filled with musicians such as Joni Mitchell, Steven Stills, Neil Young and many more.

One day, while the children were having a nap, I stood by the front door at the top of the steps, watching a man laboriously climbing towards me, placing one sandaled foot in front of the other, while keeping his head buried in a black canvas bag strapped across his chest. He stopped halfway up, his hands still shuffling in the bag before pulling out a large envelope. Leaning the bulk of his weight against the iron railing, he wiped a hand across his forehead and then, looking up momentarily, gave a wide smile. "Boy it's hot today," he said, closing the flap of his satchel and taking another step. "How you doin?"

This was Herbie. He was not at all what I'd expected. I thought he'd be a jeans and T-shirt kind of West Coast guy, but instead he looked more like a big hippie bear left over from the sixties. He wore loose white muslin pants, an Indian shirt down to his knees and with his beard, shoulder-length hair and biblical sandals, reminded me of Arab from San Francisco.

I put out my hand. "Hi, I'm Jenny," I said. "Come in."

His eyes glistened when he smiled. He put both his hands together as if in prayer. "Hi there," he said, bowing, "I'm Herbie, and aren't you just so cute Miss Jenny!" We both laughed. "I'm here to see your husband." As he stepped into the house, a waft of incense trailed behind him. "I've got some photographs to show his lordship for the new album cover." He looked at me as I stepped past him, and into the small galley kitchen.

"Cup of tea?" I asked.

"Cup o' tea?" Herbie mimicked in a high-pitched voice. "You're all just so cute, you English." He burst out laughing, disarming me and taking away any of the formality I'd brought with me from Hampshire.

"I'm making you a cup of tea and biscuits, English style," I said, thrilled to have found someone I felt at ease with.

"No, I won't honey," Herbie said, suddenly serious. "Thank you very much, I'll take a glass of water instead." He placed his shoulder bag on the wooden chair, then grabbed a corner of his shirt and wiped his face. "Man, it's hot out there," he said, "Don't know why you'd be drinking hot tea in this weather. Crazy English." He looked over at me as I continued filling the kettle. "You guys need to get yourselves a fan in here, this summer's going to be hotter than hell." He wiped his face again.

I handed him a glass of ice water and watched as he drained the contents in four gulps. He wiped his mouth with the back of his hand and offered me the glass.

"Thank you, ma'am," he said and sat down on the sofa. "So, what do you think of LA? Pretty different from little ol' England, right?"

"I love it," I said. "It's got a great energy; makes you feel like anything's possible."

Herbie's face became serious. "It is possible," he said. "Anything's possible if you believe." He stopped and then stared at me as if looking for something behind my eyes. He took a deep breath then slowly released it and was about to announce something seemingly of great importance when Mick appeared at the front door.

"There you are my man!" Herbie jumped up and held out his hand. "How you doin' Mick? Been talking with your old lady here." Herbie grabbed his satchel from the chair. "Got the contacts, I think you'll like them," he said as he opened the folder.

Mick glanced at me, smiling. "So, you've finally met Herbie. He's our new great friend."

I watched both men from the kitchen as they leaned over the table, studying the different photographs for the album cover. The warm, funny man I'd met a few minutes ago was now serious.

Mick stood up straight. "You're a genius Herbie," he said. "That one looks great, just what we wanted."

Herbie stayed in our lives for many years. A self-proclaimed 'Seeker of the Light', he would meditate every day, and introduced me to an inspirational bookshop in Hollywood called The Bodhi Tree. Mick fascinated him, even more so after being asked to photograph the album cover for *Heroes are Hard to Find*; the first record since moving to Los Angeles. The picture was of Mick wearing a pair of Sandra's white lacy underpants, puffing up his ribby chest, and holding three-year-old Amelia's hands as she stood on his feet. Herbie couldn't believe it. It had nothing to do with the usual Los Angeles glamorous photographs that most people wanted and was a very different image than the more refined photographs he was later to take of Fleetwood Mac. Herbie became part of the family, he loved the children, and filled Amelia's head with slogans like "God loves you." He lived in a gothic-style house in Hollywood, with his two large and graceful Saluki dogs. As well as being a brilliant photographer he was a real character, a "one-off" and we all loved him.

Another person that was now very much involved in our lives was Judy Wong. I suggested to Mick one day that she might be very good as a secretary for the band - she was loyal and had known Mick and John for years.

After the band had recorded their first album in LA and toured throughout the States, Bob Welch decided he'd had enough, and wanted to leave the band. At this low point, while listening to the sound quality of a particular studio he was keen to rent, Mick came across the voices of Stevie Nicks and Lindsey Buckingham. On enquiring who they were, he was told they were a couple from San Francisco, and that they had an album out called Buckingham Nicks. He arranged to meet them a few days later and not long afterwards, they both came to our house in Laurel Canyon. They were a very attractive couple, enthusiastic and friendly. Stevie was very chatty, very pretty, and had a great sense of humor. They were easy to talk to, and I warmed to them immediately.

In January 1975, four weeks after Bob had left, Stevie and Lindsey joined the band. While listening to their rehearsals I could sense the chemistry at work between the five of them; the sound of their voices singing together, their harmonies mixed with the solid foundation of Mick and John's rhythm section, brought chills down my spine. I knew they were onto something big. They were dynamic! The beginning of the new Fleetwood Mac sound had begun, and with all of this came the parties, and what was later to become the enormous Fleetwood Mac entourage.

At these parties I drank along with everybody else, no longer the shrinking violet, and would occasionally take cocaine. The following day, under the weight of a hangover, I would feel tremendous remorse, knowing I'd drunk too much and had used drinking as a way to escape from my shyness, to be lighter, talkative and amusing. Meanwhile Sandra had begun a brief affair with John McVie, her old friend, and would often call me in tears. Everywhere old-time friends were changing partners. Partly because of the breakdown of inhibitions through drugs and alcohol, and partly because long term relationships held together by a flimsy cord were unable to handle the new fast world we were now inhabiting.

Sandra and I maintained a strong bond, a lifeline throughout my turbulent Fleetwood Mac years. With her as my constant companion we took the children to Disneyland, Universal Studios and any other amusement park we could find. With Sandra I could be light and silly as well as having more meaningful conversations. More than anyone she understood the bane of living with a musician; and how lonely it could be at times.

After a happy few months of living in Laurel Canyon, Mick decided to rent a house up in the hills of Topanga, about an hour's drive from Hollywood. We took over a rustic 50s building from a couple of hippies, who left for us not only the house, but also their two dogs. We kept one of them, named Zappa, who snarled at the children to begin with and refused to come into the house, preferring instead to sit on the mat outside the front door, come rain or shine, looking like a bedraggled bundle of fur. Gradually, with a lot of love and patience, she began to follow us everywhere, lying in front of the fire, looking after the children and becoming the most treasured animal, loyal and trustworthy, living with us for many years.

The house looked as if the rain had swept it away down a gully, with a steep path leading up from it to Topanga Boulevard. Across the road was the old Topanga market, surrounded by longhaired hippies, barefoot women with naked children, bikers and stray dogs. I felt as if I was back in the sixties, with people still wearing bells and beads, and longhaired guys with cowboy hats. It was all a little unnerving to a mother of two very English little girls.

Our new home was like an elongated log cabin – the wood floors were scuffed and faded by countless traipsing of cowboy boots and in the main room was a window that ran across the entire wall looking out onto the trees and the Santa Monica Mountains. We placed our garage sale sofa and rustic looking coffee table in front of the fireplace, with two armchairs on either side. It created a cozy atmosphere on chilly winter evenings. A serving hatch on the wall, above the dining room table, revealed part of the small galley kitchen next door. The back door to the house led out from the kitchen to an empty horse corral.

Even though we were only an hour's drive from Hollywood, it felt as if we were miles out in the wild. Sandra wasn't able to visit so often, and Mick spent most of his time at Sound City Studio in Hollywood, where the band had begun recording their new album, *Fleetwood Mac*. And so began the initiation into taking cocaine in vast quantities, to fuel long hours of work, day and night, keeping up the pressure to complete the album on time. It was part of the culture at that particular studio, everyone took cocaine, and rapidly it spread throughout LA penetrating all levels of the entertainment industry.

My younger sister, Paula, was living in Los Angeles at the time, with her young son, William, and her recording engineer husband. Sadly, her life was completely awry, and so I found little comfort during her visit, but felt only compassion. One night as I watched her drink herself into a stupor, she told me not only was their marriage on the rocks, but her wedding ring had just fallen down the toilet. The night ended with me scrabbling as far as I could to reach down into the 'S' bend, while she stood beside me sobbing. I retrieved the gold band, but the marriage finished soon afterwards.

Apart from Sandra and the rest of the band, the few people I knew lived in Hollywood. Yet the entourage associated with the group was getting larger every day. Everyone was so friendly, as if they'd known us for years. Everyone who came in contact with the band were fascinated by Mick and spoke constantly of his many attributes and quirks. Not only that, but we were fast becoming part of a huge organization that was taking over our lives.

Andy, Mick's old friend and our flat mate in Kensington Church Street came to stay at our house in Topanga for a couple of weeks with his girlfriend. They were good company for me, and they loved playing with the girls. I bathed in their Englishness and their dry sense of humor. During the day, we often took the children and Zappa for a walk in the Topanga State Park. Occasionally Paula and her son William would join us.

Most of my evenings at home with the children were quiet and gentle: chamomile tea, classical music, meditation, reading, writing poetry and early to bed. But on the occasions when I joined Mick in town, when Andy and his girlfriend would baby sit, I joined in with the party-like atmosphere. Either at the studio, at a restaurant, or at someone's home - every occasion became a party. There I drank, took cocaine along with everyone else and felt free from all my inhibitions and my spiritual searching. It drew back curtains and made me feel I had an identity. I became funny and made people laugh. The energy was always palpable as we talked, laughed, and got high. Often, I wouldn't remember the end of a party, or the end of yet another huge dinner, filled with people from Warner Brothers, the tour management, lawyers and the usual friends of friends. In my attempt to mask my shyness I would drink as soon as I sat down for dinner, and then after getting the nod from whoever was holding the coke, I proceeded to pick at yet another expensive meal.

Even when we lived in England, I silently had an underlying fear of Mick becoming famous and wealthy. Although I loved him and wanted him to be successful, I was scared that if it were to happen, it would tear us apart. This fear that things would change was heightened when we visited a numerologist not long after arriving in LA. She predicted that the next Fleetwood Mac album would be big, and that Mick would become a millionaire. But success didn't impress me. It didn't make up for the fact that the children and I were seeing less and less of Mick. And yet when I did see him, we never talked about anything other than the mundane, his energy sapped from the previous day at the studio while he got himself ready to drive back into Hollywood.

Mick's parents came to stay. They loved being in California, and I had missed not having any of our family nearby, especially for the sake of the children. When the Fleetwood family were together, I knew what it was like to have a mother and father, and to feel part of a family, especially now that I was back in the fold. Forgiven but maybe not forgotten. I had felt the extent of their bond when I broke up with Mick; they had rallied round and their solidarity was formidable. I had never experienced that sense of a united front in my family. My mother's reaction to anything upsetting was to not speak to me.

I drove them to the recording studio one evening, where the band members greeted them with great affection. Biddy and Mike were enthusiastic about the music having been hugely supportive of Mick throughout his whole musical career since the age of fifteen and were very proud of his achievements. I knew they saw nothing wrong with Mick rarely being at home, believing that it was the wife's place to be there looking after the children, keeping everything ticking over for whenever the husband returned.

Life had changed dramatically for me since the innocence of the 60s. Then I was smoking pot and experimenting with LSD in order to expand my consciousness. Now, in the 70s, I was drinking alcohol when we were all together and taking cocaine, nothing to do with expanding consciousness, more like running away from myself, to numb and push away feelings of loneliness. Whereas Mick loved the countryside and being in a rustic setting, like Benifolds, for me, although I loved living up in the hills of Topanga, I would have felt less isolated, given the circumstances, if we'd stayed in Laurel Canyon. The problem between us was exacerbated by my not speaking up, not understanding that I had just as much right as he did to discuss where we could live. I accepted the situation and was left stewing inside. In that sense nothing had changed.

But the giant Fleetwood Mac wheel was now in motion and speeding up faster than anyone could have imagined. Recording to deadlines, meetings with Warner Brother's, preparing for their first tour with Stevie and Lindsey, over-seeing the new album cover, having photographs taken, and Mick, now the band's manager was caught up in this fast turning wheel more than anyone. But I felt left out in the cold, not able to see beyond my own needs for family connection, looking for the Mick I knew who was rapidly becoming swallowed up by this gigantic ride, with no way to slow down. The cocaine and the big wheel needed each other. They fed each other. The dream was coming true but at such a cost. Mick was consumed with the band and its success and there was no space for anything or anyone else. I looked to him for my support and nourishment while he looked to the band for his – we weren't aligned and looking at each other. The more emotionally distant and unavailable he became the more I craved what was being withheld. I yearned for a close and intimate connection with Mick, but he was better loving from afar, making sure we were all safe and protected.

What I perceived as his aloofness stabbed at my heart, and yet my response was always to keep a cool exterior, my insides in turmoil. It was difficult for us both, at only twenty-seven, to suddenly find ourselves in this rapidly evolving environment, but unlike Mick, my facade eventually cracked under the strain.

The dam broke one afternoon at a barbecue with the band and friends at our house. We sat outside, eating and drinking, while everyone talked excitedly about their recording and up-coming tour. At one point, after a few drinks some of us were standing and chatting in the small narrow kitchen, reminding me of a ship's galley. Mick was next to me, talking to someone, when, John Courage, one of Fleetwood Mac's road crew from England, and the one whose job it had been to tell Bob Weston to leave the band, began taunting me.

"You don't really love Mick, do you? Come on Jenny, you don't really love him."

His voice went on and on, until I exploded. I wheeled round to Mick and with all my might began pounding his chest in front of everyone in the kitchen, releasing all the hurt, anger and frustration I'd held in for years, in sobs, saying, "I can't fake it any more." I continued until someone pulled me away. Chris McVie put her arm around me and led me outside into the corral, where we walked round and round as I continued to sob hysterically repeating the words "I can't fake it anymore." I knew what I meant; I could no longer pretend that everything was okay.

There was so much unspoken pain inside me. The shame of my affair was deeply embedded, as was what I saw as the irreparable damage it had done to our marriage – a wound that could never be healed. I carried the enormity of this burden in my heart, believing it had all been my fault, discounting Mick's part in our relationship and his inability to see the imbalance, that something needed attention. All I could see was his aloofness towards me, and I interpreted his obsession with the band as his way of turning his back on me. The pain of that was unbearable. I couldn't forgive myself.

I was taken into my bedroom to lie down. Curtains were drawn and I heard Sandra and Judy talking softly while trying to soothe me. My body shook uncontrollably. While lying there, I saw a little figure in a long white nightdress. It was Amelia. "God loves you," she said, coming up to me and giving me a kiss, before disappearing back into her bedroom. She'd heard these words from Herbie on numerous occasions but had no idea how soothing they were at that moment.

The next day, much to my surprise, I woke up feeling light and clear-headed instead of the usual hangover. I looked back at the previous evening knowing I had well and truly opened Pandora's box, and now I had to sweep up the pieces. Although I felt delicate, every nerve jangling on the surface, inside I felt complete peace and calm.

Despite this feeling of peace, my sudden breakdown had frightened me. Mick didn't mention anything, dismissing it as an emotional blip, and he didn't want anything to hinder the upcoming tour. It wasn't until I told him I was scared of a similar thing happening again, that he realized I was intent on separating.

"You have a roof over your head," he said, "What more do you want?"

A cardboard box would have been fine, I thought to myself, if we were actually in it together. Nothing more was said. He went off on tour, carrying on as if nothing had happened. I couldn't get a reaction from him; so we didn't discuss it. When I told him I was looking for a small apartment in town, he seemed indifferent but

I knew I had to get away from Mick. During the course of the tour, the couple of times he asked me to visit him out on the road, I developed a high fever and was told by the doctor to go home.

Three weeks later, a few days before Mick returned from the first leg of the tour, the children and I moved into a one-bedroom apartment in town. We had an allowance from Mick of $80 a week, and a bunk bed for Amelia and Lucy. The flat was on the ground floor of a modern house with a strip of grass in front of the pavement. Zappa came with us and we began our new life.

Mick told me to get a job, so while both girls were in the local nursery school, I made handbags out of velvet and brocade, with Bakelite handles from the thirties, which I sold for very little money. Everything continued to feel unreal, as if there was no solid ground beneath my feet, and no one to ask for help. Sandra was wrapped up in the impossible affair she was having with John McVie, and Pattie seemed so far away, in another world, with Eric. I felt beholden to Mick as I desperately tried to keep things together for the children, believing he had all the power and I had none.

Pattie and Eric arrived in Los Angeles for a few days that summer as Eric was scheduled to play in Inglewood with his band. When they weren't touring, he and Pattie lived in the Bahamas, so I hadn't seen her for a year, and we'd hardly been in touch either. Eric was very possessive of her, and they both drank heavily. One evening, Pattie and Paula, who was still living in L.A. with her son, came to visit me at my little apartment. We drank quite a bit while we caught up on each other's news, and I watched as Paula became more and more unhappy, crawling across the carpet and crying as she told us she'd fallen in love with Mick's friend Andy Sylvester and her marriage was over.

I'd seen Andy every now and then once he'd moved into Hollywood. He felt familiar, reminding me of a time that seemed long ago, when life was happy and simple. During my separation with Mick, I began to rely on his friendship, going on walks with the dog, sitting in coffee bars or spending hours trawling through albums in old record shops.

While Fleetwood Mac were back in town for a two-week break in order to finish the album, Mick came to visit me in my apartment while the children were at their nursery school. We sat facing each other on the sofa. He looked so stern and frightening as he sat there in his beautiful dark green silk shirt and embroidered waistcoat, smelling of musk and patchouli oil. I hardly recognized this person; I couldn't believe he was still in there.

"I've filed for divorce," he said in a cold clipped voice. I just stared at him, not able to utter a word, watching his face as he spoke, feeling as if I was in a dream. My heart was broken, our marriage in tatters, but inside I felt numb. We had grown so far apart, and it all felt so unreal.

Fleetwood Mac went back out on the road from July 25th until October 26th. They had records in the charts, had toured successfully for four months around the States, and were now a big name. By September Chris's single *Over My Head* was in the American top ten, and by December 1975 their album had gone gold, selling one and a half million copies. The dream had indeed come true.

Towards the end of that year I noticed my scapula was protruding two or three inches out of my back, so I was admitted to the neurological ward at U.C.L.A. hospital for tests for a suspected tumor. The children went on the road with Mick and his parents, while I went into hospital. As I lay on my stomach, strapped to a slanted board, and with my head tipped towards the ground, I was told my spine needed to be injected with dye, so the tumor, or whatever it was, would show up in the scan. And there was a possibility, they said, I could end up in a wheelchair for the rest of my life if they didn't get all the dye out.

If I'd been scared before, I was now terrified. The doctors wanted to try out a new dye that was meant to disperse after a while, taking away the danger of any traces left behind, but which might cause brain damage. A consent form was put in front of me to sign and I had no one to ask for help or advice. All I could think of saying was I didn't want them to scan my brain. I felt as though I was teetering on the edge in this new world, so ungrounded and alone, with no husband to look after me. I signed the form and was then given Valium intravenously to numb my fear.

My head was then placed in a long, narrow, metal tube, I thought I was going to suffocate, as my head was going further into the tunnel and just before I screamed, they stopped, and turned on the machine.

"You might get a migraine after this," the nurse informed me.

The migraine lasted two days, a blinding pain that nothing could get rid of. In the meantime, I heard from no one. I felt alone and forgotten, at an all-time low.

A few days later, I was told to follow the doctor into a room where there were about seven young interns who studied my protruding scapula, while my hospital gown, tied with a string behind my neck, revealed all. I felt like a guinea pig. The next morning, a very stern doctor questioned me about basic American history, to check that my brain was working normally. But given my limited knowledge of American history, I got most of the questions wrong, which confused them all further. More tests were carried out throughout the week and at one point, a serious and efficient doctor stuck electronic needles into my body. I'd had enough. I broke down, endless tears running down my face. I missed my children, I had lost the Mick I once knew, and my world had fallen apart.

After a week of confinement, I was allowed out for the weekend. Sandra came to pick me up with our friend Nancy, Bob Welch's ex-wife. She was driving John McVie's car, and had just come back from The Record Plant in Sausalito. The band had just started recording *Rumours*, later to become their all-time bestselling album. I sat in the back of the car, relieved to be away from the hospital, even if only for the weekend. Or so I thought.

As we were driving across the intersection, we were hit broadside by another car, the sickening sound of metal crunching and Sandra screaming obliterated all thoughts of a pleasurable weekend as the impact threw me across the back seat and the metal ashtray cut my knee. I got out of the car, dazed, while someone called for an ambulance. As I was carried into the ambulance, I heard Sandra wailing, "What will John say?" I was whisked back to the same hospital, given stitches for my knee, had my head x-rayed, and told to stay. Thankfully, both Sandra and Nancy were unhurt.

I succumbed to more tests at the hospital, until, finally, I found the strength and courage to say, "No More!" and got up and left. Their diagnosis was not a tumor, but trauma and yet I had felt more traumatized in the hospital than at any other point during the last six months.

Soon after I got back from the hospital, I heard from Sandra that Mick now had a girlfriend called Jinny who was staying with him, his parents and the children at the Record Plant in Sausalito. I was so stunned already by all the changes that were now part of my life I could hardly react to this information, everything to do with Mick now felt so dream-like. I said nothing about this to Mick when I spoke to him on the phone. He sounded cold and distant, and seemed annoyed that I'd been in a car crash. The children were sent back to me.

I wrote many letters to my mother during our time in LA, telling her about the children and our lives in California. After writing to her about my ordeal at the hospital, describing, not in too much detail, how frightening it had been and how much I missed her, she wrote back saying she would fly to Los Angeles and visit us at the beginning of June.

Fleetwood Mac recorded their album, *Rumours*, as each member of the band went through their own emotional crisis, all of which had an influence on every song.

Chris and John were breaking up, and Lindsey and Stevie were doing the same. With the chaos surrounding these two relationships, Mick became even more the grand mediator and father figure to everyone. The Record Plant was thick with emotion, with people walking in and out of rooms, apologizing, as couples were seen in deep discussion or in floods of tears.

After Mick stopped seeing Jinny, he asked me if I would drive up the coast with the children and stay with him at the Record Plant. He wanted to see if we could patch things up. I was used to being in the studio while they were recording, and it was as if none of the events of the past few months had happened. We slipped back into a lifestyle we knew well. However, we were still unable to talk to each other about our relationship, and neither of us had changed. We both wanted the marriage to work, but we didn't know how to make that happen. Despite this, we decided to try again. There were no rules in our relationship and the fact that divorce proceedings were underway, or had now been finalized, didn't mean a thing.

Mick had bought a house further up in the hills of Topanga, surrounded by the Santa Monica Mountains, and on returning from Sausalito he asked me to come over with the girls. We spent a day there with him, wandering around the grounds, and admiring the view. Once again, we believed that our little family could live together. There were times when Mick and I regained a sense of closeness similar to when we were young and naive, talking and laughing with each other, remembering funny little things, him telling me his plans for building a studio in the house, me chatting about the girls, and on these occasions, I believed we would always be together. But they were so fleeting, lasting a day or two at the most, and then he'd slip back into not coming home at night and disappearing into a place that I could never reach.

A few weeks after we'd moved into the house Mick's parents came to stay with us again. I could see they were filled with adulation for their son and hung onto his every word. As soon as they heard him stir, they would rush around to make freshly squeezed orange juice. It was a loving thing to do for one's son, but I saw it as just one more example of their pride in everything he said and did and their blindness to his over-indulgence in cocaine. The closer they stuck together the further I felt from them all. The very nature of cocaine brings with it illusions of grandeur and a numbing of the heart and Mick's sense of detachment to those around him was like a shell that masked the gentle, sensitive person I loved. It felt impenetrable and drove me to distraction. The connection I'd felt on the first few days we spent at the house had now disappeared. And yet again I had no one to talk to, Sandra had flown to England to visit her mother and pick up her green card and so I called Andy, describing the difficulty of living with someone who was a complete stranger, and watching people I'd known and loved, hovering around him, like slaves to his every whim. I drove into town to get away from the feelings of imprisonment, and from Andy's apartment I called Mick to say it was not working. I told him I intended to move back to my apartment with the children.

In a cold, aloof voice, he told me that he and his parents had decided I couldn't see our children again until I'd got myself together. I was devastated. He was all-powerful, and with the strength of his parents backing him, even more so. I felt I was finally being driven to the edge. My kids were everything to me. It didn't occur to me at the time to demand to see my children; I didn't realize I could have fought for them. Finally, I came to the conclusion that the only way I was ever going to prove myself worthy was if I went to England for a while, away from Mick, and looked after his sister's children. I'd always felt close to Sally ever since Mick and I started going out together, and she'd always been very supportive of our relationship.

Now, with hindsight, I feel more compassion and understanding towards Biddy and Mike, who were obviously out of their depth in this crazy world, a million miles from their life in rural England. They clearly wanted to support their son and to protect the children from any further disruption, but the way this was accomplished was devastating.

As planned earlier in the year, my mother arrived in LA. Her timing couldn't have been worse. It was not the sweet trip I had envisioned; she didn't get to see the girls and I was a wreck, preparing myself for my trip back to England. My mum couldn't understand how our lives had become so entangled since we'd moved to Los Angeles, and it was hard trying to explain without wanting to upset her. Even so, she could tell I was deeply unhappy, and her response was to help me as much as she could to get back to England and away from Mick. Together we emptied out my apartment. I felt as if I was going around in circles, looking for a way out, but not finding one. I was torn between the dream of Mick and I living as a family, and the reality of the all-consuming world of the Fleetwood Mac machine we'd inhabited. Looking after Sally's twins who were the same age as Lucy was the closest I could get to my own children, so I humbly complied, feeling deeply unhappy, and knew that if I was to see my children again I would have to swallow my pride, even though every nerve in my body rebelled, and learn to accept I had no choice.

I am five years old and standing with my brother and sister outside our house in Kenya. My brother is seven and my sister is nine. We've been told to stand at the top of our gravel drive and to alert our parents when we see the visitor's car. It was not often that visitors came to our house, but when they did we could see them for miles before they actually arrived, a whirl of dust would suddenly appear followed by a little dark speck slowly moving in the distance with the black and silver metal shimmering under the hot African sky. As this gleaming object grew in size, the chugging sound of the engine would drift lazily up the hill, blending with the songs of birds and cicadas. It was mesmerizing, something we children loved to do, often counting how long it would take for a car to reach the Jacaranda trees that stood either side of our house.

Once we had sounded the alert, and the greetings were over with, family and guests all trooped out of the mid-day sun and into the shade of our house for lunch. After the afternoon had rolled on and away, and it was time for the guests to leave, we all stood at the top of the driveway to say our goodbyes. I could see my brother and sister giggling and whispering to each other and I longed to be like them, longed to be part of their private games. The husband and wife opened the doors of their black shiny car and sat down in the hot brown leather seats. As the engine jumped into life my brother and sister ran to the back of the car and grabbed onto the silver metal bumper, giggling to each other as they pretended to push the car down the hill. As it inched forward, I ran to where they were, stood in between them and, like them, held onto the bumper. The clutch was let out and the tires crunched on the gravel. We squealed with delight as we watched our stumpy bodies in the chrome of the bumper, elongated arms, strange shaped faces, lips and noses jogging up and down. The car jerked and gathered speed and we ran faster, my bare feet running on the gravel. Another jerk followed, and then more speed. First my sister, then brother gave a final push and let go, standing up straight and away from the car. But as for me, and much to my horror, I was running too fast to be able to let go and so I clung on fiercely, listening to my parents' screams as they mingled with the sound of the motor, "Let Go! Let Go!!" But I could only hold on tighter. Finally, my legs were dragging on the gravel, and my feet felt as though they were on fire. The car accelerated again, faster down the driveway while my hands remained glued to the bumper. "Let go!" was all I could hear. At last I did, and tumbled down the hill, legs and arms whirling, to a bruised and bloody stop.

The sound of the engine grew fainter and fainter and the dust began to settle, until finally I felt familiar arms wrap themselves around me. My father carried me up the drive and to the safety of our home.

Was I doing the same thing now? Had I held onto Mick for too long, unable to let go, my sense of self slowly being chipped away, leaving me like a wounded animal, rolling down the hill, cast out from my family home?

A journey beyond the muse

SUMMER '76

As the plane took off from LA airport and climbed into the night sky, I lay back in my chair and sighed. The last week flashed through my mind: the shock of being banned from seeing my children and the awful sense of helplessness. The outrage and anger I should have felt towards Mick and his parents might have given me the strength to stand up to them, but I felt worn down, the three of them standing together was just too much for me to handle. All I wanted was to be with my children, but the seemingly indivisible and merciless trio held all the cards. As we climbed higher, I wrapped the blanket around me, pushed back the seat and closed my eyes. Ahead of me lay England, my home country and my hope for solace.

Ten hours later, having spent the last two years longing for the sight of cows and sheep grazing in green pastures, I was amazed and disappointed as we began our descent into a grey polluted haze over the parched brown fields below. Things picked up with the appearance of my brother Colin's smiling face, greeting me in the arrivals lounge. He looked well and happy. His partner Sheila had just found out she was pregnant. We went to their local pub, where the jukebox played the latest English hits, none of which I recognized. When I told them a little about LA and the children, not going into too much detail, Colin responded by putting a comforting arm around my shoulder and saying, "Well it gives us a chance to see you, Jen." It was very comforting to feel even a tiny bit wanted, at last. For the next few days, they looked after me in their little flat near Tower Bridge, while I got over my jet lag and thought about my next move.

The first thing was to find somewhere more permanent to lay my head, so I called Sally, Mick's sister, and asked if I might stay with her and her husband in their flat off Kensington High Street. Sally and I had always been good friends and we had known each other for so many years. Despite her closeness to Mick, I had never felt any coolness in her manner during the rough patches he and I had experienced. I thought of her as an older sister and suggested that I could help look after her little children, maybe I could take them to the park each day. Sally welcomed me with open arms, telling me I could come for as long as I liked, if I didn't mind sleeping on the sofa bed in their sitting room. When she picked me up from Paddington Station, I must have looked a sad figure, in my leather-strapped wedgey shoes, Indian multi-colored calf-length cotton dress and long curly hair. The sight of her immediately made me feel better and I was delighted to discover that she'd brought her children along with her. Kells, aged thirteen, and Tiffany, eleven, were from Sally's previous marriage. I had known them both all their lives and was very fond of them. The twins, Alice and Lizzie, were from her second marriage and were almost three, a few months younger than my daughter, Lucy. It was a bittersweet reminder of how far away I was from seeing my own children.

Every day, in the sweltering heat of the exceptional summer of '76, I walked Sally's twins to Holland Park. The pollen was out in full and as I sat on the grass sneezing, my eyes red and tears streaming down my face, I watched the twins playing, dreaming about my own children, and trying to imagine what they were doing.

In the evenings, we sat around the long, narrow oak table in the dimly lit kitchen in Sally's flat. After a meal and a few glasses of wine, Mick's other sister, Sue, who was a regular dinner guest, would often weep as she told us of her difficulties with her boyfriend. It was a relief to me that our conversations were centered on her life, leaving my own problems out of the limelight. I would wait for everyone to go to sleep before retiring to my sofa bed, where I composed letters and cards to Amelia and Lucy, telling them how much I loved them and that I would see them soon. One day Mick put a stop to this, saying I wasn't to write 'See you soon' because it would only confuse them. I realized I was writing it for myself as much as them.

The fourteen months I'd spent in LA, which had seemed such an eternity there, began now to feel like a distant dream. The one person I was still very much in need of seeing and speaking to was Pattie, but as I was soon to discover not even she could help. I went looking to her for support and found myself instead in the center of the chaos that was now her life.

The last time I'd seen Pattie with Eric was at his show when they came to LA. He had a great band and the music was fantastic. Afterwards I went backstage to say hello and congratulate him on his gig, only to find a very drunken Eric shouting and staggering around the room and Pattie laughing at him, as if it was all a game.

Now that they were back home I imagined their domestic life would be different, more sober and adjusted to the everyday. I couldn't wait to tell Pattie about Biddy and Mike, about Mick and my banishment, to go for a walk in the woods, to hear about her life and how it had changed, to ask her if she was happy. I called and was told to come for the weekend.

That Friday afternoon I took a minicab to Eric's house. As the car pulled into the familiar driveway, I was reminded of my previous visit, when my old friend Alice was living with Eric as his girlfriend. It had been a sad time for her, and as I walked towards the house that day I couldn't help wondering, now that Eric had the woman he'd longed for, if things would be happier in this household.

I was shaken out of my thoughts by bursts of laughter and the sight of Pattie, Eric, and two friends filing out of the front door towards Eric's car, laden with bags, glasses and bottles of champagne. After much hugging I was told we were heading to one of England's stately homes on the south coast, to stay the night at the owner's invitation. As we squashed ourselves into Eric's car, the corks popped and glasses were distributed. The miles passed with plenty of drinking and plenty of laughter. My wish for any meaningful discussion had now flown out the window as I melted into Pattie's new world.

By the time we arrived at our destination we were reeling. I have a hazy recollection of being in a hall with people seated on rows of chairs listening to our host giving a talk. Eric was drinking out of his brandy bottle in the row behind me, and every so often he'd lean over and offer me a sip. The more I had to drink the more I told Pattie and Eric how lovely it was that they were together, little realizing what a raw nerve I was touching.

The drinking continued into the night. By midnight, even though our host had gone to bed, we stayed up until dawn getting increasingly plastered. I began to feel slightly uncomfortable in Eric's presence. Throughout the evening he had developed an unsettling knack of goading me, reminding me, in my deranged state, of Bobby, my stepfather. At one point, I shouted at him to stop, and banged my foot down on a tile in the hearth.

"Oh, you've cracked the tile!" Eric said with glee. I gasped, but like naughty children, we started to giggle. Eventually, we decided we all needed some fresh air, and so, sometime in the early hours of the morning, we staggered out under the black sky and onto the sand. Eric had a brotherly arm around me as we stumbled along the empty beach. The following day I felt like death, hardly able to move with a hangover that could only be relieved by the hair of the dog! Throughout the weekend we all got progressively worse as we continued to drink and take drugs, behaving like children, no boundaries or borders, cocooned in our own little world.

That evening, once we were back at Eric's house, Pattie and I got changed for a summer party they'd been invited to in the next village. An extremely drunk Eric drove us in his large Mercedes at a terrifying speed along the narrow country lanes. I sat in the back, one hand on the door handle as I contemplated the best alternative. Was it safer to jump out and be maimed, or stay and risk being killed? By some miracle we got there in one piece and the car slowed to a halt on the gravel driveway. As Pattie opened Eric's door, he passed out. "Leave him," she said, obviously used to this sort of thing, and we walked into the house.

The sound of laughter and voices greeted us as we entered a room full of people standing, chatting, with drinks in hand and wearing brightly coloured clothes. Pattie disappeared into the kitchen to get us a drink and to chat to the host. A few minutes later Eric appeared at the front door, slightly hunched, hands in pockets and laughing. Once he'd got himself a drink and was sitting down, he looked at me and shouted, "Come and sit on my knee, Jen." I didn't know what else to do, not wanting to attract attention in front of the gathering, so I walked over towards him and perched on his lap. Next thing I knew, Pattie was walking out of the kitchen towards me, a glass of wine in each hand, her face suddenly like stone as she threw the entire contents of her wineglass in my face. I looked at her in shock; she knew what Eric was like, that me sitting on his knee meant nothing. I walked outside onto the patio, feeling the warmth of the summer evening, and wondering what had happened to everyone. Pattie's life seemed just as crazy as the one I'd left in LA. I realised there was no safe harbour for me to retreat to – I was on my own. Suddenly Eric appeared, his body swaying as he walked towards me and then just as Pattie came out, he put his arms around me. She pushed us hard, shouting, "There you both are!" I was mortified. The whole scene was beginning to feel like a performance from a play, in which I was the unsuspecting bystander. Eric walked away.

Pattie and I stood motionless, staring at him as he staggered off (stage left!). We both turned, looked at each other as if nothing had happened, and then, arm in arm we walked out into the garden and strolled round and round the lawn for I don't know how long. The lights spilled out from the house and showed us the way, as we talked about her life with Eric.

As dawn broke and once we realized Eric had already driven himself home, one of the guests gave Pattie and me a lift back to Eric's house. I found my allotted bedroom - one of the many off the narrow main corridor upstairs - and drifted off to sleep. We were all exhausted from lack of sleep and over-indulgence. Hardly anything made sense anymore, but I also knew that next to nothing would be remembered the following morning.

Throughout the weekend Eric systematically attempted to cut through the bond between my sister and me, trying to make her jealous as he paid me unwanted attention. He had been used to having Pattie to himself, in his world, while I was desperately seeking her in mine.

By the time I left on Sunday afternoon, I was exhausted and stunned. It was as if reality had been completely suspended. Later, Eric told Pattie that he'd been trying to tear us apart because he knew how close we'd always been, and he didn't like it. In years to come, Eric and I would often grate against each other because of our different relationships with Pattie. I had never been attracted to Eric. I had watched him, over the years, hurt two of the people closest to me - Alice and Paula - and now I wondered if he'd do the same to Pattie. I decided to stay away.

Back in London, the day-to-day routine grounded me and was just what I needed. It gave me the time and stability to think about my future, and to build a firm determination to commit myself completely to my life with Mick and the children. Although Mick called me from the road from time to time, he always told me not to call the children. I missed them and thought about them constantly, especially at night as I lay waiting for sleep to take over. It was a great comfort to be able to stay with Sally's family; it helped to provide some sense of normality in this ghastly situation. I felt very close to her eleven-year-old daughter Tiffany, who was finding it hard living with a new stepfather and told me one day, as we stood in the bathroom, how sad I always looked, and how she too missed Amelia and Lucy. I promised I would make sure she came out to visit us in Topanga the following summer.

My month in England had given me the strength and the will needed to start my life with Mick again. Because, ultimately, we both wanted it to work, one day I called him to say I was ready to try again. "Fly to Philadelphia," he said. "You can join up with the tour."

A smart black limo met me at the airport and drove me to The Spectrum, where Fleetwood Mac were playing that night. The luxury of the car, the tinted windows, the little bar enclosed in its wooden casing: I was right back into that other world I knew so well yet filled with anxiety about how this would all work out. The grounding and steadiness I'd found while staying in London seemed far away already.

When I arrived, I was let into the backstage area right away. I could hear the sound of guitars being tuned, voices testing the microphones and the occasional hitting of drums and cymbals on the other side of the wall, as the roadies prepared the stage for that night's gig. Walking towards me along the curved concrete corridor, drumsticks in hand and wearing his black knee length breeches with wooden balls hanging between his legs, was Mick. I felt a surge of happiness. We hugged, both a little nervous as he held my hand and led me towards one of the dressing rooms.

"How are the children?" I asked, desperate to get news of them as soon as possible.

"I spoke to them today," Mick said, squeezing my hand, "and told them you were arriving this evening."

"I'm nervous Mick," I said, as we carried on walking.

"Why?" He stopped and looked at me.

"I'm nervous of seeing the others in the band, nervous of what they might think of me."

Mick hugged me again. "Don't worry," he said. "Let's go and find John to give you some coke so you will be able to stay awake for the show."

Suitably reinforced, I sat on the side of the stage that evening, watching Mick's facial contortions as he drummed, his mouth wide open and his eyes staring into mine. With relief I felt a connection. I was home on familiar territory. After each song, the lights dimmed and the Road Manager walked on stage holding a tray, like a butler, with bottle tops filled with cocaine for each member of the band and as usual, girlfriends and wives had theirs allotted to them in the backstage dressing room. I began drinking vodka and orange and continued to watch the show from the side of the stage, now a little bit tipsy.

As always, there was a party in the hotel, after the gig. Everyone was throwing glasses of wine over each other, and I clicked right back in, throwing a glass of wine over John Courage and getting soaked myself. By the time I got to bed in the early hours of the morning, I'd been up for over twenty-four hours, but was still flying high. We walked to our room in silence. The door closed behind us and Mick sat on the side of the bed with his hands covering his face. I looked on in a state of drunken confusion: he was crying. I felt so ashamed and immediately thought it must be my fault. Had nothing changed? Or was it just relief? I never found out because, as usual, we didn't talk about it. That much, at least, would never change.

When I woke up, I wondered at first where I was. Not even a crack of light seeped in from behind the thick floor-to-ceiling curtains. I opened my eyes wide wallowing in the total darkness and then reached out to feel the slumped body beside me, listening to the gentle rise and fall of Mick's breath. I was aware of the familiar pervading sickly smell of stale alcohol and wondered if I smelt the same.

The sounds from the outside penetrated the steady buzz of air-conditioning, clicking on and off every few minutes like a time bomb. It must be early morning, I thought, as I listened to the whirling sound of a dumper truck hurling trashcans onto the concrete outside. Glass bottles smashed on the sidewalk below; and then a high-pitched siren screamed, sharp and piercing, getting closer and closer before fading into the distance.

I felt my way across the room in the pitch black over the crumpled clothes towards the bathroom. I turned on the light above the mirror, looked at my red, puffy eyes, took a deep breath, and splashed cool water over my face. The very thought of going into the restaurant downstairs filled me with dread, but I needed to eat.

I heaved as I passed a table of large men stooped over their plates of steak and eggs, slurping down cups of foul-smelling coffee and guffawing with laden forks in mid-air. I turned the other way and found an empty table in the far corner. As soon as I sat down, a waitress holding a glass jug of coffee made her way over to me.

Chewing on dry toast and honey, interspersed with sips of hot tea, my mind drifted back in full Technicolor, to myself, wild and crazy, running around the room pouring glasses of wine over anyone who came near me. I moaned as I relived the splashes of vodka thrown in my face, down my t-shirt and into my hair. I'd been oblivious of Mick, knowing he was in the room somewhere, talking, talking; always talking, as I released all my pent-up sadness and loneliness that had kept me silent throughout what felt like a long and painful separation. I groaned as another wave of nausea swept through my body.

After breakfast, I made my way back into the elevator and along the corridor, thinking of the endless times I'd crept out of our room early in the morning, baby in arms, and later toddlers, keeping everyone quiet so as not to wake their father. After making sure the 'Do Not Disturb' notice was still in place, I quietly pushed the key into the lock and then held my breath. The door closed behind me with a loud click. The cold air was still pumping out from the wall above the door as I tried to adjust to the dark.

I stood motionless, scared that I had blown it on my first night back, behaving as if nothing had changed and yet I knew it had. Inside I felt stronger. I hate being on tour, I thought; my life is never my own. I'm completely at the mercy of Mick and his band.

I sighed once more as I felt my way through the darkness and lay beside the stirring body.

"I've missed you," I said. My voice sounded hollow as it reverberated in the room. The mixture of shame from the previous night coupled with little sleep and a crippling hangover made me feel as though my voice was no longer mine. I ignored the smell of cocaine and alcohol as I stroked Mick's hair away from his face while trying to block out the little voice inside that asked, 'has he been true to me?' I knew the answer. The only rule on the road, the sacred rule that everyone had to live by, was to show up for sound check and show up for the gig. He held me in his arms and then the phone rang.

"I'll be there in an hour," he said, and then turned on the light. "Sound check. They're meeting downstairs, better call room service and then get myself into the shower and out of here."

I went over to the window and drew back the curtains, my mind still befuddled, but as nothing was said about the previous night, I let it go and carried on as if nothing had happened. We were together now, and that was all that mattered.

There was just over a week left of the tour and I fell back into road life as Mick and I began to work our way closer to each other. It was somehow less complicated to do so on the road, cocooned against the outside world. But I was counting the days, each one bringing me closer to seeing my little girls and so it was a terrible shock when, just before the tour finished, Mick told me he'd sent the children off to Hawaii with Biddy and Mike for a fortnight's holiday. My spirits sank; clearly the children were being kept away from me until Mick was sure that he and I were going to be all right. When the tour finally finished, with everyone in need of a rest, Mick and I made our way home, ready to start our lives together again.

My spirits rose as we arrived at Topanga - I was home at last. Signs of our children were everywhere, all the familiar toys, books and drawings. I walked up to their bedroom, with the bunk beds against the wall. At the head of the bed hung a framed sepia photograph taken by Herbie in the old Topanga house. It showed Mick sitting in a chair with Amelia in front of him, with me standing to his left holding baby Lucy in my arms, my head to one side and leaning towards Mick. On the opposite wall I noticed a large map of America with little red pins dotted all over it - markers showing the places their daddy had been touring. It made me smile. I walked downstairs to Mick, who was already busy on the phone, scribbling on a note pad, straight back into business. I felt very different from the person who left here six weeks ago. Now, feeling stronger from my time in England, I was ready to set up a home for our children and to commit to our marriage, however difficult it might get.

Builders were due to start structural work, and a young, bald-headed man called David had been hired to create a soundproof studio for Mick downstairs. The outward signs of change helped me feel as if a new era had genuinely begun. More importantly, Mick and I were getting on well in these first few days. Little things, like having lunch together, something we hadn't done for years. I would drive down to meet him in Hollywood, where the band was finishing the *Rumours* album, and off we'd go. He took me to buy new clothes, a welcome change after spending most of the last month in jeans and T-shirts.

It was like being part of a real couple, full of hope and excitement and interest in each other but unfortunately it didn't last long. Just beneath the surface, the old habits were bubbling away. The band were under a lot of pressure from Warner Brothers to finish their album on time, and Mick quickly went back to staying up all night at the studio, taking coke and not coming home. In fact, nothing had changed, and nothing would. Mick was still being Mick and Fleetwood Mac was still all consuming. Maybe I was the one that needed to change; if so, I was determined to try.

On a couple of occasions, I dropped by the studio to hear how the album was sounding. On one of these visits I was walking along the corridor and came across a drunk, rather belligerent sounding John McVie. His marriage to Chris was over and he made some sarcastic, barbed comment about Mick's and my relationship. It touched a nerve. This time I didn't cave in. I wheeled round and socked him on the jaw as hard as I could. We both stood staring at each other. He put his hand to his chin. Chris was talking to someone behind him. He turned around and told her I'd hit him, but she ignored him and carried on talking. John came back, put his arms around me and thanked me. He said no one had ever hit him before, and he knew he deserved it. He carried on walking through the studio, with his arm around my shoulder and proudly telling everyone in sight that I'd slugged him.

The night before the children came home, Mick came back from the studio early. We were both excited and nervous at the thought of seeing them, knowing how much we wanted this to work. Amelia ran straight to me as I bent down to hug her skinny brown body, pressing my wet cheek against hers, overwhelmed with joy and relief. For little Lucy it was more bewildering: I looked up to see her clinging on to Biddy's hand, not sure for a moment what was happening. But soon she too was in my arms. We went inside so they could show me all their Hawaiian shells, flowers and little grass skirts. They showed me the little Stevie Nicks outfits that had been made for them, five-year-old Amelia looking so sweet in her black chiffon skirt and little black bolero top with long flowing chiffon sleeves. Lucy, at three, was a bit chubbier and her costume was held together with big safety pins. I bathed in the ecstasy of hearing their sweet voices and couldn't let them out of my arms.

Shortly afterwards, Biddy and Mike left for England and our reunited family settled into its daily routine. I would drive Amelia and Lucy to the Montessori school in Malibu, a twenty-minute drive from Topanga on Pacific Coast Highway and pick them up in the afternoon. I was delighted by the bits of artwork they brought home, bright paintings, little paper sculptures. The house wasn't particularly comfortable once the builders started work on the studio, knocking out the front door and leaving us with only plastic sheeting in its place. It was a comfort to know we still had our faithful dog Zappa to protect us at night against any less-familiar intruders. Still, I tried not to spend too much time there during the day, instead popping into town or going to visit Mick's new office.

He and John McVie had recently formed a management company for the group, called Seedy Management and he was justifiably proud of the fact that Fleetwood Mac were one of the few bands in the business to manage themselves. The offices were in Hollywood and were run by Judy Wong. They also housed another branch of the operation, called Penguin Promotions, which oversaw touring. One of the employees at Penguin was a woman called Gabriele, who had previously worked at Warner Brothers.

She was slim and pretty, with long blond hair, and was highly efficient. Mick spent many hours with her, plotting his strategic moves and endlessly discussing his growing empire. It made me wish I could be a workingwoman. She was present at all the meetings, she was slick and cool, and - far, far worse - Mick would continue to be with her way after office hours. Sometimes around midnight, he would call me, saying he was on his way home from her house, and then he'd ring every hour or so afterwards, saying he was just leaving. Eventually he'd roll in around five or six in the morning, completely wasted, stumbling through the plastic sheeting.

"Do you fancy Gabrielle?" I whispered one night as we lay in bed.

"I don't like her teeth," he said, and then, leaving me with my doubts, he promptly dropped off to sleep. I never asked again.

The most pressing engagement for the office to organize was a short European promotional press tour, beginning in October, to publicize the band's new line-up and the tour scheduled for the following spring. It was brought to our attention that the British members of the band would all need green cards if they were to return to live and work in the States. The normally lengthy process of application could be shortened by a good word from a politician. One was easily offered, in return for the group's promise to play a fund-raising concert the following year. But there was one further problem: in order for the children and me to be included as part of the green card package, Mick and I had to be husband and wife. A ceremony was quickly convened in the office of the band's lawyer, Micky Shapiro. Lindsey was our best man, and Amelia and Lucy our supporters. Always the optimist, I hoped this second marriage, even though I knew it was forced upon us, would bring us closer together.

Together we left for England and stayed at the Montcalm Hotel near Marble Arch. Peter Green came to visit us there. He had long straggly hair, was overweight, and looked generally disheveled. It was sad and uncomfortable to see him. It seemed to me that as far as Fleetwood Mac had ascended, he had gone just as far the other way. Danny Kirwan showed up too, and that was equally disturbing. He was very bedraggled and still filled with anxiety. He spent the whole time scratching himself; balls, bottom, head, he didn't care. Other faces from the past appeared during the few days we were in England, and although I'd been in London only three months earlier, we all somehow felt this time around as if we'd landed from the moon. For Amelia and Lucy though it was exciting. They longed to ride in a double-decker bus.

"We always go in limos," they moaned, "why can't we go on a bus?"

Back in California ten days later, work on the house renovations had by now rendered it virtually uninhabitable and so, shortly after our return in October we moved to a rented house in the Malibu Colony. With the move, life for me became more sociable. Instead of being isolated up in laid-back, spread-out Topanga Canyon we were now at the heart of the Colony, a row of about thirty exclusive houses, all close together, all backing onto a private beach. Walking down the steps from our rented house brought us right into the middle of the beach life. A couple of houses away from us lived Ronnie Wood and his wife Krissy with their new baby.

Now we were in Malibu, it was easy for people to drop in - and certainly more pleasant than visiting the building site in Topanga. My friend Sandra spent a lot of time with the children and me. She would stay overnight with us, and we'd take Amelia and Lucy to school the next morning or go to the swings and slides in the park. Ronnie would often pop round during the day, his black spiky hair, and the grin that reached from ear to ear, became a familiar sight. He always wore colorful clothes, like a harlequin. His humor filled my heart with joy. It helped, I think, that we were both English - for being English in Los Angeles gave us another reason, apart from the music world in which we moved, to gravitate towards each other. It gave us a sense of stability, not least because we spoke the same language and understood the same jokes.

Sandra and I would sometimes go out in the evening, but getting babysitters wasn't easy, and most evenings I stayed at home looking after the children. One night, for the first time, Mick was obliged to take the job. Sandra and I were talking to Ronnie and Krissy, who had popped over for a drink, when Mick appeared unexpectedly. It was a rare and relaxed evening as we exchanged stories about life on the road. Around midnight, hot for more action, Ronnie suddenly said,

"Let's go to Neil Young's recording session, it's not far."

I jumped up, feeling far too merry to stay in the house by myself and turned to Mick and asked him to baby sit. For once our roles were reversed and he had to agree, unused though he was to being left behind.

Occasionally I would drive into town with Mick to the recording studio. I remember one day as we drove along Pacific Coast Highway listening to the tapes of the still unfinished *Rumours* tracks. I loved all the songs on the album; they were all so beautiful and so emotionally charged. Every time I heard Chris's haunting song 'Oh Daddy' I felt a knot inside. That is exactly what he is to them I thought, he is their Daddy and I wished he was ours. I sometimes felt I was with someone who had completely turned off and it reminded me of a fairytale I'd read as a child, called, The Snow Queen. Gerda's once loving brother gets a slither of ice into his heart given to him by the Snow Queen, which turns him cold towards his sister.

The constant use of cocaine, although it helped with the crazy hours they spent in the studio, created what I believe was an impenetrable wall around his heart. But we didn't know that in those days, it was just part of this lifestyle. Mick was completely absorbed by the whole process of finishing the album, going on tours, keeping the band together, and being 'Big Daddy' all of which took every bit of his time and energy. But something inside me rebelled, even though I admired him for what he was doing in the band.

Even though the rest of my life felt good, I was desperate for some kind of acknowledgement from Mick, with the inevitable result that I often went about trying to get it in the worst, most counterproductive way possible.

Matters reached an alcohol-accelerated head one night at a party at Chris McVie's house in Hollywood. Over the years I had admired Chris's artistic ability to turn anywhere she lived into a warm and welcoming home. Her grand piano took pride of place in the sitting room, with a beautiful pre-Raphaelite painting above it of St. Cecilia, the patron saint of music. The sofas and chairs were deep, fat and comfortable, and placed equally well for intimate conversations or large groups of people. Flowers and bowls of fruit and nuts sat on tables around the room, and the kitchen was big enough for helping hands, or just sitting and chatting while Chris cooked her delicious meals. She lived there with her boyfriend Curry, the Fleetwood Mac lighting director, and our friend Sandra with her new graphic designer boyfriend, Larry Vigon, who went on to be the art director and designer for six of the Fleetwood Mac albums.

I was feeling happy, we'd had a lovely day with Chris while getting the house ready for the party and I was looking forward to seeing Mick later that evening. Sandra and I had gone shopping for party clothes, and I bought a pair of scarlet red high heels and a beautiful new dress. I wanted to look pretty for Mick; I wanted him to notice me. We went back to Chris's house, opened a bottle of champagne, and Sandra set to curling my hair. With my very high heels, my new dress and my curly hair we all decided that a black beret would just add the finishing touch.

We were all fairly tipsy as the house filled up with the usual friends, most of them connected with the band. Every so often I would cast my eye towards the front door or look around the room to see if Mick had arrived before having another drink or a dance and chatting with Sandra and her new boyfriend.

Around midnight Mick arrived, looking cool and aloof. It was the moment I'd been waiting for but by now I was quite inebriated. I walked up to him, not quite sure what to say having not had a greeting from him, when out of my mouth came the fatal words:

"Do you respect me?"

He stared down at me with disdainful stone cold eyes from his full height of six-and-a-half feet, indifferent to my high heels and curly hair, and without a moment's hesitation said, "No."

I was crushed, but I'd have been astonished if he'd said anything else and I didn't know why I'd asked. I wobbled off and proceeded to get plastered, hiding my pain behind laughter and jokes with Sandra, Chris and Curry. I joined in with the dancing, losing myself in a Stevie Wonder record, until I bumped into a wooden cupboard that came crashing down to the ground, and almost took me with it. It was a humiliating end to a desperate evening. I had made the fatal mistake of asking Mick the one thing I couldn't bear to hear the answer to. The truth of it was that my self-esteem was completely bound up in his regard for me. If he didn't respect me, I could not respect myself. But confronting the truth of it didn't alter anything between us; it just made me feel sad.

The suppressed anger that covered the deep well of sadness was never far from the surface and would instantly be fuelled and magnified by alcohol. One night while Pattie was visiting us for a few days we arranged to have dinner with Chris. Mick joined us at her house later in the evening. I was feeling rather tipsy as we sat around the coffee table after the meal, chatting before going home. As we said goodbye to Chris, she handed me a couple of china ramekin bowls filled with chocolate mousse left over from dinner.

Mick had arrived in his own car, the black Porsche, and as he crossed the road towards it, I suddenly knew he wouldn't be following Pattie and me back home. All the hurt and anger welled up inside, loosened by a few glasses of wine, and I hurled first one and then the other ramekin dish as hard as I could at his dark retreating body, missing him by inches but smashing on the wheel of his car on the other side of the street. He got in and drove off without a word or a backward glance while Pattie did her best to calm my rage.

But these occasional outbursts, that I had never experienced before, had absolutely no effect on Mick at all – he was impenetrable and carried on day after day, doing whatever he needed to do to keep the big Fleetwood Mac wheel turning, completely and utterly absorbed in his own world and seemingly oblivious to his wife who was crying out to be seen, to be heard and acknowledged.

Whenever I was with Chris and Sandra, the rejection was not so hard to bear. We would share boyfriend and husband stories and make light of them. On another evening at Chris's house, when Mick was due to pick me up on his way home, Chris and Sandra came up with the idea of dressing me in one of Chris's sexiest lacy black nightdresses, to see if Mick would notice. I went along with the idea, feeling rather self-conscious. After changing into my new attire, I took a seat, the low-cut nightdress strategically arranged, and waited for the bell to ring. We tried not to giggle on hearing the footsteps outside the door. As things turned out, Mick walked into the room without even looking in my direction and sat next to Chris for about half an hour, talking non-stop about the band. Sandra and I tried as hard as we could to have a normal conversation until, finally, after having felt invisible long enough, I got up and changed into my jeans and waited for the silent ride home. In the face of such complete and public indifference, it was hard to know what else to do. Mick wasn't interested in playing these silly games; he was only interested in how the recording was going or plans for the next tour.

There were some occasions when Mick and I felt like a couple, when he was able to allow himself to enjoy the ever-increasing celebrations and the success of Fleetwood Mac. At these times our differences were forgotten and together we joined in with the feelings of joy and pride that reverberated around everyone that was part of the band.

We went to the Rock Awards in the New Year, where the band walked off with best group and best album awards for their Fleetwood Mac record. Three of their hit singles had stayed in the charts for eighty weeks and they were riding the crest of a wave that would peak with the major awards at the Grammies a year later. At the party afterwards I was thrilled to see Mae West and asked her for her autograph. It was something I had never dared do before. She seemed almost to be glowing, and her skin looked unbelievably youthful; it was only when I looked down at her wrinkled hands signing the autograph that I noticed her age.

There was a tremendous excitement in the air all evening, and a wonderful sense of mutual respect among all the musicians there. I felt compelled to go up to Stevie Wonder and shake his hand, telling him how much I admired his music, and it made me smile to see Chris walk over to Pat Boone and tell him how great he looked, and so young. We all felt enormously intoxicated by the evening. Fleetwood Mac had received the acknowledgment they deserved and had worked so hard for, throughout all the heartache and pain. They had, between them, now achieved their dream.

Rumours was released in February 1977 and with it came yet more of the endless publicity photographs and press articles. There was another shoot at Topanga when a crew came to take more pictures of Mick. He put on a nightshirt and jumped into our bed with a nightcap on his head. The children loved it, laughing and scrambling all over him. With his beard and hair, he reminded me of the big bad wolf dressed up as the grandmother. Other sessions took place at various photographers' studios, and one of these - for the cover of Rolling Stone Magazine - continued, as so often, through the night. Mick arrived home early the next morning, just before the children got up. I could tell it had been a night of drink and coke, and he was elated.

He described the idea they'd had of being photographed in bed together, him and Stevie cuddled up at one end with Lindsey and Chris together at the other, and John alone reading the paper. The intention was a spoof on the rumors about their private lives, and yet, symbolically, the picture showed them exactly as they were. All married to each other. But during the session, Mick told me in all seriousness, he had realized one thing for sure: "Stevie and I have definitely known each other in a previous life." I was later to see the photograph of the two of them snuggled up together, a large satisfied smile on Mick's face and Stevie giggling beside him, and wished I'd understood then what he had meant by that remark.

A journey beyond the muse

RUMOURS FLYING

Next on the agenda for Fleetwood Mac was a tour to support the release of their new album. Rehearsals began in a large studio lot behind the office. Mick was there every day, and from time to time I would drive down with the children to watch them. There was a buzz in the air, and a whirl of activity as every aspect of the stage show was honed and people rushed around, finalizing all the details for the road. They knew they were onto something big this time, even bigger than the last album. Mick predicted that sales would reach around nine million.

Everything to do with Fleetwood Mac felt so huge, so all-absorbing, that I found myself quite surprised when Mick could spare time to be home from his frenetic round of rehearsing, getting tied up in the office or making plans to manage Bob Welch. Any moment when we could be like a normal couple, seeing friends at our house together, was to be treasured. It was a rare thing for us to invite people to our home for dinner. The people Mick wanted to see, he saw every day, and the others he would bump into at parties or backstage at a gig.

One evening, when I knew he was on his way home, I invited Ronnie Wood over and he brought his old friend Keith Moon, from The Who. It was the first dinner we'd had together with friends in our home, an evening I will always treasure, when a bit of normality of ourselves as a couple crept into our lives. Keith and I reminisced about old times at the Scotch of St. James's nightclub back in the sixties, and he told me how difficult he found life at times. Because he was a funny man, and often very silly, he had built up an image over the years that had grown so large he felt trapped inside the persona. Since everyone expected it of him, he couldn't help but play the fool, which meant his more introspective side hardly got a look-in; only on rare occasions such as this. He didn't feel the need to be a clown that evening. Over the years, the memory of our talk has become more precious and meaningful to me, for it wasn't long after this conversation that I heard he'd died.

With the tour preparations complete, the band went out on the road and the children and I settled down to life without Mick. It was easier in many ways when he was gone. None of the anxieties about whether he would be coming back at night, no reminders of the gaps in our relationship, none of the pain of not communicating. My own routine remained centered around the girls, and seeing Sandra at Chris McVie's house, and Ronnie, who would often come up to visit me in Topanga. Sometimes we'd go for a ride along Pacific Coast Highway, visiting other friends of his, and talking into the night. He was a good friend, and although I never talked to him about Mick, I always felt he knew. Whenever he would pop over to Chris McVie's house where Sandra and I would be swimming with the girls, he was full of apparently inexhaustible energy and an endless ability to make us all laugh. He would stay for hours, and after I'd put the children to bed, we would have dinner and stay up late talking and listening to music.

Seeing Ronnie was innocent fun. He loved simply hanging out, and it stopped me from feeling lonely. I was about to meet up with him the following day when, out of the blue, Mick called from the road, saying he wanted the children and me to join him in Austin, Texas. We flew out to meet him and settled back into the touring circus of hotels and planes and one-night stops. But the children were used to being on the road, always carrying their little canvas bags filled with colored pencils and paper, quite unfazed by the sense that tens of thousands of people were queuing up to see their father and his friends every night.

A couple of months later the children and I went to London with Mick and the band and stayed at the Royal Garden Hotel in Kensington. It was good to be back in England. It was very different from the year before when I had felt so lost and alone. Now I was married to Mick again and we were united as a family. Countless friends and family came to visit us at the hotel; all eager to see Fleetwood Mac play at Wembley - their first ever gig back home with the new line-up.

One night I went to the show with Pattie and a rather drunk Eric. We stood at the back of the hall. Stevie looked magnetic, singing and dancing in her black chiffon outfit and high-heeled boots. The lights changed color as they followed her across the stage and when she grabbed the microphone and yelled out 'Rhiannon' I could feel the pulse of the audience rise. But Eric was not impressed. I was aware of him shuffling and mumbling beside me.

"He's a good guitarist," he said, nodding his head in the direction of Lindsey, "but he's too tight, too locked inside himself to be great."

I think Eric was in some ways genuinely upset by what he saw. The Wembley show was worlds apart from the old Fleetwood Mac days with Peter Green. Eric had known Peter; they were like two musical peas from the same blues pod. Mick, John and Chris had strayed a long way from the roots that sustained Eric; they had become an American super group, with a snazzy, slick West Coast show, set, lights and all. After a couple more numbers I could see Eric was getting increasingly impatient with Stevie, calling her a dark witch. Finally, he walked out of the hall and waited for Pattie and me by the bar. I wasn't entirely sure if he really didn't like watching the band, or if he simply wanted a top up.

While the band was touring England, I arranged for Amelia and Lucy to be christened along with two of their cousins. Among the guests were my mother, Biddy and Mike, and my sister Paula with her son William. Paula's drink problem had escalated by then and it was while sitting at the table afterwards, she passed out face down right into the middle of the christening cake. The children thought it was very funny. It was in fact terribly sad. Although we'd had fun only a few days before walking through Kensington Gardens, I could see things had got worse since I last saw her.

I felt a large gulf between us and a lot of the people we saw in England on that trip, people we hadn't been in touch with for many years who now wanted to see Mick and me, and get a feel for what success was like in California. I felt as if we were somehow larger than life in their eyes, rich and famous and a little bit glamorous - part of the bright, Californian circus that had come to town - and there was an element of awe in their attitude towards us that made it difficult to feel entirely at ease. We had become different, alien; we were now visitors in our own country.

It was with an unexpected sense of relief that, a short while later, I flew with the children to join Mick in Paris along with Biddy, Mike and the rest of his family. We stayed at the George V hotel, in a magnificent suite with two bedrooms and a huge sitting room, luxuriously furnished with gilded sofas and chairs and enormous French windows. I perched on the window sill, watching Biddy and Mike as they sat by Mick, laughing at the almost excessive splendor of the room and then falling about as he pulled two pencils from a pot and knocked one against the other, saying, "Look at me, I've got all this money because I can hit two bits of wood together!"

Mick's sister, Sally, knew Paris well, and after dinner one night, took a few of us to a nightclub. We danced until dawn. I had always loved to see Mick dance, and we hadn't danced together for so long. With Sally around, he seemed to become more like the Mick of old, and I'm sure the unavailability of cocaine helped. We were the last to leave the club, and I have fond memories of the four of us, including Mick's old bass player, linked arm in arm, strolling through Paris in the early hours of the morning under a fine mist of rain.

Once the European leg of the tour was over, we returned to Los Angeles for a few days before Mick set out again with the band to carry on touring through the States. They met with sell-out audiences everywhere, and sales of *Rumours* continued to rise. In May of that year it hit number one in the Billboard charts, replacing The Eagles' *Hotel California* and stayed there for the next eight months.

Since returning to Topanga, Mick and I could only share his triumph by telephone. So much of our life was centered on the phone that we had developed a kind of telepathic instinct for when the other was going to call. He was usually the one to ring while on the road, but one evening I needed to speak to him and when I was put through to his room a woman answered the phone. I held my breath. There was nothing I could do - it was part of the hazard of having a husband on the road. I held firm to my commitment to our relationship and hung up.

I had other distractions too. That summer, while Mick was still on tour, Sally's daughter, Tiffany, came out to stay for a couple of months as we'd agreed the previous year. Although she was only twelve, I felt a deep connection with Tiffany. She was unhappy living with her stepfather and loved being with us. We had sweet little dinner parties, just the four of us, Amelia, Lucy, Tiff and me. It was a special world, being with them, soft and gentle and full of love; I'd rarely felt happier.

Not long after she left a thunderbolt struck! Mick called me from the road, more upset than I'd ever heard him. His father had been diagnosed with cancer and given only six months to live. We were both devastated. Mike had been told that conventional medicine could do nothing for him, and he was about to start trying alternative treatment; beginning with a homeopathic doctor he'd been seeing in London. Mick wanted his parents nearby and asked them to stay with us. He told me urgently, to find someone who could help his father.

I had no idea where to start, but then I remembered a friend telling me about a Dr. Mark Holmes, an acupuncturist who lived in Malibu. We arranged to meet at a coffee bar on Pacific Coast Highway. At first sight, I had my doubts. He looked so thoroughly Californian with his brown face and sun-bleached hair, and he seemed far too young to have much experience. As it turned out, however he had spent a considerable amount of time in Japan studying acupuncture and traditional Chinese medicine, and his youthful thirty years belied a remarkable wisdom, sympathy and maturity. We sat at a table in the corner of the coffee bar as I told him about Mike and asked if he thought there was any hope. He assured me there was always hope, and suggested we meet his Japanese master once Biddy and Mike arrived.

I had always been interested in homeopathy and other alternative ways of healing and began asking him questions about his work. As we got up to leave, I made an appointment for myself to see him at his office in Santa Monica, probably more out of curiosity than anything else.

Over the next few weeks, in the interval before Mick got back from tour, my visits to Mark became more and more important to me. It would be no exaggeration to say they began to change my life. Between the acupuncture, and with the aid of his gentle and supportive manner, I didn't feel the need to drink when in social situations. I felt I had someone who was completely on my side, who cared about me and wanted to help. The positive effect of feeling supported gave me even more confidence in suggesting he look after Mike. Equally important, I found the strength and comfort within myself that I had been so desperately seeking in Mick. The consequence was that not only did my perspective on our relationship change, but so too did my sense of the balance of power within it.

Mick had realized that Topanga was not big enough for Biddy and Mike to stay and, with Fleetwood Mac doing so well, he was able now to afford a larger house in a very exclusive part of Beverly Hills. I found a beautiful white New England Colonial-style house in Bel Air, into which we moved while Mick was still on tour. It was much closer to Hollywood and far less cut off than Topanga. The house stood on top of a small hill and was reached by driving through two big electrically operated iron gates. The driveway led up to a double garage, and a large space for Mick's ever-increasing number of cars. From here there was a little path to the front door, with a garden on one side and a swimming pool on the other. On the ground floor was a large sitting room, elegant with oriental rugs covering polished floorboards. It looked more like a house from England rather than Los Angeles, and as soon as we bought additional furniture, it felt like our first real home.

It was here that Mick joined us for a short, ten-day break before embarking on the next stage of their tour, around New Zealand, Australia and Japan. He looked dreadful: exhausted, pale and pasty with dark circles under his eyes, his beard long and unkempt. His clothes - the Chinese silk shirts and tailored waistcoats - looked very smart, but inside I knew he was frayed, that his internal seams were coming apart. Still, he loved the house, its big rooms and the sense of space, and we decided to celebrate my thirtieth birthday with a house-warming party. Inevitably, because it was November 1st, it turned into a Halloween fancy dress party for the extended Fleetwood Mac family. I was still not drinking, and loved dressing up, dancing and letting go without the fear of losing control. During the evening a very drunk Stevie came up to me and secretively pushed a pill into my hand. "A birthday present for you," she whispered. I knew Stevie took uppers and laughed later when she told me that she'd given me a slimming pill by mistake. I hadn't taken it anyway, already feeling happy without the need for stimulants - I loved dancing, and it was enough for me to enjoy taking the floor with a smooth-looking Boz Skaggs in a room full of friends.

Mick spent most of his days during this time off in a blacked-out bedroom, never getting to bed before morning. His cocaine intake had rocketed, and I watched unhappily as he delved into his big plastic bag of powder before going out to meetings with lawyers or Warner Brothers. It was in stark contrast to Mike, who arrived with Biddy, looking healthy and cheerful, as he always was, making it impossible to imagine he'd been given only a few months to live. I think it was a shock for them to see the state their son was in, he looked more like Rasputin these days. His hair was long and straggly, as was his beard. I found his appearance upsetting and at the same time I felt sad for him; it was obvious that he wasn't in a good way, and I desperately wanted to help.

One night, after everyone had gone to bed, I followed him into the sitting room. I felt much stronger in myself now, having given up drinking and with the immense support I was getting from Mark Holmes. I wasn't frightened of Mick anymore; I no longer needed to ask him, "Do you respect me?" This time I was able to speak to him from a place of strength and caring, of inner calm and self-respect. We sat together on the sofa, and I held his hand.

"Talk to me," I whispered, "I'll support you with whatever you need." I thought I understood the depth of his pain - his dream had come true after years of work and heartache, and Fleetwood Mac had finally made it; and yet, at exactly the same time, came the nightmare of his father's impending death. It seemed so sad.

After a moment's silence, Mick looked up at me and nodded.

"Go to bed," he said, his voice husky and hardly audible. "I'll be up in a few minutes."

I went to bed and waited; and when the waiting got too long, I crept downstairs again to see if he was all right. The sofa was empty, the front door was wide open, and his car had gone. He had vanished. I felt as though I'd been slapped in the face, and stupid for believing after all this time that I had got through to him, that maybe just this once we could have talked about all the things that were keeping us apart. But with Biddy and Mike there I saw the full impact of Mick's behavior afresh, for they were certainly seeing it for the first time. They had always thought their son could do no wrong, but now they felt compelled to talk to me about how strange Mick had become, and how they understood at last how difficult it must have been for me. Their understanding meant a great deal. I was no longer the unreliable element in their eyes, the tables had turned; Mick was falling apart while I was holding things together.

With Biddy and Mike now living with us, we spent many happy hours talking and playing with the children. Mick became the wayward son, rarely home in the evenings and spending little time with any of us, until he went off on tour again.

Three weeks later, after the band had completed its swing through Australia, New Zealand and Japan, I flew out with Biddy, Mike and the children to meet up with Mick in Hawaii. There were presents for us all - Amelia and Lucy looked sweet in their little Japanese kimonos - but Mick continued to seem distant and distracted, and physically just as wretched as before. It was all the more startling in this paradise, and I remember thinking what a contrast he made to the black-belt karate bodyguards the group had now retained, one for each of them. The children and I would get up early and watch the karate guys working out on the beach at the water's edge. They looked so graceful as they practised in their loose-fitting outfits, silhouetted against the pale silver sunrise and the palm trees.

From there we flew back in time for Christmas at our house in Bel Air. In the past we had always gone to Chris McVie's house, so it was to be our first Christmas at home, and all of Mick's family were invited. I knew how much they were looking forward to seeing Mick; I knew too how little of him they were likely to see. Sally arrived with her husband and children, and Mick's other sister Sue, and his aunt Nora. Nora was Mike's elder sister and she came from Liverpool. My first impression of her was of an elegant-looking sixty-year-old, tall and slim with thin red lips and a pale powdered face and short white hair. She would sit on the edge of a chair as she chatted to us in her Liverpool accent, her back ramrod straight with both knees to one side and holding a cigarette in a hand stuck in mid-air. Nora looked immaculate, with nothing out of place. But she had never been to California before, and had spent very little time with her brother and his family.

On that first night we all went to a very glamorous and famous restaurant in Beverly Hills called Chasens, where all the movie stars would congregate for the

Academy Awards parties. Mike hadn't seen Nora for years, but as she became more inebriated, a mixture of jet lag and lethal cocktails, she got up from the table where the whole family was sitting, insisting on dancing to the Spanish Fandango. In just one evening Aunty Nora's straightlaced English reserve had become completely undone as she started to turn decidedly Californian. Much to his distaste, when it was time to leave, Mike had to almost carry the drunken Aunty Nora out of the restaurant in full view of the paparazzi with their light bulbs flashing. But the final straw, and what sent Nora on the next plane back to England the following day, was when she peed on the seat in the limo. That was the last we ever saw of her.

It should have been a perfect family Christmas. All Mick's nearest and dearest were there and the house looked festive and welcoming with a large Christmas tree in the sitting room and masses of presents underneath it. The children played and swam outside while the grown-ups cooked and talked and laughed and drank to good health and good fortune. But for me it was marred by my growing sense of detachment from and disenchantment with Mick. Apart from the odd evening out, none of us saw much of him that holiday. He would make the occasional appearance, his face haggard, buried under his long scruffy beard, blowing his nose and smelling strongly of patchouli oil. Since I'd stopped drinking the gulf between the two of us had continued to widen, and after all the rebuffs I had ceased reacting to his behavior. My pain and confusion had been replaced by a far colder, clearer feeling of disdain.

Nevertheless, the New Year started brilliantly for the group. Fleetwood Mac received all the music awards, and in February *Rumours* was pronounced Album of the Year at the Grammy Awards. Rolling Stone magazine had nominated them Band of the Year, Best Album and Best Single (Dreams). While they were flying high in every way, my feet stayed on the ground. Looking around me with a sober eye, my dissatisfaction had come to a head and I decided it was time to leave. I could no longer get through to Mick, I no longer respected him, and I was beginning to feel worried about the effect of seeing him this way was having on the children. I wanted them to respect their father at least when they grew older. I'd made my commitment, and worked hard at it, but the reality had become intolerable. Late at night, when everyone had gone to bed and the two of us were sitting on the floor in the den, I told Mick of my decision. He'd been drinking and was slumped against the wall, a glass of brandy in his hand. He pushed the glass in my face and said, "Go on, have some." I backed away. "You've changed," he murmured, slurring his words. "You've become strong."

He was right. I had made up my mind to leave Los Angeles and take the children back to the saner world that England represented for me. It wasn't so much that I wanted nothing more to do with Mick; more that I hoped it would shock him into changing his lifestyle, into bringing him back to reality. I didn't know in those days about psychotherapy or Al-Anon (a program of recovery for the family and friends of alcoholics), I didn't know how to live with an addict. I was stumbling around in the dark.

By now my mother was living in Scotland. I called and asked if we could stay with her. She was thrilled and told me to let her know as soon as we arrived. I was unable to leave immediately because my youngest brother, Boo, and his wife, were due to visit, so I waited for them before packing our bags.

I hadn't seen Boo for a long time and his work as a chef had taken him and his wife to the Bahamas the previous year. It was good to see him, and I tried to make his trip as enjoyable as possible, given the circumstances, and without putting too much of a burden onto his young shoulders. Even so, those last few days weren't easy and the night before we were due to leave for England all the tension seemed suddenly to explode in my head. My brother told me he'd overheard Biddy and Mike telling Mick, as they sat out in the garden together by the pool, that I was basically the same unreliable person I'd always been. I was stunned. There were times in the past when I might have reluctantly accepted this, but not now. In the last few months I felt I had achieved so much and now had such a strong and clear sense of purpose. I'd been the sober, stable, central anchor for everyone. Now I felt they had completely betrayed me. Once again, they'd closed ranks along family lines.

That evening I sat alone with Mick in the dining room in a cold fury. I was so angry, so consumed by the absolute injustice of it all that I wanted to pick up the large oak table and throw it across the room. I wanted revenge, however irrational, and told him I would stay if his parents went back to England. It was a knee-jerk reaction, and of course he refused. And of course, too, I wouldn't on reflection really have wanted them to be sent back.

I barely slept that night, and when morning came Mick helped us load our luggage into the limo. Nobody objected this time, as if it was perfectly understood by all three of them that me leaving and taking the children with me was the right thing to do. I was never to find out what they really thought; there was no discussion. The actual parting, though, was painful, even harder than deciding to go. It took all my will to see it through. Mick hugged both the girls, and took me gently in his arms, his tall body leaning over mine. Then he looked me in the eyes, his hands grasping each of my shoulders, and whispered, "Take care of yourselves." As in times past, I was only a hair's breadth from staying. If he'd said, "Please don't go," I would have changed my mind in an instant. It was unbearably sad, only this time the anger I felt towards Biddy and Mike helped sustain me. The sense of betrayal had hit deep.

The children didn't know exactly what was happening, only that we were going to England. I hoped they wouldn't miss their father too badly and tried to reassure myself that they were used to being separated from him. But that didn't mean they didn't mind. As we were preparing to leave, I couldn't help remembering a day, a few weeks earlier, when Mick's Porsche wouldn't start. After a few tries he called for a tow-truck to come and take it to the garage. Lucy and I had stood in the driveway, watching the truck chug up the hill. A man got out and fixed the Porsche onto a big metal hook, then he turned and drove slowly back through the wrought iron gates with the car hanging behind the truck. Lucy burst into tears. She'd had little time with her father, and she didn't want any more taken away. I prayed this next move would not cause more unhappiness.

We arrived in London and stopped overnight at a hotel where Paula and her son William joined us. The cousins played together while Paula and I talked, and gradually the enormity of what I'd done sank in. I was relieved to have escaped from Los Angeles, but the future was a complete blank. Apart from catching the train to Scotland the next day I had no idea in which direction to go. But I was determined to hold on to my resolve. Hiding my fear and mustering some courage, I told the children we were all off on a big adventure and they would be having far too interesting a time to worry about anything sad. But in my heart, I knew I was doing the very thing I never wanted to do to my children.

A blanket of snow greeted us once we arrived in Scotland. The girls were delighted; perhaps it really was going to be an adventure. My mother met us at the station and bundled us all into her car. After the warmth of the train it was startlingly cold and blustery. My mother lived in a bleak-looking tenement block, with tiny rooms, suitable at a pinch for one person. Outside was a yard in which countless little neighborhood kittens scampered around. For the first time, it dawned on me that my mother had in fact very little money, and that she lived extremely frugally. It was a far cry from Bel Air, in every possible way. Very generously, she turned the heating on full for us, but we stayed cold, unused to February weather in the Highlands. We had lived in the Californian sunshine for the last four years and for the couple of weeks we stayed in Scotland, the three of us were sick with flu, laryngitis and chest infections.

Soon we were to become a burden for my mother, but I didn't know where else to go. Although I was determined to keep going, I was groping in the dark and full of regret and sorrow. It took an effort of will to remember that the Mick I missed so much bore no resemblance to the Mick I'd left behind, made all the harder still when the girls told me, as they so often did, how much they missed their Daddy. Keeping up their spirits was a never-ending pursuit. All I had only ever longed for was for us all to be together as a family, but that now seemed impossible.

I called my friend, Alice Ormsby Gore. She and our old friend, Kelvin, were living together on the border of Wales, in Shrewsbury. Alice told me she'd heard of an old farmhouse for rent not far from where they were living. It sounded ideal, and I was thrilled at the thought of being near Alice and Kelvin, so I bought an ancient Morris Traveller with moss growing inside the windows and began the four-hour journey to Shrewsbury.

When we arrived, the house turned out to be both beautiful and absurdly impractical. An old stone cottage at the end of a mile-long driveway with everything covered in snow and surrounded by sloping fields. It was completely secluded and had no central heating. I loved the countryside, but that didn't help us get warm. Fires in the kitchen and sitting room stayed lit from early morning to late at night and we all took hot water bottles to bed. Alice brought bits and pieces over from her house in an attempt to make everything as comfortable as possible. She had definite views on my situation and kept telling me I'd done the right thing. It was a comfort to hear, but inside I never felt quite as certain as she did. It was impossible not to have doubts, and I still felt a very long way from knowing what to do next.

I found a school in the town where the children could start the following week. At least something was organized now, I thought; but after only their first day, Alice told me Mick had called and wanted to speak to me. I felt relieved; news from the home front. Four weeks had passed since leaving Los Angeles, and it seemed just to have dawned on him that we weren't there. When Mick called back it was comforting to hear his voice and immediately some of the old fondness flooded through my veins. I could tell he'd missed us, perhaps more than he was saying, and I knew I'd had moments of uncertainty during our separation too. He wanted to talk things over in person but wasn't allowed to step foot in England for tax reasons, so he asked if we could meet him in Southern Ireland. The children were over the moon about seeing their father, longing to tell him about their adventure.

I looked forward to it too, although with some trepidation. Alice called her sister Victoria who lived in Ireland with her husband and small children and asked if we could stay with them for a few days at their house in Dublin.

Mick looked better than when I last saw him and we immediately relaxed in each other's company. Over a long and happy meal in a Dublin restaurant, while the girls played under and around the table, Mick told me how much he'd missed us and asked if I would come back to LA with the children.

"I know it's been difficult Jenny, but I'll buy a house in Malibu for you and the girls," he said, fiddling with a napkin ring. "It'll allow us both more time and space to think about our future."

Without a moment's hesitation, I said yes, feeling instantly that I owed Mick another chance. I was also beginning to dream in those few hours of seeing him that maybe, just maybe it could work. My most favorite moments in the world was when the four of us were together, it felt so complete, and happened so rarely.

The signs seemed hopeful, and Mick and I took ourselves off to the West of Ireland for a couple of days alone, leaving Amelia and Lucy to stay in Dublin with Victoria and her family. After hours of driving along the country roads in our hired car, we spent the night huddled close, shivering and happy in a cold little room above a rowdy pub. It was as if the magic of Ireland had worked its tricks on us, as if the years had dropped away as we slipped right back into our best and most comfortable way of being together. There were no distractions, no work, no coke, nothing but for us to enjoy ourselves; and as we grew accustomed to each other, and laughed and joked and marveled at the countryside, I felt the chances of getting back together grow ever stronger. What I didn't know then, but was shortly to discover, was that Mick was harboring a secret that would have instantly deflated all my newly found optimism.

Mick returned to LA and we began our time in the holding bay while he looked for a house. All my previous plans were abandoned. I immediately did an about-turn based on the strength of a few words from Mick. There was no point in the girls going back to their school, and I wasn't even sure I wanted to stay in Shrewsbury. Pattie had returned from being on tour with Eric and asked me to bring the girls and stay with her before our trip back. As far as I was concerned, it was just what the doctor ordered, so I sold my car and settled in to wait for the summons from Mick.

After the rigors of the last few weeks it was an enormous relief to know that he had taken over the reins, and that the responsibility of finding a new life for the children no longer rested solely on my shoulders. Lucy was still badly affected by the English winter and I longed for us all to be back in the sunshine. Up until this time I had remained sober, but on seeing Pattie I immediately fell back into our familiar pattern of celebrating our reunion with a bottle of champagne. I was still very influenced by her, so much so that I lost sight of my resolve to stay sober.

A few weeks later Mick called to say that everything was ready. We packed our bags, said our farewells to Pattie and with a renewed spring in our step made our way to Heathrow Airport and the long flight back to Los Angeles.

Much to my surprise and delight, as we came out of Customs I saw Mick standing by the barrier at LAX. As soon as he saw the children, he bent down with his arms stretched out and his fingers twitching.

"Ah," he said, as they ran into his arms, "my girls!"

As I got closer, he stood up, stroking the top of Lucy's head, and with his hand resting gently on my shoulder, kissed me on the cheek.

"You made it," he said, and then smiled. He bent down, scooped up little Lucy in his arms and reached out for Amelia's hand. "The car's nearby."

I followed along, feeling happy to see the children with their father, looking elegant as always in his jeans and white silk shirt with a red and white spotted silk scarf around his neck. Mick was still very slim, and I noticed people sneaking glances at him as we walked past. As soon as we were on the freeway both girls fell asleep.

Finally, we got onto Pacific Coast Highway with the ocean on our left, past the main drag in Malibu and into Ramirez Canyon. As we made our way along the canyon night was falling, a warm breeze was blowing, and I could hear a little stream trickling along the side of the road. Through my jetlag, I felt again the hope that things would finally work out between us. It had been a long way round, but I knew somehow we were coming home.

And suddenly there it was, the sweetest little house surrounded by pungent smelling eucalyptus trees. We walked up the stairs to find one long room that had been divided into a sitting area and dining room, a kitchen and two bedrooms. It was perfect, and the smell of wood permeated everything. Mick had furnished our new home with care, bringing rugs from our house and some of the beds. The children ran around, excited at seeing all their old toys and books. Mick had chosen well for us. It was a place to begin again.

A little while later, after we'd tucked two happy children into their beds, Mick got out the vodka and we sat down together:

"Do you like it?" he asked, pouring himself a drink.

"It's great Mick, I really love it," I said, looking around the room. "You've made it so homey, it's like a little treehouse."

When he pulled out a white packet from his waistcoat pocket, I tried not to show my disappointment. While we were in Ireland he'd been more his old self, not taking cocaine, and I suppose I had naively thought that he'd still be the same Mick once I got back to LA. Now he carefully unfolded the packet and then scooped some of the white powder under his fingernail, brought it up to his nose and sniffed hard.

Oh God! I thought, that means he's going to be up all night.

He slowly folded the packet and then slipped it back into his pocket. "Ah," he said, letting out a deep sigh. He reached for his glass and took a drink. I noticed now, in the time it had taken me to sort out the girls' night things, his eyes had become bloodshot.

"How are you?" I asked.

He shrugged his shoulders. "I'm fine," he said, "lots going on."

"What's going on?"

"Usual stuff." He took another gulp from his glass.

"Any more thoughts about us?" I asked, and then bit my tongue. "I guess we'll just take it as it comes, right?"

"There's something I ought to tell you," he said, leaning back against the sofa. "I've been having an affair with Stevie for the last few months. Since we were in Australia."

At first I didn't understand what he'd said. It took some seconds for it to sink in. I stared at him in silence, feeling as though I'd been kicked in the stomach; my mind and heart in complete turmoil as I struggled to make sense of his words. He had asked me back and I had lowered my guard. It had taken so long and cost so much strength to build it up. And now I had let him in. I had given him my trust. I had believed in him and he had betrayed my naivety. I was here under false pretenses. A surge of anger welled up. Why had he not told me before bringing us out here? And then I remembered, he hadn't said come back and we'll be together, he'd just said come back, I'll buy you a house so we'll have more time and space to think about our future. Had I misread the signals?

"Does anyone else know?" I asked.

"Everyone."

I felt so stupid, so humiliated, and so foolish. And then I remembered Stevie's

New Year's Eve party, and the cloak she'd given Mick that night. "For my wizard," she'd said while draping it over his shoulders. I had put it to the back of my mind. The photograph of them all in bed for Rolling Stone Magazine, Mick and Stevie snuggled up together, his sudden disappearance in the middle of the night before I went to England. She had finally got her hands on him, I thought bitterly, and I had never suspected.

Mick continued to drink himself into oblivion as I sat and stared at the floor, the silence making a whirring sound in my head.

"I'm going to bed," I said, knowing there was nothing left to say.

"No wait." Mick grabbed my hand. "Don't go yet. I'm confused."

I started to cry. "Are you staying or going home?" I asked. "You can sleep on the sofa."

I wanted him to go but I was frightened at the thought of him driving. He followed me along the passage to the bedroom. I put my hands over my ears as he carried on talking.

"I have nothing more to give!" I sobbed.

With the combination of jetlag, exhaustion and shock I could feel myself verging on hysteria. All I wanted now was for him to leave me alone and let me sleep.

"The trouble is," Mick said, "I can't make up my mind if I want to be with you or her."

During the six months the children and I lived in Malibu, Mick and I reconciled our differences, but it slowly petered out into a sort of no-mans-land; Mick in his house in Bel-Air and me with the girls in Malibu. It was far from clear where we stood with each other. At times, once the shock had subsided, Mick and I would chat about his falling for Stevie as if we were old friends. "Oh well," he said one day, as we were walking towards my house, "she wrote some good songs because of it all." We looked at each other and laughed. Even now, it was all about Fleetwood Mac.

But there were other times, when I found myself relying on that friendship and the connection we were trying to re-build, but there was no consistency. I sat around our dining table with the children one evening in June, having prepared a special meal for our wedding anniversary. Candles were lit and the children dressed in their finest, expecting Mick to join us as planned, but he never showed up.

It was around this time that the children and I went to John and Julie McVie's wedding reception in Christine's house. Mick didn't show up, and I realized not long after arriving that Stevie was hiding in the broom cupboard. I could see people being dragged in one by one to talk to her, but she couldn't face me. I ignored it all and talked instead to sympathetic friends who knew about the affair and were not supportive of it.

During our time in Malibu I received a phone call from Mick's father while we were living in Malibu. He and Biddy had returned to England a few weeks after we'd arrived and I was still feeling upset by what I perceived to be their betrayal, and deliberately hadn't invited them to Lucy's birthday party at our new home. But when I heard Mike's voice calling long distance, sounding just as he always had, my heart melted.

"Jenny old girl," he said. "How are you all? I hear from Mick you've settled into your new home."

I smiled. "Lovely to hear from you." We chatted for a short while and then I asked him how he was.

"I can't eat," he said. "I don't seem to have much of an appetite." Neither of us spoke as I took in the enormity of what he was saying. I knew what that meant; he had managed to outlive the doctor's prediction, but against all our hope, maybe the cancer had taken hold.

A journey beyond the muse

Above: Los Angeles, 1974 (photo by Herbie Worthington)

Right: Faithful dog Zappa

Below: New beginnings, Los Angeles, 1974 (photo by Herbie Worthington)

Left: Second marriage,
autumn 1976 (photo by
Mary Torry Devito)

Below: On tour, festival in
Austin, Texas, September 1976
(photo by Sharon Weisz)

Lucy in Stevie outfit and
me, 1976

Sandra and me with Bob Welch, for a possible album cover shoot (photo by Oliver Ferrand)

Judy Wong, Los Angeles

Boo, Colin, Me, Paula, Pattie, David
and new wife Ruth at their wedding,
July 1978

Colin and Debbie's wedding,
Cranleigh Village, 1983

Me and Mick attending Pattie
and Eric's fancy dress party, 1980
(photo reproduced with the kind
permission of Pattie Boyd)

Amelia, Ian and the dog in the pool cooling down!

Me, Don Henley, Chris McVie, Mick Fleetwood, Jeff Lynne, Ian Wallace at a Musicians in Tune book signing, Book Soup in Hollywood 1992

In conversation with Princess Diana at Kensington Town Hall, April 1993

Above: Nepal, overlooking Tibet, 1995
Right: David and me, 2009
Below: Appearing at the Whitstable
Literary Festival with Andy Miller,
May 2014

My dad's membership card for The Guinea Pig Club

THE GUINEA PIG CLUB

THE QUEEN VICTORIA HOSPITAL
EAST GRINSTEAD, SUSSEX

MEMBERSHIP CARD

Name: *Jock Boyd.* 28/2/945

Jock Boyd, my father,
Nairobi, 1954

Above: Book signing after giving my talk in 2018 (photo courtesy of The Beatles Story, Liverpool)

Left: Wolf & Izzy, Ojai, California, 2019

WILLOW COTTAGE

And so, without my realizing it at the time, this four-year chapter in Los Angeles came to an end. I had been happy in our treehouse; the children had made friends and life could almost have been idyllic were it not for the uncertainty surrounding Mick's and my relationship.

The girls and I would sometimes stay with Mick in Bel Air, but nothing had changed. Stevie was still in the picture, alcohol and cocaine were still in charge, and blacked out curtains in the bedroom allowed Mick the sleep he needed to face each day. My ability to react to Mick's relationship with Stevie, or his lifestyle as I had in the past was now exhausted, and so we drifted in and out of each other's lives.

Despite moments of frustration and confusion, I felt no need to make a drastic decision. Nevertheless, without me initiating anything the situation took care of itself. In June 1978 I received an invitation from my younger brother David, to attend his wedding on July 15th. Even though I was tempted to go, it was only when Pattie called me a few days later that I gave the possibility more thought.

"You, Amelia and Lucy have to come!" she pleaded. "The whole family will be there. It's such a great opportunity for us to all be together and you can stay with us." I smiled. The thought of seeing my family and taking a break from LA for the summer appealed to me.

Between us we concocted a plan. The children and I would go to England for a month, arrive three weeks before the wedding and then meet up with the family in Bristol on 15th July.

As arranged, Pattie met us at Heathrow Airport, and drove us to their house in Surrey. Amelia and Lucy were thrilled to be staying with Pattie again and as soon as we arrived immediately made a fuss over Willow, the large grey dog and Eddy the cat.

At the top of Eric's driveway was a lodge where an old married couple had lived for years. It had always been their job to look after Eric's house and garden while he was on tour. Pattie and I asked the husband and wife if they would baby-sit Amelia and Lucy in the main house the following evening since a friend of Eric's was due to arrive and we'd planned to go to the pub for supper. The friend arrived fully loaded with bags of groceries the next day, and I watched him as he placed packets of cupcake mix and butter on the kitchen table.

"What are you going to make?" I asked.

"Hash brownies," he said with a crooked smiled. "They should be ready by the time we get back from dinner."

Before leaving the house, he gave strict instructions to the old couple to take the brownies out of the oven at a certain time and to place them on top of the cooker. We then made our way to The Parrot, a pub in the next village owned by a friend of theirs, Gary Brooker, the keyboard player and singer from Procol Harum. After exchanging greetings, we took our drinks outside and sat under the pergola, where we waited until our table was ready. By the time the meal arrived, and we'd all sat down back inside the restaurant, Eric was still standing out in the garden, his head poking in through the window, with a lace curtain surrounding his face. He talked to us as we ate our meal, making Pattie laugh with his silly jokes; his behavior didn't seem to faze her at all. I laughed with everyone else, but it made me feel uneasy.

Returning later that evening, along with some friends from the pub, we found the little brownies neatly placed on a plate, but with a piece missing from one of them. Where was the other half? How would the old folks handle being stoned, I wondered, as I watched the woman approach me. I studied her face, trying to detect any telltale signs, but all she said was how lovely the girls were and how good they'd been.

Looking at the dish she said, "I didn't think John would mind. I gave the two girls a small piece of this cake with a cup of milk before they went to bed. They had a bite each but left the rest." She shook her head. "They didn't like the taste."

I quickly ran upstairs to see if the children were all right and found them sleeping peacefully. Once the old couple had left, we all took one of the brownies. Even though I only ate half of mine, fifteen minutes later Pattie and I stood by the cupboards in the kitchen rooted to the spot as the effects of the hash got stronger; neither of us able to speak or move. I hated this feeling! It reminded me of my San Francisco days of smoking pot. The rest of the evening was spent staring at people as they wandered in and out of the kitchen, looking a little self-conscious under our stoned gaze.

Early the following morning, when I heard Mick's voice on the telephone wanting to speak to the children, I panicked. He was calling from LA and hadn't yet gone to bed. I felt concerned about the children as they continued to sleep until later that morning. It could easily have been jet lag, but I immediately put it down to the piece of brownie. As always Mick had a knack of calling at the worst moment, and never when I wanted him to.

That afternoon Amelia and Lucy came with Pattie, Eric and me to meet his grandmother Rose, who lived in a village nearby. She was a wonderful old woman, and much to the children's delight had a big Macaw parrot in her kitchen. As we sat in her garden drinking tea, Rose pointed to a small plum tree.

"I planted the stone from a plum I'd eaten," she said, looking at Amelia and Lucy. Amelia looked at her in awe and then turned to me and said, "I want to be somewhere long enough so I can plant a stone and watch it grow into a plum tree."

Having spent so many years, especially the last four-and-a-half, in Los Angeles, immersed in the rock and roll lifestyle, it was easy for me to fall into a similar way of life here in England. Added to this was my absolute joy in spending time with Pattie. And because I loved her, and she Eric, I gradually accepted him as part of the family, a sort of teasing older brother. There was also a familiar sense of being part of a family when touring with him and his band, which I knew only too well, when everybody becomes a tightly knit unit all with the same goal in mind: the concert.

Two weeks before David's wedding Pattie and I went with Eric and his band to Germany where they were scheduled to play at an open-air concert in Nuremberg. Bob Dylan was headlining the show.

After arriving at the venue in the afternoon, Pattie and I sat in the Clapton caravan on the grassy backstage area and opened a bottle of vodka. She was still my drinking buddy and together we egged each other on. It was part of our rock and roll connection. As preparation for the show got underway, I caught the occasional glimpse of Eric's road crew running around the surrounding area or poking their head through the door of the caravan. Throughout all of this Pattie and I lounged back on the seats, chatting together, doubling over as each one made the other laugh. It was infectious and spread to anyone who came into the caravan. On being told Eric was about to start we walked towards the side of the stage where I saw Bob Dylan. Pattie spoke to him briefly, and then introduced me. He put his hand out to shake mine, but to my dismay I was given a limp handshake. I was devastated. He was one of my heroes.

The more I had to drink that night, the more upset I was about Bob Dylan's handshake, which of course gave a drunken Eric all the ammunition he needed to goad me until I cried; an ability he displayed on numerous occasions as I got to know him better. He loved to see how far he could push me, then, when I broke, his arm went around my shoulder and there was no one sweeter.

Carl Radle, Eric's bass player, spent a lot of time talking to Pattie and me, and making us laugh. He was one of Eric's greatest friends and had played with people such as Delaney & Bonnie in the late sixties, Joe Cocker, and Leon Russell. He was a musician's musician, and, like the rest of Eric's band, was from Tulsa, Oklahoma. He was in his early forties at the time, and quite a bit older than the rest of us, slim, with a balding head and glasses. He had the sort of humor I liked: dry with a touch of wisdom. Everyone thought Carl was the most together and balanced person they knew, meaning, he never drank the same drink, or took the same drug for more than a couple of days at a time. Because the band had a few more concerts to play before going back to Tulsa, Eric asked Carl to stay at his house.

The day of my brother's wedding, which was the reason I came to England, happened to be on the same day that Eric, Bob Dylan and other great musicians were playing at a Rock Festival in Surrey, The Blackbushe Aerodrome. When we found out, Pattie and I were devastated. We'd had so much fun watching Eric's band in Nuremberg and seeing Bob Dylan play, that we began plotting ways we could go to the gig, as well as make an appearance at the wedding. Pattie decided the only way we could do it was to get a helicopter from Bath after the service and before the reception and fly to the show. And so we arranged for a helicopter to be on stand-by.

After the wedding service, our ever-increasing extended family was made to stand in a line for the customary photographs. Amongst the guests was our stepfather Bobby and his wife, who I hadn't seen since he'd left our mother. My youngest brother Boo and his wife had flown in from the Bahamas. He and Colin stood beside Pattie, Paula and me, looking like a couple of Mafiosi standing tall in their dark glasses and smart suits. It was the first time my mother's children had all been together since we were young, and I loved it. We watched my brother, David, and his new wife step into the Lord Mayors carriage and get whisked away by two large horses to the reception at the Guildhall. Pattie and I had been certain by that point we would be on our way to the concert, but as we watched our family walking towards the wedding party, we didn't have the heart to bail out. The helicopter was cancelled.

For the next few days the children and I hung out with Pattie, Eric and Carl. We created our own little world; playing pool in the games room, listening to music, watching films on television or swimming in the pool with the children. Now that my sole purpose for our visit to England had come and gone, it dawned on me that finally I'd had enough of living in LA. I was ready to start a new life in England, near my family and close to Pattie.

While looking for a cottage to buy, the girls and I moved from Pattie and Eric's house to a hotel beside the A3 motorway, with a crumbling out-door swimming pool and a couple of ponies in the field. Two weeks later, Mick arrived in England. His father was dying. One evening he made his way to the hotel, drunk and high on cocaine, and tried to persuade me to go back to LA with him. Nothing he said made sense or convinced me to return. I am sure he was tortured by the impending death of his father and was very confused, but this time around it was not difficult to tell him our life was now in England. Helped by the beginnings of a long-distance romance with Carl, even though he'd left for Tulsa by now, I had no desire to try again. The following day, I went with Mick to see his father in hospital and as I stood at the end of his bed, he smiled at me and said in a clear voice, "I love you Jenny." He died the next day.

As soon as Mick returned to Los Angeles, he began a relationship with one of Stevie's best friends, Sara. He had introduced her to me the night before my departure to England. While Mick and I were having our last meal together with the children in LA he had spied Sara Recor, the wife or ex-wife of a friend of his, sitting at the bar and had got up to say hello. In those few minutes I sensed an attraction between them but chose to ignore it.

After some searching, I found what would become our home for the next four years. Willow Cottage was tucked away up a narrow lane – the trees on both sides meeting overhead formed a shaded tunnel in the summer. It was a 1930s red brick house with a stony driveway that sloped down to the lane. Around the house was a large garden overgrown with bushes and overhanging trees, and to the right and behind a hedge was a field full of black and white cows. I walked up the gravel path, listening to the cows munching, watching with delight as their heads, and occasionally only their large pink noses, poked through the hedge. This was everything I'd missed while living in LA and I knew at once it was the perfect house for my children and me. It was a five-minute drive along the lanes from Pattie and Eric's house, and close to what was to be Amelia and Lucy's new school.

I met the elderly couple who owned the cottage. The wife hardly said a word as they showed me around the house, but it was obvious to me she had loved living there and was sad to be leaving. There were four little bedrooms, a dining room, sitting room and large kitchen. Above the garage was a ladder strapped to the wall with a secret den at the top, perfect for children to play in. I called Pattie and Eric for a second opinion and waited while they zoomed over. It was early evening, just before supper, and so with a combination of empty stomachs and the smell of bacon frying in the pan, we all decided this was the cozy house I should buy.

Before we moved in, I found a local builder to make a few alterations. Over the course of several weeks, while we chatted over cups of tea, I found out most of the local gossip. Amongst the many tales he delighted in telling me, was the reason why the previous owners had left Willow Cottage. The neighbors next door were proud owners of a swimming pool in their garden, a rare thing in Surrey at the time, and the wife had often heard them splashing around during the summer. One stifling hot day, while the neighbors were away on holiday, she stripped off her clothes and bravely crept through the thick hedge. Once through she jumped into their pool and swam in the icy cold water. All would have been fine, and she would have had a carefree day, if it hadn't been for the fact that the gardener was pruning roses and with eyes out on stalks, watched with glee at the boldness of this naked woman swimming up and down the length of the pool. As soon as she saw him, her moment of reckless wild abandon turned into unbearable shame and embarrassment. It was just too much for her stiff English upbringing.

Once we moved into the cottage, I realized pretty quickly that I was in a completely different world to the one I'd left behind, especially living in Surrey. People were guarded and hid behind a veneer of respectability, unless they'd had a few drinks. Then anything was excusable - "Oh, I must have had one too many!" Even so, compared to Los Angeles, life at Willow Cottage resembled something closer to normality as far as the children were concerned. Together with a few other local mothers, we set up a school car-pool to ferry the children back and forth, and I began to feel like part of the community. As each day blended into the next, I started to relish this life of routine, far from the emotional roller coaster that had previously kept me constantly on edge. Not many people here, in the midst of Surrey, had heard of Fleetwood Mac, which gave the children a chance to grow up like all the other kids, except that their father lived in America.

My main companions to begin with were Pattie and Eric. Eric had grown up in the nearby village of Ripley, and so Pattie, Eric and I often went to his local pub in the evenings and met up with his mum and his old school friends who still lived there. The cricket club on the village green also became a place to congregate on Saturday evenings or Sundays before lunch. It was village life. No matter that Eric had become a world known guitar player, here he was still known as 'Rick'. They were like one big family, and for now I was part of it. Apart from my old friends Liz and Kellogs and their children, who lived three hours away, I didn't know anyone else. Even so, although at times I felt rather lonely, I began to feel more settled in my new environment.

Over the next few months I heard very little from Mick. Periodically I would call him and let him know what the children were doing. One day he called to say he wanted the girls to stay with him and Sara at our old house in Bel Air and that Biddy would look after them. I felt uneasy letting them go, knowing what state their father was in, but I didn't feel I had a right to refuse. I felt guilty enough knowing I'd taken the children to England, even though I believed I was doing the right thing. A week before Christmas, I put our daughters onto the plane bound for the 'City of Angels', desperately holding back the tears so as not to alarm them.

Feeling bereaved without my children running around the cottage, I made plans to spend Christmas with Carl in Tulsa. While he was staying at Eric's house, he had startled me one day by telling me he took heroin occasionally, as well as other opiates. This was different to the world I had known in LA. Although I didn't know much about it, I knew Paula had taken heroin on and off for a number of years. "It's fine," Carl reassured me. "You just have to be careful how long you take it for." I was deeply shocked. This was the heavy stuff I vowed I'd never mess with. He became my introduction to that other world but thank God it was only a glimpse.

A few days before Christmas, Carl met me at the airport in Tulsa. We drove through the town with fairy lights twinkling in every shop window and passing streets and sidewalks covered with snow until we reached the countryside. A bumpy track took us to Carl's big, rather deserted-looking house. I walked into a large room downstairs lined with bookshelves and apart from an old sofa and an over-sized television there was very little furniture. On looking around, it became clear to me that I didn't really know Carl, except in the context of being with Pattie and Eric in our familiar surroundings, and even then for just a few days at a time. Most of our contact had been long distance telephone calls. There was a feeling of emptiness everywhere. It was not a house that felt lived in but was more of a barricade from the wild lifestyle of each tour. During the week I stayed with Carl, he introduced me to a liquid form of morphine called Delarda, which he injected into the muscle of my arm a couple of times while I was there. On voicing my concern before he did so, he told me the effect would be soothing and gentle.

By now I had allowed the information he'd given me about his opiate use to sink in, and even felt rather childish that I'd been so shocked. As we sat on his bed, watching comedy programs or old films on television the effects of the drug took hold. I could feel myself sinking into a mindless state; my emotions numb and even the pain of missing my children at Christmas began to fade.

Carl knew all the musicians in Tulsa, but his best friend was a woman called Emily. On Christmas Day, we drove over to Emily's house to have lunch with her and her family. As we walked through the front door Emily greeted us with open arms. She was a large woman and very motherly. I looked around the room, at the Christmas tree in the corner decorated with lights and ornaments, green pine branches above the mantelpiece and candles on the wall in metal brackets. I could tell Carl was very fond of Emily; they were good friends and had known each other for many years. I was introduced to the members of Emily's family and a couple of her friends; all sitting around the dining room table. After being offered a drink Carl and I sat down with them and watched as the turkey, followed by heaped bowls of vegetables and stuffing were placed on the table in front of us. A real Christmas feast, candle-lit faces, warm and glowing, but inside I felt empty.

Because I hadn't eaten much for a few days, it didn't take long for the alcohol to have its affect, and, excusing myself with glass in hand, I walked upstairs to Emily's elegant bathroom. A large mirror hung above the basin. After washing my hands and looking into it I saw the reflection of a white, tortured face with vacant and hollow eyes. I watched as tears welled up and black mascara rivulets rolled down my face. A wave of sadness engulfed me. As kind and friendly as everyone downstairs was, I felt so lost and lonely in this strange place and away from my children. My first Christmas without them!

The children were flown back to England in the New Year just in time to celebrate Amelia's birthday. Pattie joined us as we all sat cross-legged on the floor in the sitting room, next to an upside-down empty cardboard box, with her birthday cake with eight candles balanced on top. Even though our dining room table hadn't arrived yet, it still felt like home. The children loved our cottage and over the next few years spent a lot of time running around outside, exploring, making camps and enjoying the sense of freedom. In the field beside the cottage was a big barn filled with straw bales and a swing attached to a wooden beam. Gradually, during the months that followed, the place became filled with Amelia and Lucy's school friends, running and squealing around the house and out into the fields.

Once the tea parties came to a close, it was usually the fathers who arrived to collect their darlings. The usual glasses of wine were offered to them, while the children continued to play. We would chat about village life or they would ask me questions about Los Angeles until irate wives began to call, demanding that their husbands be sent home from the newly divorced woman from America. Surrey was very different from LA and although I loved the quaintness of it all, I did at times feel a bit out of place.

Later that year, my brother Colin moved in with us after separating from his partner. His young son, Alex, spent every other weekend at the cottage, where he got into the habit of calling me Mum. It was here too that Paula and her son, William, would occasionally come to stay. One evening, I watched in dismay while William and the girls, in fits of giggles, pushed a drunken Paula up the stairs. She was showing all the signs of alcoholism that evening, stealing drinks in the middle of the night, or when no one was looking. She and William lived in London with Eric's right hand man, Nigel, so I didn't see her very often.

Alongside this idyllic existence with my children, which formed a deep and integral part of my life, and without the roller coaster, came a feeling of restlessness, a need to focus on something other than the children, the cottage and the surrounding social distractions. I didn't need to get a job, but the idyllic life wasn't enough. I needed a sense of purpose and longed to feel connected to something or someone. Alcohol allowed me to connect to people I would not necessarily feel I had much in common with and it became a bridge, releasing, on a superficial level some of this frustration and restlessness. Writing poems helped; thoughts and feelings were easier to write down than to share verbally.

Most Sundays the children and I drove over to my mother's house twenty minutes away in Haslemere, where we would meet the rest of the family. After a few drinks while our mum was cooking the 'Sunday Roast' we often reverted back to behaving like children. I would flick a Brussels sprout at Colin, or he would have a fight with Paula, then everyone would join in, and yet, my mother completely ignored it all as if there was nothing unusual in this behavior. I loved being with my family. No matter how wild and unbalanced we got, in a very dysfunctional way, that's where I felt secure. It was so different to living in Los Angeles, where nothing ever felt real, or down to earth.

Pattie spent a lot of time with us at Willow Cottage. I spoke to her, or saw her, almost every day. She would come for tea or help me with the children's birthday parties, and I felt inseparable from her. She was very gentle with the children and they loved her. Eric was away touring a lot of the time, and at one point was seeing one of Pattie's young women friends. During this time, she stayed with me for a couple of nights, sad and angry, and then left for Los Angeles to stay with friends of hers who lived in Hollywood. Pattie had always been very civil to any girl who was after Eric. One actually arrived at their house one day while Paula was visiting. As soon as the girl pulled out a cigarette, Paula offered her a light, and with the flame 'accidentally' on high, singed off some of her eyelashes and eyebrows.

Towards the end of March, Mick called to say the words I dreaded hearing: he wanted the girls to go to LA for three weeks, to spend Easter with him and Sara. I panicked. Mick was still 'out of it' most of the time and I knew Sara was not that popular with the children. My only compensation was the knowledge that I still had many friends there who could keep an eye on the girls and Mick's sister Sally knew of a schoolteacher friend who could go with them. Again, I believed I had no choice.

I knew Mick missed Amelia and Lucy, and I would either hear nothing from him for weeks on end, or he'd call three of four mornings consecutively and speak for hours. I would hang onto these conversations, often filled with sentimental memories of past times together. Even though I was aware he'd been up all night and was riding high, they touched a part of me that still held on to the dream of being a family. But then he was gone, disappearing behind a haze of cocaine, just like a genie from his bottle, into a cloud of smoke. Our nerves were still raw, and our hearts still broken.

It was with a heavy heart that I put my children on the plane to the States for their Easter holidays. I went with my brother Colin to the pub that evening with one of his friends, trying to cheer myself up or drown my sorrows. The following morning, I was woken by the piercing and relentless sound of the phone. I could hardly lift my head off the pillow as I fumbled for the receiver. It took me a while to recognize the voice of the landlady from Pattie and Eric's local pub.

"Jenny," she said, "I've just heard from Pattie and she wants you to fly to Tucson right away so you can be her bridesmaid. She's getting married to Eric today in Tucson and asked me to make sure you get there in time."

I let out a moan. "I can't," I said, my mind whirling as I tried to think of an excuse. "I haven't got any money and I won't have time to go to the bank."

I felt torn, I knew having me there would mean so much to Pattie, but her timing was bad. I felt as though I was stuck to my bed, too much to drink and too little sleep.

The landlady had arranged everything. "We'll lend you the money," she replied. "There's a flight on Concord to New York, and then a connecting flight to Tucson. You'll make it with a couple of hours to spare." With a sinking feeling in my gut I realized there was no getting out of this. "You have to go," she stressed. "She really wants you, and I've told Joe to come and pick you up."

I slithered off the bed and with a thumping head prepared to pack my bag. I moaned and groaned my way into the cab, telling myself, at least this time I might not miss my children so much if I'm with Pattie.

Eight hours later, I arrived in a daze at the selected hotel in Tucson where Pattie and Eric were staying, and where, just as the landlady had said, I had two hours to spare before the ceremony. Pattie looked beautiful and overjoyed to be surrounded by her dear, and old friends, Miel, Rob Fraboni and Chris O'Dell. I was given some coke to keep me going, and together we fluttered around Pattie before making our way to the Bethel Temple. There was Eric and his road crew waiting for our arrival. Miel, Chris and I were Pattie's bridesmaids. I felt tears well up as Pattie said the words she'd longed to say, and I knew how happy this was making her. We all celebrated after the service in one of the small ballrooms at the hotel.

After the wedding, at Carl's request, I agreed to join the tour for the next two weeks. Muddy Waters was opening for Eric on this US tour, starting with their gig at The Tucson Community Centre Arena the night after the wedding. Pattie and I went to the show. On one of the days off Pattie and I went with Eric to Muddy Waters house where we were given lunch in the garden and swam in his pool. It felt so easy, so natural to be with Muddy and his wife and yet here we were with one of the greatest Blues musicians of our time, and one of Eric's heroes as if it was no big deal at all. It felt very special to me.

I spent a very colorful Easter Day in New Orleans with Carl and then, as arranged, left for LA the following day with the hope that this time I might be able to see Amelia and Lucy. Pattie had arrived in LA a few days before me and was staying with her friends Rob and Miel.

It was an automatic response while in LA to call Mick. I wanted to reach out, to re-connect in some way, having not seen him for almost a year. With trepidation and shaky fingers I dialed the familiar number.

"Hi," I said, trying to sound jolly and feeling relieved it was him that picked up and not Sara.

"Jenny?" His voice never changed. It was so easy to imagine we were still both eighteen." Are you in town?" he asked, sounding surprised.

"Yes," I said, "And wondered if you and Sara felt like meeting up this evening. We could go to Something Fishy in Malibu?"

"Sure."

"I'm with Pattie and her friend Miel," I quickly added, wondering if he could hear the quiver in my voice. I felt fragile.

"Sounds nice," he said. "We'll see you there this evening." I waited, knowing he hadn't finished. "But just want you to know," he continued, "it's not a good idea for you to see the children while you're in town. Too confusing for them."

I just listened and said nothing.

We arrived at the Japanese restaurant on Pacific Coast Highway and made our way to the sushi bar. Pattie ordered sake as soon as we sat down. She and Miel were on a high, laughing and drinking as they remembered one funny story after another about the wedding. I hid my nerves behind cups of sake, trying to join in every so often, but filled with anxiety at the thought of seeing Mick. We'd never spent this much time apart and what was worse I was about to see the father of my children with another woman on his arm. Was it too soon? Should I not have called him?

I turned my head in mid-conversation; I knew Mick was standing by the door. My heart sank when I saw him. His white silk shirt, brown velvet waistcoat and jeans looked immaculate as always, but his hair was long and lank and his beard bushy and full. He had a thick white brace around his neck, and large, dark rings under his eyes. When I went up to him, every nerve in my body was shaking; he leaned over to give me a hug. Standing beside him was Sara, who smiled sweetly and said hello. She was very pretty, tall and slim with dark hair. They both sat down on stools further along the bar next to Pattie. I felt sick and allowed Pattie and Miel to do all the talking.

After dinner we drove in convoy a little further up the coast to visit Mick's friend, Gary Busey, whose film 'The Buddy Holly Story' I had watched, and, having been a great Buddy Holly fan in my teens, thought was wonderful. Even so, I didn't want to be there, I hadn't bargained for anything other than a meal together and even then, I hardly said a word all evening. My nerves felt raw. At some point in the early morning, after a night of partying, everyone in the room decided to take a walk along the beach, leaving Mick and me alone, rooted to the spot. We stared at each other from across the room.

"You're too thin," he whispered.

I could hear the room buzzing in the deafening silence that followed. Then it broke. I watched, as if in a dream, as Mick buried his head in his hands and sobbed. We were still in the middle of our nightmare, even though he was now with Sara, but I still couldn't let go of the dream of us all being together as a family.

After what felt like an eternity, we finally left the party. Miel drove her Porsche along Pacific Coast Highway, with Pattie joking and laughing, and me crunched in the back feeling heartbroken. They wanted to watch the sunrise from the top of Mulholland. I didn't see Mick for the rest of my stay there.

I arrived back in England a few days before Amelia and Lucy, and life carried on as normal. Pattie and I had started tap dancing classes in Guildford and would meet up each week to practice our moves in the dance class and to the sound of an old upright piano. We soon discovered that the best place to practice in between classes was out on the veranda at her house. After a few drinks and while everyone played pool in the room upstairs, Pattie and I would rehearse our routine. The night before our Level 1 exam it poured with rain. We changed into our costume, high as kites, and tapped on the wet terracotta tiles with our metal-toed shoes, black top hats and silver canes. We danced, Fred Astaire style in the pouring rain, in front of the flood lights, and to the sound of Eric and all his mates jeering and shouting obscenities as they leaned out of the top window.

During that summer, when the children were with Mick for two weeks, I visited Carl at his house in Tulsa once more. This time it felt even stranger than my first visit. Eric had fired his band, and so Carl spent most of his time in his house, high on Delarda. I didn't join in this time. After a week where there was very little said between us, I got a ticket to LA to be near my children and to see my friends Sandra and her husband Larry. It was while I sat on the plane going over Carl's parting words - "Bring the girls back with you next time" - that I knew with complete clarity there was no way I would ever bring them with me to this house. Crying at the thought of where my deep loneliness had taken me, I knew I would never see Carl again.

Later that year in November, Mick called to ask if I would like to come to New York. Fleetwood Mac were on tour, promoting their latest album, Tusk, and were scheduled to play at Madison Square Gardens. My friend Liz and I booked a room at the Carlyle Hotel in Manhattan where we were joined by Sandra and Larry. Having been given the use of one of the limos, we spent the following day being driven around Manhattan, looking at the sights, shopping and finding exciting places to eat, while Mick got ready for their first night. As always, the show was dynamic, making it impossible to sit in our seats, flooding me with memories; heart breaking, heart-warming while all the time Mick's steady beat never stopped.

The following night, after watching the show for the second time, a whole group of us, including Mick's sister, Sally, and her son Kells, went to Studio 54. It was like old times with everyone there, dancing, drinking and chatting to people, still buzzing from the show. Mick and I left the club in the early hours of the morning and made our way back to his hotel. As I got into bed, Mick told me he just had to have a word with Lindsey and would be right back. I lay there and waited. As time went on, I began to feel angry. I had walked into the same old trap, he was loaded, and getting more so, while talking about Fleetwood Mac. Part of me felt humiliated and angry, stood up, but another part was laughing. We were still dancing the same old dance, but for how much longer would it last?

The band congregated in the hotel lobby the next morning, ready for their trip to Boston. Mick and I held hands, still up in the air about our relationship as we said goodbye

Bob Welch had been playing in New York and asked me if I'd like to go for a ride that evening in one of the horse-drawn carriages through Central Park. Bob had been showing interest in me since the days we were in old Topanga, but very mildly. Then, when I left for England, he started writing long letters to me. I was surprised to begin with, he had always kept so much of himself to himself, mentally very quick and clever, but tightly buttoned up. Reams of prose came reeling out of his pen, and, as well as this, I heard a song on his album, called, Jenny Don't You Cry. He had obviously watched me from afar for many years, aware of the ups and downs in my relationship with Mick.

I agreed to go with him for the carriage ride. The trees were filled with little twinkling Christmas fairy lights, and the air was crisp and cold. A warm woollen rug was put over our knees, and bells jingled as the horses trotted through the park. All was fine, until in mid-sentence Bob made a lunge across the seat towards me, while, at the same time I slipped onto the floor, trying to avoid the lips that were puckered together and making their way across the carriage. I liked Bob and found this situation horrible. Of course, I realized afterwards, a night ride in a horse drawn carriage was a romantic gesture, not something you would want to do with a brother. And that's how I saw Bob.

The first time Mick came to visit us at Willow Cottage was December 1980. He was on his way to Ghana to fulfill a dream he'd held onto for years, to delve into the rich musical culture of that country and to record and play on an album with some of Ghana's pop and folklore musicians. He hadn't seen the cottage before, and, as I stood in front of the Aga in the kitchen, Mick did something he'd always done in the past, which never ceased to fill me with shame. Without even thinking, he lifted his arm and ran his finger along the surface of a picture frame and inspected the dust. This time I laughed and said, "I'll never change Mick." To my surprise he began crying. Even though he'd been living with Sara for over a year, unexpected bursts of sadness were not far from the surface for either of us.

During his visit we went with our children to my mother's house for Sunday lunch. Pattie and Eric had already arrived plus my brothers Colin and David with his wife and rather formidable in-laws. After lunch and quite a few brandies later, while we were all congregated in the small sitting room, Eric went over to the armchair my mother was sitting in, sat on her knee, and with his arm around her shoulder, and face up against hers, started teasing her, testing her limits of politeness in front of the in-laws. She tried to lighten the situation by laughing and saying, "Oh Eric, don't be so silly." He carried on; he was having fun seeing our mother squirm. Mick, who had been watching this charade and feeling for my mother, stood up tall, grabbed Eric by the scruff of his neck and frog-marched him outside the front door. Pattie and I watched in amazement; nobody had stood up to Eric's drunken behavior before. Good old Mick, I thought to myself.

Later that evening, after returning to Eric's house, I left with the girls and described to Mick how to get back to Willow Cottage: a five-minute drive along the lanes. Mick continued in party mode with Pattie and Eric and his friends from Ripley – all heavy drinkers. I got a phone call from him some time in the early morning.

"I'm in a phone box. I've been driving around these lanes for the last two hours and I still can't find you!" He sounded exhausted. "I've been to the police station in Guildford to call Biddy to get your number, my fuel gauge is almost empty and a guy on a motorbike is trying to help me."

"I'll stand by the front door," I told him, after trying to calm him down and then spoke to the motorcyclist.

As dawn was breaking, I heard the sound of a motorbike and then tires on the gravel as Mick's rented Jaguar pulled into the driveway. I stood in the doorway, freezing in my white cotton nightdress as I watched him walking towards me. He turned to thank the motorcyclist for his help and then almost collapsed on the mat.

I enjoyed having Mick at the cottage, believing at times I could easily live with him in this environment; it was so much more low-key than Los Angeles. But I knew he had another life there and his time at Willow Cottage would only sustain him for a short while.

On the 8th December I heard on the radio that John Lennon had been shot. I had just taken the children to school and was driving home. So as not to let this dreadful news register, I went back to bed for another hour in the hopes I hadn't heard it correctly. Hearing Mick in the next room blowing his nose, I called out to him,

"John Lennon's been shot."

The shock of this sudden news had a profound impact on Mick, it was only then I allowed the possibility of his death to sink in. We both rushed out of our beds and turned on the radio. He was dead. It was too shocking to take in. How could it have happened? There seemed to be no reason for this. He had recently started recording again, the most beautiful songs of love, an obvious new beginning for him that had now been cut short. George called me a few days later. His response to John's death was to double the security around his own house. It must have been what every well-known musician feared.

In complete contrast, a few nights later, Mick and I went to Pattie and Eric's fancy dress party dressed up as two school children, which, in many ways, was not that far from the truth. Mick was dressed as a schoolboy with his long legs sticking out of his little grey flannel shorts, and a cap on his head. We had spent the whole morning in Guildford, trying to find a school blazer that would fit him. I was in a school skirt with my hair in bunches. Pattie was Minnie Mouse, her little red skirt with white polka dots, and her long black skinny legs, and black little hands that she held close to her mouth as she giggled. Eric wore one of Pattie's black see-through mid-calf dresses with his white Y-fronts showing underneath. On his white hairy legs, he wore short black socks and shoes. He'd cut and spread a bath sponge over his head, like an old lady's tight perm and with lipstick smudged over his beardless face, a cigarette in one hand and a glass in another he laughed his way through the evening. Amongst other local musicians at the party was Phil Collins, with his small children, wearing knee length trousers, braces and a knotted handkerchief on his head. He was a regular visitor to both our houses and someone who Mick enjoyed talking to. My brother Colin came as the Jolly Green Giant.

Because it was so different to his life in the States, Mick relished his time in England with us all. He liked the fact that it was low-key country living. Eric's gigs were purposefully low-key. One concert he liked to do was the 1500-seater in Guildford, our nearest town. Another was in our local village of Cranleigh. It made everything more real, not so distant and unapproachable. I took John McVie and his wife Julie to the Cranleigh gig when they came to visit me. It was a real eye-opener for John; so different to the Fleetwood Mac shows, and something he would have loved to do. It reminded him of his old days playing with Eric and John Mayall.

I took Amelia and Lucy to Eric's concert when he played in Ireland. Pattie and Eric loved having the children nearby and Eric had nicknamed them 'Double Trouble'. Even so, he was happy to have little Lucy sitting on the side of the stage, just a few feet from where he was standing, in full view of the audience. After the show the children were tucked up in my hotel room as a large banquet was being prepared for us downstairs. In the middle of the private dining room was a long table covered with flowers, silverware, candles, glasses and plates all neatly arranged on a crisp white tablecloth reaching down to the ground. The room quickly filled up with the band members, the road crew and friends.

Patties and Eric's old friend, Rob Fraboni, had just arrived from the States. He was a very interesting man and fun to be with, someone I was to see a lot more of in years to come. As the evening wore on, and after lots of food and alcohol, I have a distant memory of Pattie, Rob and I sitting under the table with our pudding and glasses of wine, hidden from sight by the long white tablecloth. That was the extraordinary thing about this world we inhabited - nobody seemed to think twice about three guests who came to a meal and ended up sitting under the table. Where, one minute we were talking about the cosmos and our spiritual beliefs, and the next guessing whose shoes belonged to whose feet.

During the four years we lived at Willow Cottage I had a couple of short-lived dalliances. Both men were younger than me, and often behaved like children, which made it easier not to commit. Although there were many happy times at Willow Cottage, and I loved living in the country and near my family, even so, the emotional drain that my relationship with Mick over the last few years had taken on me must have had a deeper effect than I realized. I began losing clumps of hair from my head and noticed ever-increasing bald patches.

As my hair loss turned into full-blown alopecia, I consulted a dermatologist in Harley Street. I was told a lot of men had developed alopecia during the war and that there was no known cure, or any certainty that more hair would grow back. After showing him my bald patches and my thinning hair, he said, "Don't worry, they make wonderful nylon wigs these days, any color, and you can just bung them into the washing machine." That did it! I saw the funny side, and knew, without a doubt, I would go bald before wearing a nylon wig that you can just bung into the washing machine. I told my friend Liz, and we just laughed. In more serious moments, though, I realized the alopecia was just the tip of the iceberg and I needed help. I contacted a Jungian psychotherapist and began taking the first steps towards some self-awareness.

My therapist was a softly spoken woman, gentle but also penetratingly direct. I saw her for a year. Although I still continued to drink and sometimes took cocaine when offered at social gatherings, as the weeks went by I noticed a subtle difference. So much so, that, at one of the parties at Willow Cottage later that year when someone gave me a packet of cocaine for my birthday, I secretly emptied it down the loo. Initially I had been scared of going into therapy, thinking I might retreat inside myself, and just sit there with nothing to say. My fear was that I would only find emptiness.

As I drove along the A3 into London every week to see my therapist, I sometimes cried, sadness unexpectedly taking over at the loss of Mick. With time I realized that as much as I loved Mick, I was not able to be in a relationship with him. The two didn't necessarily go hand in hand. The most powerful thing I experienced during these sessions was that of feeling heard, something I had unconsciously been craving all my life, and desperately sought in every relationship. It got me in touch with feelings I didn't know I had, and gave me the confidence, in the therapy room, to speak from my heart. I didn't know then quite how important the effect of being in therapy was having on me. Always a slow starter, it cranked open a door that had been tightly shut most of my life, and although I had a glimpse of my inner life during that year, it wasn't long enough. I still had further to go.

In November of '82, after being in therapy for a year, I went with Mick's mother, Biddy, and my daughter Lucy to New York to see Mick. Fleetwood Mac's Mirage tour had finished, and he was at a loose end. The three of us spent most of our days sightseeing, while Mick lay in bed recovering from nights of revelry. I felt better and stronger than I'd felt for years, and my hair had started to grow back. One afternoon, I gently knocked on the door to Mick's darkened hotel room where he lay sleeping, hung over from the previous night. After entering I sat on his bed, my hand resting lightly on his arm and asked him if he would like to try again. I really believed that with me feeling stronger I could make it work this time.

Mick opened his blood-shot eyes and whispered, "I'm no good to have a relationship with," and then turned his head and drifted off to sleep.

His words stunned me. For the first time it became clear - this really was the end.

Without realizing it I had been driven for all these years to keep us together, not only for my children, but also for myself. I had been determined not to follow the same route as my mother, and yet, given the circumstances, was it so surprising? I wanted to glue all the fragmented bits together again, as if the cracks had never happened. But in reality, I couldn't live with this man. I couldn't find my way back through the layers of drugs, alcohol, fame and exhaustion, to the man I had once known.

11
BACK TO SCHOOL

With the on-going support from my therapist, and the realisation that what Mick had said was true, I felt a deep sense of relief as I made my way back to England. Now there were no more threads left hanging from our relationship, no more possibilities. Mick had finally severed the last ray of hope for both of us and it was time to let go.

That Christmas, I decided to take the children to Los Angeles. They could spend some time with their dad, and I could see my old friends. Christine McVie had called me asking if we would stay with her in her warm and welcoming home in Beverley Hills.

The Christmas decorations sparkled in the unseasonal sunlight when we arrived at her house, and the warmth of a log fire in the sitting room gave the feeling of an English winter, except for the knowledge that the air conditioning was on full blast. Chris was thrilled to see us, telling me we could stay with her as long as we liked, and we were just in time to start rehearsing Christmas carols.

That evening, once the children were tucked up in bed, we all gathered in a circle around Chris as she played the piano. Her new friend, Ian Wallace, was the conductor and played spoons, clicking them against his arm or hip in time to the music. Sandra and I giggled as we watched Mick and his musician buddy Billy Burnette obediently singing from their hymn sheets, looking like two choir boys. It lifted my spirits to be with everyone, and even more so having now almost recovered from the debilitating effects of alopecia.

While we stood around the piano, I hardly noticed Ian. A few nights later, though, when Chris and I went to a club to watch Billy Burnette and his band performing, I recognized him playing the drums. We went backstage after the show and Chris introduced me to him.

"I met you before," he said with a crooked smile, still holding his drumsticks and with a small towel around his neck. "In Germany with Pattie, when I was playing with Bob Dylan."

I felt surprised and a little flattered that he'd remembered me. I had no recollection of him at all from that time. After the show I left Chris at the club and went back to her house to sleep off my jet lag. It wasn't until the following morning, when I saw Ian and Chris chatting in the sitting room having just got back from the club, that I noticed something familiar about him. The fact that he was tall and a drummer didn't seem to hit home; it was more the feeling of cool air between us when he shook my hand before leaving.

If anyone had told me I was exceedingly vulnerable at that time I wouldn't have believed them, I felt on top of the world. I had spent my first year in therapy, which in England in the early 80s, was seen as not that different to seeing a psychiatrist for some debilitating psychiatric disorder. I didn't know anyone who saw a therapist. My weekly sessions had affected me deeply, and though the unraveling process was still in its early stages, it was enough to unconsciously send me running in the opposite direction. I had uncovered a few layers of defenses, leaving myself soft and vulnerable. Mick had rejected me only four weeks before, his flame finally blown out, and I was left searching for him in the dark. Meeting Ian was a perfect case of being on the rebound.

When the day came to sing our carols, everyone was sporting a long white T-shirt with the words 'Yule Tide Ding Dongs' written in big red letters across the front, a name conjured up by Chris and Sandra one night when deciding who could pick the silliest name. Amelia and Lucy's T-shirts looked like little dresses. We rehearsed a quick run through of *Away in a Manger* and *Good King Wenceslas*, then everyone piled into a small van, driven by one of the carol singers, and we headed for the elderly people's residential home in Santa Monica. Mick and Chris sat on the front seat with the driver, while the rest of us sat squashed together on seats along the side of the van, or on the floor. Sandra was sitting on the floor with her back against my knees and her legs outstretched towards Ian who was sitting opposite her. After a few miles, and many jokes and much laughter, Sandra suddenly realized she had her toes resting in between Ian's legs. "Oh, I'm so sorry," she cried, putting her hand up to her mouth and laughing, "I didn't realise." She turned to me and whispered, "I was wiggling my toes." Quick as a flash, Ian responded, "Does that mean we're engaged now?" We all laughed. I liked his humor. As the happy campers kept on going, someone shouted, "How much further?" "It's a good league hence," came a reply from the quick-witted joker.

On Christmas Eve Mick, Amelia, Lucy and I stayed the night at Chris's house and were given one of the large sitting rooms to sleep in on the other side of the house. The children slept on sofas, me in the beautiful ornate red Chinese opium bed and Mick on a camp bed between us. Father Christmas visited the children that night, which wasn't the only reason they were so joyful the next morning. It was enough for them to wake up to both parents in the same room, even if they were in separate beds. Smells of the turkey cooking wafted in from the kitchen, and the sound of friends arriving heralded the beginning of the festivities. After making some breakfast for Mick and the girls amongst the hustle and bustle of people preparing Christmas lunch, I noticed Ian had arrived and was standing in front of the fire.

He was from the north of England and had moved to LA in the mid-seventies. While living in London he played drums in the band, King Crimson, but soon after becoming Bob Dylan's drummer, he moved to Los Angeles. A wild person in England, he drank and used drugs, leading the life of a hardcore rock and roller. During our discussions throughout that Christmas period, I found it hard to believe the stories he told were about the gently spoken, tall, dark-haired man in front of me. In some strange way, while playing games throughout Christmas day we always ended up on the same team. I could feel a little buzz forming between us by the end of the evening but gave it no thought until a few days later at a party given by Judy Wong.

A large crowd gathered for her Christmas bash, many of who were people I hadn't seen for a long time, and yet, much to my surprise, I found myself looking towards the front door each time the bell rang. He didn't show up. On the day before New Year's Eve I called Ian and asked if he'd like to have dinner and go to a jazz club with Chris, Sandra, Larry and me. I wasn't a big jazz fan, but I knew I only had a few days left before returning to England, and so I took this opportunity to see him again. By this time, I was back into the old way of life, drinking in the evenings and staying up late with everyone on the nights the children were with Mick and Sara at his house in Malibu. The four of us went out to dinner that night in a very smart restaurant. It was agreed that Ian would join us later at the club once he'd finished his gig. By the time he arrived, we'd opened another bottle of champagne and I was feeling more than tipsy but keeping myself upright thanks to visits to the bathroom for a line of coke. At the end of the evening Ian drove me back to Christine's house where we continued to drink and talk long after everyone had gone to bed.

A few days later I flew back to England with the children. I was on cloud nine. Although I hadn't spent much time with Ian, I could feel an attraction growing, enhanced by my intoxicated haze. My friend Sandra made it very clear she was not happy about this attraction; she knew me too well and could tell I was running down a fast track to nowhere. In my mind I had broken out of the Surrey routine, feeling high after the excitement of my two weeks in the States, and the familiar world of rock and roll. Although I had spent a couple of nights with Ian in his flat, and he seemed to be just as taken with me as I was with him, my biggest fear with this new romance which stopped it from being a holiday fling, was the thought of Ian spending the night with another woman while I was so far away. I became hooked on this possibility, knowing if it happened it would render what we had meaningless, and my ego was too fragile for that. I knew what guys were like on the road. We stayed in touch through phone calls and I suggested I come out again in a couple of weeks. I had never been so bold. He seemed delighted that I was the driving force in the relationship. All he did was sit back passively, as I set about altering his world.

With Pattie's help in making sure the girls were looked after, two weeks later I flew back to Los Angeles. As I sat on the plane, I told myself that if this relationship didn't work I would never try again. I had already cemented it, not knowing who he was, or if we were even compatible, let alone the fact that he lived five thousand miles away. I didn't give that a second thought. By the time I arrived in LA Ian was recording with Bonnie Raitt and her boyfriend Rob Fraboni, Pattie and Eric's old friend, who was producing the album. The studio was rife with drugs and alcohol, and I immediately began covering up my shyness and vulnerability by joining in. During the whole week of my stay, we lived, ate and slept at the studio. I was back in the same lifestyle that was the total opposite to my life in England with the children.

As fate would have it, a short while later, Ian was touring around Europe with slide guitarist David Linley, and they were scheduled to play in the UK. I knew I was dropping a bombshell by continuing with our relationship. My mother was very angry when she heard. "You have a home, money and wonderful children," she said, "why do you want more?" She was so upset that she even refused to speak to me a few days later when she saw me at my brother Colin and his girlfriend Debbie's wedding in our local village of Cranleigh. I justified it by telling myself I deserved to be with someone, even though I had a niggling feeling it wasn't right. Really, I was just lonely. I thought Ian was a safe bet and I knew the world he came from; it was the same one I'd been in for the last eighteen years, familiar territory, part of the same tribe. While chatting with Paula after the ceremony, she asked me if I would ever consider marrying him. Her question came out of the blue, and it was only then I realized I would. As Ian and I had arranged previously, I flew out to Munich to spend a few days on the road with him and the band.

Compared to Fleetwood Mac, life on the road with this group was very low-key. We travelled in a tour bus with bunk beds, stumbling out at four or five in the morning once we'd arrived at our destination. After a few days I felt exhausted. One evening after sound check and while the band were waiting to go on, I watched Ian walking towards me with a bottle in his hand, and thought, who is this person? Quick as a flash I covered up the feeling of doubt and changed my expression.

At some point during the visit we discussed plans for me to move to Los Angeles with the children and set up home. For this to happen we would have to get married, so that Amelia, Lucy and I could apply for green cards. Although Ian was still married and had lived apart from his wife for a couple of years, he asked me to marry him. I said yes. It was not a decision made with a clear head. I had started the ball rolling and I wasn't looking back. It was two and a half months since we'd met.

Amelia, Lucy and I left our Willow Cottage life in the summer of '83. Pattie was very sad to see us go. Since I'd moved back to England, we had seen each other just about every day, each of us relying on the other's support throughout the crazy, fun and sad times. But I didn't take time to look over my shoulder and took no notice of anyone who tried to dissuade me from going through with my plan. I pretended I didn't care about my mother's disapproval. The ruthless way in which I axed our life was so extreme; it was as if nothing or no one had any meaning. My love of the English countryside, our little home, my family and my children's upbringing were all wrapped around my heart and buried in the earth while I whirled around like an unleashed dynamo, telling myself that at least the children would see more of their father. With a ruthless precision and hardly a backward glance, I put my house up for sale and coldly severed the ties to our gentle life in England.

In its place I rented a small, bare, house in the desert heat of the San Fernando Valley, with a meager swimming pool in the yard. I bought a Mazda two-seater sports car and armed myself with maps of the area. It all felt so different from where I had lived previously. Amelia, at the age of twelve, had decided she wanted to continue her schooling in England with her friends who were all transitioning to the same boarding school. She wasn't ready to break her English ties. Lucy came to live with Ian and me and went to Lawrence 2000, a private school in Van Nuys. She missed Amelia and with an awful twang of guilt I watched her become more introverted each day. Not even the fact that she lived near Mick brought her any joy.

He was a stranger to her in many ways. His and Sara's habit of staying in bed most of the day, hung over, left her wandering around by herself on the few occasions she visited him.

Because Los Angeles is such a transitory place, with people coming and going depending on the work that's available, once I'd sold Willow Cottage, I decided to buy a house in Sherman Oaks, a safer and better area. I wanted to give Amelia and Lucy a sense of permanence, and a home that was our own. It was a couple of streets north of Ventura Boulevard, the main road that separates the valley from the hills and the ocean. The valley can be up to fifteen degrees hotter than the ocean side, which was a forty-minute drive away. It is flat land with rows and rows of similar houses and condominiums, separated by small roads running down and across in grid form. The one I bought was a long one-story house, with four bedrooms, a den, kitchen and sitting room. Some of the furniture had arrived from Willow Cottage, but because I wanted to protect Ian from feeling he was living in my house and surrounded by my furniture, I sold most of it and bought what he wanted. But at least there was a garden behind the house, with two big lemon trees and a huge swimming pool, where our dog, Ben, who I had flown over from England, swam lengths barking at the water.

Ian had begun touring with Bonnie Raitt and wanted me to join him on the road. As in the past, I still didn't like road life. It's fine if you're a musician - the travelling, the sound checks and the hanging around - because you get to let off steam on stage during the show. I would travel with them, go to sound checks, sit at the long trestle tables eating a meal with everyone else, then, after more hanging around I would stand on the side of the stage and, although I loved listening to the music, watch the same show every night. After the show we would all congregated in one of the band member's room and there we'd all drink and get high. On one occasion, after being on the road for a while, we arrived in Albuquerque, New Mexico. That night we all drank tequila. I had seen one of the musicians in Bonnie's band get off with a girl the night before, after the show, and was appalled to witness how different he was once his long-time girlfriend arrived the following day. I had seen all this so many times and the hypocrisy scared me. I realized I was walking on thin ice by putting myself back into this world, heightening my feelings of vulnerability, knowing the very nature of rock and roll life on the road rarely included being true to the wife or girlfriend.

Bonnie managed to fit in easily. Through her sense of humor, her consumption of alcohol at that time and her language, she could appear as hardcore as the guys.

But underneath she was sensitive, a deep thinker and I enjoyed talking to her. She cared deeply about the under-privileged and minorities. In her younger years she had been completely caught up in the civil rights movement, and the blues and folk music that represented it. On some occasions I would walk into the dressing room and see her curled up on the sofa or cushions on the floor, moaning and nursing a headache or stomach pain. Half an hour later she was up on stage, looking sexy, dancing, singing and playing her slide guitar. I was full of admiration for her. She was buoyant and bouncy most of the time, but still capable of being reduced to tears.

Ian and I got married in April '84. As I stood in the Presbyterian Church about to walk down the aisle, I kept thinking, "Am I making a huge mistake?" The last year had been filled with uncertainty about Ian's divorce, which finally came through, allowing us to get married so we could apply to get our green cards.

The church was almost full with my family and friends and all the different band members Ian had played with over the years. Pattie and Colin and his wife Debbie had flown over from England, bringing Amelia with them as well as my friend Liz. All of them had made such an effort to be there for me. Suddenly the music began and Colin, looking very stern, took my arm as we walked down the aisle towards Ian. Pattie, Amelia and Lucy stood next to him, ready to stand by my side.

The reception was held in our garden, with colorful round tables beside the pool, covered with flowers and food. Amelia and Lucy stood by me in their long white and yellow dresses, looking like innocent angels and watching as I cut the cake.

Two days later my family left for England, taking eleven-year-old Lucy with them. She had pleaded with me ever since we'd arrived to let her go to boarding school with Amelia, and so, even though Amelia had by this time decided she'd had enough of boarding school and wanted to live in LA, I'd already arranged for them to spend the last term of that school year together. I missed them badly and longed for the time when they could live with us. I knew Ian wanted me to be available to go on the road with him, and it was an automatic response for me to put his wishes before my own. I decided the next best thing to having the children with me, and a way of bringing them closer was to send them, once they returned, as weekly borders to a school in Ojai I'd seen and liked, run by an English headmaster. It was an hour's drive up the coast and there were horses for them to ride, which Amelia, like the grandfather she never knew, was crazy about. I told myself that the air was clean and fresh compared to the LA smog and enrolled them to start the following September.

John McVie offered Ian and me the use of his house on Maui for our honeymoon. Once we arrived, I contacted George who was staying at his holiday home in Hana, on the southern tip of the island, to tell him we were on Maui. He was delighted and asked us to drive down and stay the weekend with him. He told us that Olivia, his wife, and their little boy Dhani had just left for England and he would be happy for the companionship. The house was on a cliff, overlooking the sea and as we walked around the grounds together, the three of us sat in different nooks and crannies amongst the rocks and talked.

"I know it's even more beautiful than this," George said, waving an arm in the direction of the mountains and the ocean, at the sun bouncing off little ripples on the water's surface. "But I can't see its pure beauty in my present state." I knew what he meant. The more God conscious we became, the more beauty we saw in everything. He was referring to Maharishi and his teachings about the seven levels of consciousness that become more accessible through daily meditation. As for me, I felt content with the beauty as it was. Throughout the weekend we chatted happily and caught up on all our news. He asked about Pattie and how Ian and I had first met. He knew Ian from before as he'd played drums for many of the same musicians George knew. It was a very special weekend.

Ian had asked Rob and Bonnie to join us on Maui, and it dawned on me when they arrived, that it was because he knew they were more than likely to bring some coke. The next morning, while we were all sitting on the beach together, Rob brought out some synthetic mushrooms, in the form of pills, and gave one to each of us. I had never tried mushrooms before, and except for the gig in New Orleans, had stayed away from anything psychedelic since the sixties. Even so, I took one of these pills.

It was not long before we began to feel its effect. Suddenly everything seemed very funny and we began laughing uncontrollably. Tears rolled down my face, and, feeling instantly conspicuous, I turned around and saw a couple of people staring at us from under the shade of a palm tree.

"Let's go for a swim," I suggested, when there was a lull in between the bouts of laughter. We all stood up, grabbed our snorkels and masks and splashed our way through the waves. I let the others swim on ahead of me while I walked back to the beach and threw my snorkel onto our towels before putting on my mask. The water felt warm as I swam towards them.

With the mask strapped to my face I alternated between swimming under water, then surfacing for gulps of air until I was way out of my depth. Each time I put my head down, I became more and more mesmerized by the sight of the sand shifting and swirling beneath me, the rippling effect of the dappled sunlight on the ocean bed and the brightly colored fish darting across my vision. I had entered another world and completely forgot about where I was or about catching up with the others. I kept my head down for longer as I swam further out to sea until I felt as though my lungs might burst. It became more of an effort to lift my head for air, and so I stayed down, believing in my deranged state I could breathe underwater. I released all the air from my lungs, feeling dreamy as I stopped swimming and looked around at the rocks far below, and then took a deep breath of water. I immediately surfaced, coughing and choking, my arms and legs flailing, as I struggled to catch my breath and stay afloat. I panicked as each swell of the ocean came towards me, knowing I was out of my mind. I looked for the others but only saw tiny specs far out on the horizon, too far to shout for help and so I turned around and began swimming back towards the shore, slowly and steadily, terrified of a recurrence.

As I sat shivering on the sand with my towel around me, things didn't seem so funny anymore. While I waited for the others to return and for the effects of the magic mushrooms to wear off, I kept thinking of what could have happened and thanked God I was on dry land.

This one incident proved to be life changing. Later that day, during a conversation with Bonnie about an herbal remedy she was taking, a flicker of a flame reminded me of my interests from long ago in alternative health. I felt inspired, something I hadn't felt in a long time. The more I thought about it the more I became aware of the haze I'd lived my life in, and the need I now felt to do something productive, to give back to life in some way. The near drowning experience had been the wake-up call I needed.

On returning to LA this sense of purpose continued and deepened. Having jumped off the wild emotional roller coaster and fortified by my new resolution, I now felt ready and secure enough to consider stopping drinking. It was a disturbing thought, however, as much of my identity was wrapped up in the social drinking person I'd been for so many years. And I knew Ian wasn't going to like the change.

One particular evening was instrumental in me finally deciding that I'd had enough of cocaine. It was the evening of Ian's birthday party, September 1984. The house was filled with all his musician friends. At some point during the evening I noticed my bedroom door was closed and on opening it found Ian and one of his friends huddled together leaning over a table. The atmosphere in the room was secretive as they stopped talking and a large line of coke was immediately laid out for me. I didn't know if I'd taken too much or if something strange had been mixed with it but I couldn't look or talk to anyone after that, I was too high and all I wanted to do was curl up and disappear. Thankfully it gave me the final shove I needed never to touch the stuff again.

My first step towards giving back to life was to join a drug and alcohol prevention team that I'd seen advertised in the newspaper. It was a three-month course, giving participants all the information needed to talk to ten-year-olds in the local schools about drug and alcohol awareness. I buddied up with one of my team members and together we spoke at two different classes a week during the school term. I was too shy to stand in front of the class, so my colleague did most of the talking after which I'd sit with a group of kids after the class while they asked me questions about drugs. Some of the girls would stroke my hair and touch my multi-colored bracelets.

Ian's response to me not drinking was to drink more. I had made a stand but had no support and was feeling pretty wobbly. I realized that if I had half a glass of wine with my meals, rather than abstaining completely, even though I would only have one or two sips, it was enough for him to not notice things had changed quite so dramatically.

In the fall of that year, once Amelia and Lucy were at their school in Ojai, I would drive up the coast on Friday afternoons, excited to see them, and bring them home for weekends. Ian spent a few weeks at a time touring with Crosby, Stills and Nash and then home for long stretches, either swimming laps or sitting on a deckchair by the pool sunning himself. He would play his drums in the garage, trying to write songs while waiting to be offered a tour or to play on someone's album. It made me very nervous. I had to dig deep and get silently desperate before plucking up the courage to suggest he reach out, make some calls and let people know he was available for work. It didn't't occur to me then that he'd become used to being looked after and was not as hungry for work as he had been before we met.

Because I was the one paying most of the bills, I decided it was time I found a job, a thought which had not occurred to me before. I now seriously began to think of what I could do to earn money having not worked for the last fourteen years. Armed with my early retail experience in the Foale and Tuffin shop, in the Apple Boutique and in the Chelsea Antique Market, I asked some of the assistants in the smart clothes shops in Beverly Hills if they needed anyone but became increasingly despondent at their reply. It was clearly going to be more difficult than I'd thought, especially when I had to fill out each form, and put 'none' when asked about my college education.

Someone, a friend of a friend, told me of a job available with a clothes designer in Beverly Hills who needed an assistant. I drove over to the mansion and was shown into a small office by the back door. This so-called designer, a young woman in her mid-twenties, had happened on the 'bright' idea of sticking sparkling sequins and beads on white T-shirts and putting her own label on the back. I took the job and spent my days sitting in an office with two other women, with very little to do. On Friday afternoons my 'boss' would dash in, give us last minute instructions and then fly off with her boyfriend in his private jet up to Santa Barbara. During the week, if she wasn't rattling around the house, she was off 'doing lunch'. Always immaculately turned out in true designer clothes, (none of these T-shirts for her) lots of make-up, perfect hair and nails, she would fire instructions at everyone in the office and then waltz out of the door. I felt so humiliated and cried every night when I got home, knowing I had experienced so much in life, and here I was being ordered around by someone I had no respect for and couldn't relate to. My pride couldn't stand it, and after two weeks I left. What I did learn from this pitiful experience was that I needed qualifications to get a worthwhile job.

The angels must have been smiling on me because not long after this incident I found Ryokan, a small college on Venice Boulevard in Los Angeles, that offered undergraduate and graduate courses in a variety of subjects, specifically adapted for mature students. What caught my eye was a BA in Holistic Health, which included psychology and nutrition amongst other subjects. I was interviewed by one of the board members and asked questions about my education and background.

"It would take you at least a couple of years, maybe more to get a BA in Holistic Health," she said, shaking her head as if doubting that I was ready for such a commitment. "Long hours. Lots of papers to write, and then you'd have to do some catch-up subjects for not having completed high school."

She looked at me and sighed as my brain whirled around the very idea of what committing to something as huge as this would entail.

"I think I could," I said feebly.

"I tell you what," she replied, "I'll make an appointment for you to meet Dr. Ron Alexander, our Director of Psychology."

A date was set for my interview with Dr. Alexander at his office in Santa Monica. Luckily for me my mother was staying with us at the time and was full of encouragement at the prospect of one of her children going to college. On the day of the interview I left her on Santa Monica pier and crossed the road for my appointment.

As I sat in the waiting room, hands hot and sweaty and my stomach in knots, I wondered if I was ready to take on this big commitment. I had put my name down for other classes when I first arrived in LA, classes that I never completed, even though they were only for three weeks, or a weekend. I could make my life simpler, I thought, if I walked out of the building now and never contacted them again. As I was about to get up, the door suddenly opened and a tall young man with a penetrating gaze and a mass of brown hair invited me into his office.

He sat down on a black leather armchair in the corner of the room and beckoned me to sit on the chair facing him. It was too far away. I wanted to sit closer. I wanted to sit so close that my faint voice and shaky convictions would be loud and convincing enough that he would clearly understand why I had come to see him. He was very serious and quite intimidating, mid-thirties, good looking with a Bostonian accent and piercing eyes.

"What college experience or outside college courses have you taken?" he asked.

"None," I said. My enthusiasm and excitement immediately turned into fear. What was I doing here? Maybe I was too old to start college.

"Why now? Why do you wish to attend our college at this point in your life?"

I looked into his eyes, hoping he would smile, but he continued to stare, not letting up on his intensity while waiting for my answer.

"I'm ready to do something for myself that feels meaningful," I said, feeling my eyes welling up. Suddenly I knew, deep in my bones, that more than anything I wanted to be accepted by Ryokan. It would be the first big commitment I'd ever made for myself and I knew it was going to be tough.

"Do you feel you can commit to the long arduous process of getting this degree?"

I nodded. "Yes," I said. "I do."

"Good," he said. "Are you in therapy?"

"I saw a therapist for a year in England," I said, feeling stronger and with more conviction in my voice. "And I'm about to find another."

I left Dr. Alexander's office not knowing how I'd fared but prepared myself for the possibility of rejection. The director called me again a few days later to say I'd been accepted, but on a three-month trial.

At the age of thirty-seven I began my college degree. The first class was on nutrition. As ten of us mature students sat around the rectangular table in the library, we were asked to give our names and a little information about ourselves. As it got closer to my turn, I could feel my anxiety building. I was different from my fellow classmates; I spoke with an English accent, had only just emerged from my rock and roll bubble, and felt as if I was five years old. My head was buzzing, and the room began to spin. I put my hand up to tell the tutor, and then passed out. I must have looked deathly pale as I slumped forward. A few minutes later I saw concerned faces around the table all looking at me. The tutor crouched down with his arm on my shoulder and a woman stood beside me with her hand on my back telling me to breath slowly. From the panic of not wanting to be noticed I now had the full attention of everyone in the room. A memorable first day at college!

Ryokan became the place where I was to learn how to speak up in front of groups of people and I even made it known at one point, when we were sharing our life stories, that my sister had married one of the Beatles. It was information I had always held back in the past, believing it separated me from others. After mentioning it in the group I felt freed from this noose and was delighted to see their response. They were fascinated but didn't treat me any differently; they could still see me for who I was.

For the first time I was not available to go on tour with Ian every time I was asked, or to parties with him and other social events. It was unnerving going against my built-in belief that if I didn't do what was expected of me, I wouldn't be loved. I felt shaky in my new identity, and yet I knew I was taking an enormous step towards finding myself.

At the end of a successful school year, I took Amelia and Lucy out of Ojai and put them into private schools in Sherman Oakes. Ian rarely got involved with the children's lives but was happy to help with homework or take them to concerts when I was busy. Occasionally he would speak up for them if I had laid down a rule that was no longer necessary. At these times they were grateful he was there, but he also irritated them with his rigid ideas, and his overly organized record collection, or the books on his bookshelf – everything in alphabetical order. I would hear Amelia continually telling him, "Ian, stop being so anal." Having tried in vain while we were in England to be both mother and father to my children, I had been harboring the impossible hope that Ian would become a sympathetic father figure.

Mealtimes were often fraught with unbearable tension. It reminded me of mealtimes when I was a kid, except the pressure around the table now was released in fits of giggles or idiotic conversation. When just the children and I ate together it was fine, we would talk about all sorts of heartfelt things, but when Ian was present, for some reason everyone would act up. I'm sure my anxiety and the children antagonizing each other created most of it. I was desperately trying to control the whole situation. Amelia usually began by giggling and would do something silly like put her foot on the table, to which Ian would respond by doing something equally silly to try and out-clown her or be judgmental and an argument would start. It was all so disruptive, with uncontrolled energy flying everywhere around the room. Lucy always took Amelia's side and I would end up feeling torn in half, stomach in a knot, and not knowing how I could glue everyone back together. Later on, when I was back in therapy, I learned not to get so distraught by trying to protect the girls from Ian and the other way round. From then on, I would just let them get on with it and they sorted themselves out very well without my intervention. But for the time being I felt desperate for everyone to get on, for Ian to accept the children and for them to accept him.

This belief that I had no voice of my own when in a relationship began early in life. It was such a natural thing to sacrifice my own wishes in favor of what the other person wanted, to put their needs before mine. Somehow their needs always seemed more important than mine. It was a very scary thing for me to actually stand up and say, "This is what I want to do." And yet I'm sure it would always have been fine; I just didn't think I had the right. I had been surrounded by people for years that knew exactly what they wanted, creative people, those able to express themselves, whereas I had lost touch with myself, and my needs, long ago. And yet the force of my own inner nature which had driven me all these years and stopped me from losing myself completely, would occasionally erupt from deep down inside, rearing its bounteous head in all its glory and destroy the situation. At these times I felt an inner strength having slain what I believed to be the jailer of my kingdom. It was the only way I knew of surviving, of not losing myself altogether. That destructive part appeared often out of the blue when I was no longer able to keep my thoughts and feelings locked inside. The severed relationship always left the other person in shock, having no idea of the rumblings that were going on deep inside. I would finally be free to be myself but left feeling mortified at the damage I'd caused. The worst of it was the belief, and my biggest fear, that if I did ask for what I wanted, or was free to be myself, I would be unlovable and abandoned. And yet, as it turned out, it was always me that left others, when in reality I was the one that had abandoned my own needs.

For the first time ever, after being with Ian for two years, I was conscious of breaking that cycle. It felt very precarious, but I managed to continue with my desire to go to college, even though it meant fighting off my negative inner voices that told me I should be at home cooking the meals for my husband and the kids, or I should be available to go on tour with him otherwise he'd find someone else.

All my fears would rear up again, but this time I rode over them, feeling each one acutely but continuing with what I was doing. It felt unfamiliar holding my own reins.

During this time, I spent two or three days and evenings at the college, taking on as many subjects as I could; acupressure, nutrition, anatomy, American literature, creative writing, psychodrama and psychology. I wrote masses of papers and studied all kinds of books. It was thought provoking and soul- searching material, and I loved having the support and friendship of my fellow students.

As I began the long solitary journey within, I could feel myself becoming distanced from Ian. Part of this process was magnified by my new life of abstinence from alcohol and drugs. I was now able to look at some of the deep, dark thoughts I carried inside; had I been a good mother? Although I was devoted to my children, had I been sufficiently there for them? My dreams of being a mother had been gentle and idyllic, leaving me unprepared for the life that awaited us. Trying to create a normal family existence while riding the roller coaster of rock and roll had been an impossible task. I grieved deeply for the way I had led my life, and for the loss of innocence and dreams. I mourned not only for myself but also for anyone I had hurt along the way. The whole process of looking within was devastating and writing the kind of papers needed for the psychology class helped to release these torturous feelings. I was in the process of a complete turnaround and realized that the compliant person who had met Ian two Christmases ago, the giggly, sociable party girl, had disappeared. In her place was someone searching for her own truth, no longer in need of any substance in order to escape from herself.

During this introspective time, I became aware of how much I missed England; the green fields, the cool air, the seasons and, most of all, my family. It was as if I had just woken up to the fact that I was back in the US, having vowed never to live there again. I wanted to take my children and go home. On one occasion, Amelia came back unexpectedly from school and found me in tears. Clearly, by moving back here and marrying Ian, I'd acted impulsively and made a big mistake. But now I couldn't allow myself to put the children through another major upheaval, so instead I decided to stay and make the best of the situation. College life played a large part in this decision, helping me to remain grounded. It grabbed my interest, challenged me and gave me a sense of purpose.

One of the many things I questioned on this internal journey was my relationship to drugs and alcohol over the years, and how different many things would have been if they had not played such an integral part. I called a friend of mine in England who was newly in recovery from alcohol addiction and, because I didn't know anyone who didn't drink to excess, at least in the rock and roll world, I asked him if he thought I might be or have been an alcoholic. He listened carefully as I listed times when alcohol had got in the way and then he finished our conversation by saying, "I don't know, Jenny, just go to some AA meetings and see what you think."

The weekly tutorial on psychology and psychotherapy with Dr. Alexander became the most meaningful of all my classes. I loved the depths of the lectures and the encouragement to speak out in class without fear. Once, while our group sat in a circle, Ron asked someone to volunteer to be a therapist and another person the client. We had performed this role-play before with different people, but this time I elected to be the client. Ron sat next to one of my classmates, prompting her with appropriate questions, with me opposite and within the circle of the group. I was asked what I wanted to talk about.

"I think I might be an alcoholic," I said, feeling a little nervous about the implications, but also hugely relieved to name the demon. Our role-play continued until the class ended. As everyone got up to leave, to my surprise a number of people came up to me to show their support and encouragement in speaking out.

Crawling through the past, writing one paper after another, brought up situations I had not given thought to before. The more I felt myself changing inside, the more I longed for a maternal figure to put an arm around me and acknowledge this soul-searching path I was on, to hold my hand and tell me how far I'd come and how proud they were of me, but there was no one who could fill that role. The people I'd held onto in the past, in the belief they were my rock, I realized now, were never able to provide me with a safe harbor. I'd always attributed that role to Pattie. All the photos of us in Kenya show me with my head either on her shoulder or leaning against her. Whenever we were together, my confidence was boosted, and my world felt safe. I never crossed Pattie. Having her approval was too important to me. But now that had changed It was an internal journey I was on and only I could acknowledge its progress.

I needed to go to England for a few days to pick up my green card. As my trip got closer, so did the fear that by striking out on my own and giving up alcohol I had betrayed Pattie in some way and altered my role in our relationship. As much as I loved her, I knew that for my own sense of self it was time to come out from under her shadow. Having made the decision to stop drinking and go to college I was now in the process of disentangling myself from being under the control of others.

The lonely journey of reclaiming the fragmented parts of myself had begun, even though they were still fragile.

We met in London. Pattie was now separated from Eric and it distressed me to see how sad she looked. At first refusing our customary bottle of champagne at dinner that night, when I saw the hurt expression on her face, I ended up agreeing to one glass. The next morning, I felt hung over and disappointed, the anxiety I'd felt in LA in anticipation of returning to England had not been unfounded. The strength I'd built up over the last year had temporarily disappeared and I was unable to let go of the co-dependent relationship with Pattie, even at the expense of my own convictions. My one glass had turned into the usual few glasses as I shared with her my enthusiasm about attending college and how much my life had changed thanks to my newfound abstinence. She, on the other hand, was relieved to know at least in this part of the relationship, she still had control.

Even so, my few days in England had been refreshing, away from the desert heat of Los Angeles in the summer and surrounded by family and the cool green countryside. Once back in America, armed with the hope that in time we could all live in England together, I walked into the bedroom one day where Ian was lying on a futon, doing a crossword.

"How about we make a four-year plan to stay here in LA, and then try living in England?" By then, I knew the children would be in college.

"No!" he said, without taking his eyes off his crossword.

It felt as though someone had slammed and bolted the prison door, and here I was trapped in this infernal desert heat. I walked into the sitting room and lay down on the sofa in front of the air-conditioner, unable to move.

Life in LA continued to have an unreal quality to it. At times I felt it was all a dream and I would wake up one morning to find myself in Willow Cottage getting the children dressed for school. I didn't't feel grounded. This feeling was heightened in October '87 when we were awoken by a violent shaking in our bed. Sleeping on a futon close to the floor made the sound and movement fierce and more frightening. The walls moved, the sliding doors to the yard rattled and objects crashed to the floor. It was all so sudden. As I was trying to get up, Lucy came running into the bedroom screaming. I clung to her and pushed her under the doorframe.

The most terrifying thing in an earthquake is not knowing how much more intense the shaking will become, or for how much longer. Amelia had spent the night with a friend, so I tried to call her, but the telephones were dead. We turned on the television and were told to be aware of aftershocks, to stand under a doorframe or crouch under a table. The earth was still quaking every so often, and apart from the intermittent sound of alarms, the air was filled with an eerie silence. We were all very frightened. There were a few more aftershocks that day, all equally scary and deeply unnerving, intensifying my hatred of LA and leaving me fearful of another earthquake at any given moment. It made my longing for England even more pronounced; I wanted to feel solid ground beneath my feet. I decided on my next trip to England that I would put some money down on an apartment in Surrey, a place where I could spend time in the summer holidays and rent out during the year. It was my way of getting my toe in the property market with the hope that one day we'd move back there.

After the long struggle to complete my Bachelor's degree, instead of feeling happy for succeeding, I felt low. Not having experienced the sense of completing anything before, it felt anti-climactic. And yet my mother, who'd made it clear how proud she was of my achievement, flew over for the graduation ceremony. My senior paper, The Orphan Mother, had opened up many memories, old wounds and unresolved questions about my childhood. I had interviewed my mother before I began writing this paper. For the first time she told me everything about our life in Kenya, a subject that she had previously refused to discuss having found it too painful to talk about. By speaking to me about the past it enabled her to release her memories, slowly allowing them to see the light of day.

It was some time after my mother's visit that she surprised me by saying the words I didn't ever expect to hear. We were sitting next to each other on the sofa at her home in Devon, having a cup of tea, perhaps talking about her recent visit to LA when she turned to me and said:

"I'm sorry darling, I wasn't a good mother when you were all growing up."

"Mum," I immediately responded, "you were young, and you did the best you could in the situation."

"No, Jenny, I want you to hear me. I know I wasn't a good mother and I'm sorry." I squeezed her hand, looked her in the eye and said, "Thank you."

Writing my senior paper was just one of many cathartic experiences during this time. I realized a couple of months before the completion of my Bachelor's degree that I wanted to continue learning and begin the Master's program in Counseling Psychology with Dr. Alexander as my tutor.

Through Ron Alexander's classes I was back in touch with my spiritual path, back to where I had been many years before. The positive and creative side of that same feeling of emptiness I had held onto for so long, the underlying longing, had now been transformed into a search for fulfilment that was not only psychological, but also spiritual. At that time, I was in touch with George Harrison, mostly through fax, about his meeting up again with Maharishi. He gave me information about the Transcendental Meditation Centre in LA. With his help I was given a new mantra and began meditating again.

I began the Master's program with trepidation. Everyone in the class had been to college before and had studied some psychology as part of their curriculum, so I felt like a true beginner. The program consisted of twelve modules, each a month long, and endless papers to write. At the end of each month I sighed with relief before moving onto the next step. We were all encouraged to start counselling in one of the many low-income counselling centres. Although I loved listening to my clients, and set up a good rapport with them, after a year I knew that being a therapist wasn't something I would want to take on as a career. Instead, on completing my Master's, I decided to take a PhD in Humanities. Working on a dissertation would allow me to do the thing I had always loved: writing.

It was after writing so many papers about my family and early life over the last few years that the idea of contacting my father came to me. I wondered if, now that he was getting older, he might have any regrets about disowning his children. My mother told me she'd bumped into him and his wife many years before while she was at a school fete in Somerset with my younger brothers. He and his wife had ignored her. It was probably after this incident she told me that Pattie, Colin, Paula and I were secrets, my father's children didn't know of our existence. As a teenager my brother Colin had made contact with our father but was given the cold shoulder and asked how much money he wanted. Pattie had seen him in her early thirties. She'd been instructed to meet him in Exeter near his office, but he steered her along the backstreets; always looking over his shoulder in case anyone he knew saw him. She felt as though she was a mistress and didn't bother contacting him again. And so it was that I wrote a letter to him and sent it to his office in Exeter with not much hope of a reply.

I couldn't believe it when a letter finally arrived. He was real! I had a father! I opened the envelope with great excitement and then read, in his small, looped handwriting, about the flowers in his garden and the two dogs he took for walks every day. That was it. There was nothing about the years gone by or about his new family. But at least I had made a connection, fragile as it was, and we were now in touch.

I kept writing. I told him about my life in Los Angeles, and about my teenage daughters, his grandchildren. For a few months we kept up a correspondence, his letters never sharing about anything more than his garden and his dogs. When I told him I was coming to England for two weeks and would love to meet him, much to my surprise he agreed to my suggestion that we meet in Salisbury, at Biddy's house. I gave him her phone number and told him how much I looked forward to seeing him.

On the morning of our meeting, as I opened her door Biddy greeted me with a look of concern.

"Jenny," she said. "I have just put the receiver down from your father."

"Is he going to be late?" I asked. But I knew what was coming next.

"I'm so sorry," she said, putting her arm around my shoulders and guiding me into the kitchen. "He told me to tell you he couldn't meet you today, and never will."

I was stunned. I had been so close. A deep feeling of anger welled up from within as it dawned on me why he hadn't come. He'd been caught out. I grabbed the local phone book and found the number for Mr. and Mrs. Boyd. A woman's piercing voice answered in a cut-glass accent.

"Hello?"

"I'm my father's daughter," I blurted out. "And I want to speak to him."

"I'm sorry, he's out!" was the brittle reply.

"I want to speak to my father." I was determined not to let her get in the way. It was my right.

"I'm sorry he's out!"

The phone went dead. I felt tears rolling down my cheeks and wondered why I cared. He'd never made any attempt to contact us throughout all these years, I didn't even know who he was. A few days later I flew back to Los Angeles, knowing I would never hear from or see this man who was obviously unable to speak up for himself.

As I sat on the plane, I realized that most of my life I'd alternated between telling myself I didn't have a father, to imagining what it would be like if I ever met him. I thought I'd seen him once, back in the 60s, wandering around Bermondsey Market; a striking blond-haired man wearing a tweed jacket and a cravat. Of course, it might also have been an illusion created by the hash brownies Pattie and I had eaten earlier that morning. As Pattie and I stood at either end of the crowded market, filled with the hustle and bustle of antique dealers, we caught each other's eye. She had noticed the same man. We acknowledged each other with a smile, knowing we were both thinking the same thing. "Our father?" she mouthed.

Then again, having only seen him in a black and white photo of our parents on their wedding day, we didn't even know what he looked like. In the photo, my 18-year-old mother looked beautiful, wearing a long flowing dress and smiling, while Jock, so serious, a handsome man in Air Force uniform, stood with his arm across his chest as if reporting for duty. I'd also seen an official family photo of Pattie, Colin and me as a baby with our parents proudly standing behind us. Even though it was almost certainly not our father we saw at Bermondsey Market that day, he was always lurking in the back of my mind.

With these thoughts whirling around as I flew to the US, I found a piece of paper, asked the air stewardess for a pen and wrote a poem:

It stirred a memory
From years gone by
A memory so faint
It only whispered
Wings touched me gently
I nearly could see
Myself as a child
And you next to me.

A couple of years later, having in the meantime achieved my dream of putting some money down on a property in England, I decided to spend a couple of weeks in the apartment I'd bought in Surrey. I was sitting in the armchair, reading one of the many books I'd bought with me, when the phone rang. Not knowing how I recognized his voice, I knew it was my father speaking. I had no idea how he got my number unless he'd contacted my mother. I was too shocked to ask.

During our conversation he told me he was no longer with his wife and would like to meet me. I couldn't believe it! Finally, I was going to meet my father. We made a plan. I was to spend the night at his new flat in Sherbourne, Dorset, and the following morning I would drive him to London, where we would have lunch with Pattie, and then put him on a train to Norfolk to stay with my brother Colin. He was finally ready to see his children.

Two days later, when I saw an old man walking towards my car, I felt nothing. There was no feeling of connection, nothing in his face that took me back to my childhood; nothing that told me he was my father. He was just an old man, wearing a cravat and with a scarred face. We greeted each other with a hug, and then he suggested going for a walk to the cathedral in town. There were enough interesting sights to keep the conversation light and focused on what we saw, and despite my neutral reaction, I was still walking on air at the thought of this extraordinary meeting which until then, I had only ever dreamed of but never imagined would actually happen. Once we returned to his flat, I noticed with a feeling of trepidation that there was only one bedroom with two single beds a few inches apart. I put it to the back of my mind and focused on my time with him.

The sightseeing trip in the town had been easy and allowed me to ask lots of questions about the surrounding area, and to keep up a pretty normal conversation. But as we sat in the small sitting room, I remembered my mother telling me once she'd separated from my stepfather, that my father never spoke, never said a word for days on end, and it would drive her mad. With gusto and determination I kept talking, saying anything to fill the spaces and to stop his wall of silence from engulfing me too, sparking off memories from childhood.

"Do you have any photographs of us in Africa?" I asked, looking around the sparsely decorated room.

He looked at me and shook his head.

"Do you remember any stories of us all in Kenya?" I continued, trying to keep the conversation upbeat.

Again, he shook his head.

I suddenly became aware of the silence hissing and swirling all around me. I could feel myself begin to panic with the prospect of a whole evening to get through and then sleeping in the same room, beds almost touching, with this stranger.

"Do you remember me as a little girl?" I asked, feeling as though I was now scraping the barrel.

"No," he said. Then his eyes lit up and he smiled. "But I do remember my horses." My heart sank.

We ate a cold tasteless quiche in silence. My head was on its way to a pounding migraine. "Keep talking," I told myself, as I said whatever came into my head, unable to bear the silence.

Once we'd finished eating, I took the plates into the tiny kitchen, and began washing them in the sink. With the tap running, a plate in one hand and the washing-up brush in the other, I felt, to my horror, two arms grab me around my waist from behind as he pulled me against his body. I jumped in panic. Then it struck me for the second time that I had to sleep in the same bedroom as this man, just one foot away from his bed.

I wanted to run right there and then, to jump into my car and keep driving until I got home. But how could I? Even though I was a grown woman and had just been groped by my father, the man I'd been searching for all my life, I had never been in this situation before and I didn't know how to handle it. The reality was that I still didn't have a voice. I didn't know how to say, "How dare you!" or "I'm leaving." It was the last thing I expected, and so I just walked quietly into the sitting room feeling horribly embarrassed and devastated. After all those years of wishing I had a father or resigning myself to the belief that I didn't have one. And now, this father I had longed for, the one I believed would help me put together the missing pieces of my childhood, was a terrifying stranger; just an empty shell with nothing to say and no memories of me as a child. As an adult I'd heard about his accident during the war, stories from my mother while interviewing her for my BA of him staring at the wall, but that did not excuse his behavior.

I willed the hours to go by, pleaded with them to move quickly so I could leave this place, and never think about contacting him again.

Bedtime came. I got myself ready and then crept into the single bed closest to the window. I lay on my side like a block of concrete, petrified to move, pretending to be asleep. I could hear my father in the room, the sound of him breathing, his footsteps walking towards me, and then bending over my bed he kissed me goodnight on the lips. "Good night dear," he said. I froze. I lay there all night feeling miserable, keeping very still and not daring to sleep until the sun came up. By 6am I was up and dressed, ready for our drive to London and to meet Pattie. I called her, as we got closer, saying we would see her earlier than expected.

As we sat in the noisy restaurant together, waiting for our lunch, I watched my sister asking our father all the questions I'd asked the day before, only this time we were able to steal surprised and knowing glances at each other. I took him to the train station that afternoon, and as he hugged me in a vice-like grip his hand crept down my back and squeezed my bottom. I watched the train pull out of the station with a huge sense of relief. That was it. Never again, I told myself. I will have nothing more to do with him.

Later that night, as I relived the desperate meeting with my father, I felt deeply hurt, disgusted and bewildered. I had hoped for so much more. I began thinking about how different my life would have been, and how different my relationships would have turned out, had I known what it was like to have a healthy and balanced, loving father. To feel that unconditional support from an early age might have given me a greater sense of substance, made me more grounded, and not so in need of projecting the father-figure role on to the men in my life. Often while growing up I had felt at the mercy of outside forces, not able to find my internal anchor. With these thoughts I allowed my mind to wander, reliving what it was like growing up in Kenya, memories of my father's all-pervasive shadow coming in and out of focus.

The only childhood memory I had of him were through the eyes of a five-year-old. We are all sitting around a large dining-room table, eating in absolute silence, his black leather-gloved hand resting like a strange totem on the table. He was always silent. A nine-year-old Pattie had the ability to send my brother, Colin, and me into smothered fits of giggles by wiggling her ears. My father's fierce blue eyes would skim from one of us to the other, baffled and unamused, searching in vain for the cause of the frivolity before continuing with the meal. I don't remember ever hearing him speak. Although I didn't know then about his accident, about his disfigurement and the trauma he'd suffered, I believed I loved him and felt the pain of his solitude.

That silent, empty figure of my father had haunted me, both literally and symbolically throughout my life, the pervasive atmosphere of rigid silence and vacancy. I had always feared that silence and yet I picked it up as if it were mine. I took it away with me into the world, so a part of me, like him, felt locked inside and longed to be released.

As I sat mulling over the last couple of days, it became clear to me how deeply I'd been affected by my father, both in his presence and in his absence.

A journey beyond the muse

12

PURPOSE FOUND

When the time came for me to find a subject for my dissertation, I remembered reading, 'write about what you know'. I had spent the last twenty years amongst musicians, and this was what I decided to write about. I had also spent most of my life believing I wasn't creative, so I put these two themes into the mix and started my research on musicians and the creative process.

I began by compiling a list of the musicians I'd like to interview and the questions I would ask them. Were they encouraged as children to be creative? What gave them the drive to create? Did drugs and alcohol enhance or block creativity? Do we all have the potential to be creative? While I was thinking of these questions, there was one that stuck in my mind: did they consider their talent a God-given-gift? Did Eric Clapton think of his talent as a gift? If so, was the responsibility of this gift too much for him to bear? Was that why he turned to alcohol and drugs? These questions affected me deeply. It made me curious about not only Eric, but also about other musicians. Were they aware of something greater than themselves while creating? Were they more in tune with their inner voice than the rest of us?

When I did eventually interview Eric, who by that time had stopped drinking, he confirmed my belief in the spiritual connection to creativity by saying that at times while creating, it can be daunting, like staring into the face of God, and sometimes it's very frightening.

The compelling drive of these musicians to express themselves was inspiring. It was ignited by a need to feel whole, to fulfill their destiny and to feel at one with themselves. I too became aware of accessing my own creativity through interviewing the musicians and writing my dissertation, it filled me with a new confidence in myself, and trust in my ability to write about this fascinating subject. I never thought I'd find a creative voice in exactly the same people I'd been drawn to all my life, who had previously represented the very reason I'd felt so out of touch with my own creativity.

On finishing my dissertation, and having interviewed forty musicians, I sent the manuscript to an agent. Her response was positive; she asked me to add thirty-five more interviews, and suggested I have a friend of hers, Holly George Warren, to help with the editing. With my counseling background I felt far more confident in asking questions, knowing when to keep silent and when to respond. Finding other musicians to interview was a breeze when they heard I'd spoken to Eric Clapton, George Harrison, Ringo Starr, Joni Mitchell and many other well-known and respected musicians. I only needed to think of someone I'd like to interview and somehow, miraculously I was able to locate them. I was in my element and completely absorbed in this project. Ian was now playing with Bob Dylan and I no longer felt the need to check up on him or worry about what he might get up to on the road. I was feeling secure within myself.

My interviews continued full time – in London, New York and LA - and once they were finished, the manuscript went to my agent in New York. Eventually my dissertation was transformed into a book, published by Simon and Schuster in the spring of '92.

Now that this task was completed, and my four-and-a-half years at college had come to an end, I needed to find a job. A friend of mine said she'd heard of an addictions treatment center in Arizona called Sierra Tucson who were looking for someone to help with marketing in Los Angeles. This time I did have the qualifications needed to apply for the job. I flew to Tucson for my interview, even though I didn't have a clue about marketing. After meeting the rest of the marketing team and walking around the facility, I was offered the job. As an introduction, I was required to spend the customary five days in their Family Program, which began the following week.

The five days was an enlightening introduction into how a family reacts to having one of their members as an addict or alcoholic. I watched the metamorphosis take place as parent or spouse began by pointing the accusatory finger at the obvious addict, only to discover by the end of the week the part they themselves played in their loved one's addiction. It was a family affair.

The evenings spent in my motel room during that time were filled with reflections about the past and my relationship, even though on a social level, to drugs and alcohol. My siblings and friends all found it totally acceptable behavior when we were together, no matter how much we drank. I now realized alcohol had given me a false sense of connection to people; it had made me feel sure of myself, more lucid, more spontaneous, and less split and self-conscious. What it excluded, though, was something much more important. A little sound, ignored for so long, stuffed deep down inside where I thought there was nothing; my own voice.

I attended a few AA groups when I got home, but they didn't feel right for me. After spending so much time at the center and going to all the therapy groups I came to the conclusion I wasn't an alcoholic, I identified more with what they referred to as a co-dependent - 'A pattern of dependence and need for approval from others in an attempt to find safety and self-worth'. I was addicted to people that felt nurturing to me, mostly Pattie and Mick. The thing that turned it into an unhealthy relationship was focusing on them for approval rather than finding it within myself. Their acceptance meant I would not be deserted. They were deep irrational childhood fears that had nothing to do with adult life, but which compelled me to believe that somewhere inside them were the nurturing parents I never had.

Every few weeks I flew back to Tucson for a marketing meeting and to spend time in the adolescent or eating disorder units. I attended lectures and another round of the Family Program. A psychiatrist called Dr. Nash gave one of the lectures. He was an elderly man with a wrinkly face and eyes that sparkled. I liked him immediately, especially when I heard him describe the difference between religious and spiritual people.

"Religious people try to stay out of hell," he said. "Whereas spiritual people have already been there."

One day, while in the middle of a board meeting, I was told there was a package waiting for me at the motel. I drove over during the lunch break and opened the Federal Express envelope. Inside was a bright orange book with large thin blue writing, 'Musicians in Tune', with smaller yellow writing underneath, 'Seventy-five Contemporary Musicians Discuss the Creative Process'. And there at the bottom, in the same color was, Jenny Boyd, Ph.D. I hugged it. It felt as though I'd given birth to my third child.

Having been part of the Family Program at Sierra Tucson had given me a greater understanding of how alcohol impacts the relationship between family members. The effect it had was powerful and made me aware of how much I cared for Mick and how helpless I felt in stopping him from drinking and drug abuse. I called him soon after one of my trips, knowing the time had come for me to talk to him.

We arranged a meeting. He lived almost opposite us at the time, a little further up the coast in Malibu. It was a small place that felt barely lived in, just used as somewhere to lay his head. He opened the door and bent down to give me a kiss. As he wandered around the kitchen, opening cupboards as if looking for something, I asked him to sit with me on the sofa. I couldn't stop shaking as I stared into his eyes. I took a deep breath.

"Mick," I whispered, feeling tears unexpectedly trickling down my cheeks. "I feel scared."

He looked startled, caught off guard. "What's wrong?" he asked.

"I love you." I took another deep breath. "And I'm scared you're going to die." My tears kept rolling. Knowing this was the most important thing I had ever said to him. I kept my eyes glued to his. People had endlessly told Mick he should stop drinking and taking drugs, but he had ignored them all. Now it was my turn. I told him in very few words how I felt without placing any blame or manipulating him through guilt. Now it was up to Mick, and a miracle. Through my work I had seen countless times that miracles could happen. At the time his sister Sue was battling with breast cancer and I wondered, once I left his house, whether it would give him an added incentive to be fully present for her, in a way he was unable to be with his father.

I saw Mick again in Hawaii a few weeks later. Ian was flying in from Japan the following day with Bob Dylan who was scheduled to play a concert on the island. Mick and I both happened to arrive on the same day to see our daughter Lucy. She had been living on Maui for the last six months and it was her nineteenth birthday. The three of us swam in one of the rock pools together, one of those rare and special moments for her; alone with both her parents. Later that day, as we sat in one of the cafes by the pool, I noticed Mick wasn't drinking.

We watched Lucy running up the beach, her long Fleetwood legs striding across the sand towards us. She wanted Mick to go for a boat ride with her. As if in slow motion Mick walked over to the canoe, his head down, with Lucy behind him. They pushed the boat into the sea and jumped in, each of them grabbing one of the paddles, both silhouetted against the setting sun. Mick had on his white terrycloth hat just like the photographs I'd seen of him as a small boy, only now he had a beard and long straggly hair. Something about them in that little canoe struck me as sad. He seemed so lonely, and at a crisis point in his life. I watched them both rowing out towards the sunset and then had to look away.

Bob Dylan's Maui concert took place in a small outside arena, packed with excited people. George Harrison and his wife Olivia had driven across the island to see the show and were staying in our little complex of beach huts. It was good to see George; it always gave me a great sense of comfort knowing he was in the world. He was a link to our younger years, when life was not so complex. After the show I walked into one of the rooms set aside for family and friends where I met and talked to Lynn Frankel, Mick's new girlfriend, and future wife. A little while later George, Olivia and I were standing outside on the terrace, looking at my book when I noticed Bob Dylan walking towards us. He took the book from George's hand and asked if he could borrow it. By the time he gave it back the following day it was curled over with most of the pages earmarked. I felt deeply proud he'd studied it so carefully.

Ian and I spent our last night in Hawaii on one of the other islands. It was our eighth wedding anniversary and he wanted to celebrate by having dinner in a fancy restaurant. I could have happily just sat on a beach and watched the sun go down. Instead we sat opposite each other in a cold and characterless room and said nothing. It was one of those moments where there was nothing to say; we had travelled in different directions for too long.

The time had come to promote Musicians in Tune. Much to my joy and amazement, Mick was still not drinking or taking drugs, and suggested meeting me in New York to help with the promotion. It felt reassuring and meant so much to me having his encouragement. He had been hugely supportive ever since I started college. He would let me know how proud he was of me, and continually reminded me to remember my own natural wisdom while learning about this whole new world of psychology.

We talked together on radio programs, appeared on television with other musicians and did interviews for magazines and newspapers. Even though I was no longer in need of it, this was the support and respect from Mick I had craved for all those years. Back in Los Angeles I did more television and radio interviews and Mick and I appeared on a television program called The Dennis Miller Show. Mick's other band, the Zoo, played a number and then it was our turn to talk. In front of a live audience, as we walked across the stage to get to our seats, we were greeted by Lucy's loud wolf whistle from the crowd, mixed with the sound of clapping.

This was followed a few days later by a book signing at Book Soup, a popular bookshop on Sunset Boulevard. A few of the musicians had agreed to accompany me. Sitting in a row with Don Henley, Mick, Chris McVie, Ian, Ringo, Stephen Bishop, Graham Nash, and Jeff Lynn made it one of the happiest evenings I could remember. Having their support felt tremendous. The queue of people waiting to have their book signed went out onto the street and around the block. George showed up later in the restaurant some of us had gone to after the signing, just to congratulate me.

After a year of working at Sierra Tucson, and getting to know the key players, the thought occurred to me that maybe I could be instrumental in setting up a similar center in the UK; an outreach program. I approached the CEO and talked to him about my ideas. To my surprise he told me I could find an office in London and start promoting their facility as soon as possible. It was not a natural thing for me to ask for what I wanted, but one of the many things I'd learned while working for Sierra Tucson was how to speak up. We decided that I would leave LA on the first day of December '92. Ian and I had been living in one of the town houses in Malibu for the last three or four years, a place I enjoyed, with the beach just across the road. Even so, I had kept the picture of England in my mind all that time and so when my request was granted I couldn't refuse. The fact that my daughter Amelia had decided to move to England at the same time was an added advantage. I couldn't believe my luck. It was everything I'd wanted, and I was getting paid to promote something I believed in.

Ian had been against going to England for so many years, but grudgingly he agreed to come if I could keep him in the style he'd been accustomed to. Boxes were piling up ready to take with us or put into storage. Ten days before our departure I remained anxious over having made this huge decision to leave our life in LA, but more than that, I didn't want to be responsible for separating Ian from a music career he'd spent the last twenty years building in the United States. This time, I wouldn't be able to support him if he couldn't find work. When I told Ian that I couldn't be responsible for him, that the weight was too heavy, I cried. In many ways, even after ten years, I didn't feel I really knew him. Maybe he'd been a pale substitute for Mick — a role he could never live up to. Once I became more conscious of who I was and what my needs were, we had slowly drifted apart. I knew my path now lay in a completely different direction and that the marriage was over. Ian stayed in LA for several more months before moving to Santa Fe.

Not long after I returned to England, I found myself in an unwanted relationship instigated by someone who was professionally involved in the addiction field. It was not something I was ready for but at the time I didn't have the strength to resist his manipulative advances. Although I had achieved success during my last few years in LA, having completed my degrees, having got the book published, spoken on national television and radio, and finally achieved my dream of moving to England, I had, on the other hand, just left my family home, a ten-year relationship and I was starting over at the bottom rung of the ladder, with no time to grieve my losses.

The positive side of this awful predicament that had me in tears most days, was a trip to Arizona to attend the five-day therapeutic program at Sierra Tucson; a workshop that as their UK marketing consultant I was encouraged to experience. Not only was I able to work on this debilitating relationship and relinquish it during my time there, but it also inspired me to create similar workshops in England, using the same facilitator, Don Lavender, to run them.

This was my way of making what I had experienced available to a larger cross-section of people, as Sierra Tucson - whether it was the in-patient program or their Quality of Life workshops - was only for the wealthy.

When I returned home, I hired a group room at a hotel in Kent, bought a rather meager database from someone who'd previously made an unsuccessful attempt at putting on workshops, and contacted the few therapists I'd got to know in the last six months of living in England. The two-day workshop was a triumph. It was filled with not only recovering addicts wanting to do some work with their family members, but also therapists. On the days I wasn't meeting new doctors and therapists, handing out brochures and giving them lunch, I would sit in my room that passed for an office in Sloane Square. Hardly anyone called, including Sierra Tucson. Some of the London doctors I'd met were polite and charming but would make no bones about asking why they would send any of their patients to an all singing, all dancing very expensive private American treatment center.

Having never done any marketing before, and not absolutely sure I knew every detail of what I was selling, I relied on my enthusiasm and belief in what I had witnessed and how inspired I'd felt at Sierra Tucson. I began developing friendships with all the local therapists based on life experiences and mutual interests as well as Sierra Tucson. Knowing that a therapists' job can be isolating, I invited them to lunch and tea gatherings where they could meet and exchange information with other therapists and doctors.

I attended the main addiction conferences in London and became quite adept at setting up my booth with its colorful photographs of blue skies, saguaro cactus flowers and happy faces. I would place piles of catalogues about Sierra Tucson on the table beside me, with my cards ready to hand out to the hoards of people as they wandered around the hall, weaving in and out of all the other booths and marketers representing treatment centers from around the world.

As each speaker was announced throughout the day I would leave my booth and become part of the audience in the hall next door. At one of the conferences I went to I came across a woman called Rokelle Lerner. She was a therapist from America well known not only as a dynamic speaker, which I agreed after seeing her talk, but also as an author on books about recovery. I saw her later that afternoon when she came up to my booth. We chatted about Sierra Tucson, about her talk and about my workshops. She was inspiring and I immediately liked her, so it was no surprise when she asked me if I would represent her in England as a speaker and facilitator of workshops. We didn't know at that time we'd be working together for the next twenty years.

I went to another conference shortly afterwards at The Kensington Town Hall. This one was set up to raise awareness about eating disorders and the main speaker that day was Princess Diana. It was the closest she'd come to publically expressing her own struggle with an eating disorder. She began her speech by saying, "I have it on very good authority that the quest for perfection our society demands can leave the individual gasping for breath at every turn."

It was a courageous thing for her to do, and because of her willingness to talk about her eating problems it allowed others to do the same and get help. It opened the door in a big way and made it okay to bring these dark secrets of addiction out into the open. After her talk she walked around the room looking at all the booths, chatting with people, until she came to where I was standing with my friend, Liz. She admired the photographs and in a gentle and unassuming way asked me questions about the eating disorder unit at Sierra Tucson. Her openess made me feel very much at ease as we talked about the struggles of addiction. She had opened herself up in front of the world that day, declared her secret, and was now interested in knowing how others could be helped.

After a couple of years in England Sierra Tucson decided to cut their ties with the UK, which meant I was out of a job. Having met all the key players in the addiction field by this time, I asked a woman I knew, a supporter of twelve-step programs, if the foundation she'd started would sponsor me in bringing more therapists from the States to put on similar workshops for people in recovery from addiction and relationship issues. Don Lavender was now working independently from Sierra Tucson, but I continued to bring him to London three times a year to facilitate his workshops on trauma. Nobody else was offering these kinds of workshops at the time and every one of them was full. I sought out different US therapists specializing in eating disorders, codependency, family relationships and shame.

Because I no longer had a Sierra Tucson office, I asked Pattie if I could work in the dressing room of her flat in London. I sat on the carpeted floor, surrounded by her shoes and bags, while I wrote in my notebook and made calls on her telephone/ fax machine as I began setting up one workshop after another. This was the beginning of what was later to become my company, Spring Workshops.

I felt inspired by the response to these workshops, getting letters and cards from participants thanking me, or hearing glowing reports from referring therapists. It was reassuring to watch people reclaim their lives either by going through treatment or attending one of the workshops. However, living in England was much harder than I'd imagined and sometimes I wondered whether I'd made the right decision in moving back. There were tough days, the only money coming from what I earned, and, apart from my family, I had very few friends. My daughter Amelia had moved back to England the same time as me, which was comforting and especially so when a couple of years later she gave birth to a little boy she called Wolf. I spent a lot of time with both, but I knew, much to my dismay, she was quietly making plans to move back to LA.

I felt in need of an adventure! Something completely different and away from my life in London, and so when my new friend Electra suggested I should go with her on a trek to Nepal I was tempted. But when I saw photographs of her previous trip I knew, whatever the cost, I had to go. Before setting up the next series of workshops, three years after arriving in England, I was on my way to a place that had always fired my imagination.

Our guide was a trekker from Germany, who at Electra's request had agreed to take a group of her friends from England. We arrived in Katmandu and met up with a Sherpa and porters before taking the perilous bus journey, a couple of days later, up the narrow winding track to our destination and the start of our ten-day trek. We all slept in tents, carried for us by the porters, along with heavy cans of kerosene, cooking utensils and food for the whole trip. They sang as they jumped from rock to rock in flip-flops, as if they were carrying nothing heavier than a bag of feathers on their back. The only other person I knew in our group, apart from my friend Electra, was our old family friend Kellogs, who had at the last minute decided to join us. Every night once the other members of our group had finished supper and were all sleeping peacefully, Kellogs and I would join the Sherpa and porters as they stood in a circle, away from the tents, singing and clapping their hands to the sound of a hand-held drum. One by one we took it in turns to dance in the middle of the circle in front of their beaming faces as they clapped harder and sang louder. They didn't speak much English but as they passed me along the trek the following day, they would call out to me and say, "Hello good dancing!"

It was a life-changing experience in more ways than I had anticipated. I lived each moment of the journey to the full, knowing that all I needed to do – both on the trek and in life - was to put one foot in front of the other. We walked seven or eight hours a day for ten inspirational days, along narrow tracks cut into the cliffs, through villages and across suspension bridges with deep gorges underneath. This was breath-taking scenery, always with the snow-tipped Himalayas high on the horizon. Among our group of trekkers was an architect called David. The attraction between us slowly grew as we walked and talked for miles and miles up and down the mountain paths, sharing our life stories. His was a life that had not always been plain sailing, but it was obvious to me he had managed throughout it all to be a generous and supportive father. What a place to meet my future husband!

The following year, on one of my trips to see my kids in Los Angeles, I arranged to visit a treatment center in Arizona called Cottonwood de Tucson. A friend of mine was a member of their marketing team and introduced me to the CEO, Ron Welch, and to their Medical Director, both of whom I warmed to immediately. Their philosophy and way of treatment was not so different to Sierra Tucson, but the campus was smaller, more contained. The Santa-Fe style buildings sat amongst Sawuaro cactus and brightly colored desert flowers and I couldn't help but notice the mountains on the horizon changing color as the sun crept across the sky.

I felt inspired by what I saw and heard that day and felt a deep connection to the people who worked there. This was confirmed by the time I was ready to leave when Ron Welch asked me to be Cottonwood's marketing consultant in London. I was thrilled! He gave me carte blanche to set up a Cottonwood presence in the UK and told me he would support any decision I made to achieve this goal. Dr. Moore, the Medical Director, and Ron seemed to see a potential in me that I hadn't recognized in myself., but it gave me the confidence and determination to live up to their expectations. I believed in the Cottonwood team I'd met that day, their pioneering approach towards treatment and their respect for their patients as well as for each other.

On returning to England, with Spring Workshops still thriving, I set to work on organizing the first three-day Family Program workshop facilitated by the very skilled family therapist from Cottonwood. I mailed hundreds of flyers as usual to everyone on my database and to all the therapists, psychiatrists and doctors. Within a week the workshop was full, with a waiting list. The UK Family Program grew and continued to flourish three of four times a year. It was the best way to promote Cottonwood, clients told their therapist or doctors and the referrals to Cottonwood for in-patient began in earnest, making it the number one choice for treatment.

UK 12-step treatment centers were light years behind the States at that time. Many of them were like old-fashioned boarding schools, a bit rough round the edges, patronizing towards their patients and stuck in the old-fashioned model of anti-medication. In complete contrast to Cottonwood which not only treated addiction but also the underlying disorders which were often the cause of the addiction in the first place, such as depression, bi-polar disorder or trauma.

Now that there were so many people from England attending Cottonwood, Ron asked me to facilitate a weekly aftercare group for when they returned. Even though I was nervous at the thought of facilitating my own group of former hard-core addicts, I was often moved to tears as I witnessed their humility, their spiritual awareness and sense of gratitude at being given a second chance in life. It was inspiring to see the change between the first time I met them for their assessment and their transformation a few weeks later, many of whom had been suffering from eating disorders, depression or addiction.

I set up breakfast meetings for the UK doctors and psychiatrists to meet and chat with all the key players from the Cottonwood facility. Dr. Moore gave talks on the latest cutting-edge information about medication and addiction. I took a group of doctors and psychiatrists, some of whom were from treatment centers in the UK, to Cottonwood for a few days. Part of the schedule was for them (and me) to experience the Challenge Course, an outdoor team-building event that had them all in fits of giggles as they tried to release their need to control every situation.

Cottonwood had become the new buzzword in the UK addiction field, and I felt proud to be associated with them. I was often asked by Ron Welch to attend marketing meetings at the facility out in Tucson and to share with the other marketers the successful strategy I used, but of course there was no strategy, I just did what I felt inspired to do knowing I had the support of the CEO. Although I had enormous respect for Ron Welch and admired the way he ran this treatment center, I was a little scared of him. His approval meant a great deal to me and I think he knew it. I looked to him as a sort of father figure even though he was a little younger than me. His strong silent support and trust in my abilities was something I had never experienced from my own father, and what it did was to ignite a belief and confidence within myself.

David and I got married in the spring of 1997. It was then, feeling secure in my life and with David's encouragement that I agreed to see my father again. Pattie had arranged a family lunch at her house, and he'd been invited. Arriving with a woman he had known many years ago in Africa, he gave me his usual hug when he saw me, with a very tight and improper squeeze. A few weeks later he came with his partner, Mary, to David's cottage in Norfolk and on a walk in the fields I told Mary about my father's inappropriate behavior. He never did it again.

It was around this time that my mother made a pilgrimage to visit the shrine of Our Lady of Walsingham in Norfolk. On her return she told me of an extraordinary coincidence; while there, she'd sat next to a woman who'd not only lived in Kenya but had also known my father and his then new wife. She confided that this woman had come from a wealthy Catholic family and would not have been allowed to marry my father had her parents known he'd been married before and had four children. She would have been disinherited and so they never mentioned our existence. At last I knew why we had been kept secret for all these years. My father had also kept us hidden - in the back of his mind. So tightly had he suppressed our existence, that as an older man, he had not remembered me as a child!

In spite of this, the longing for a father went so deep I was not able to relinquish the belief, and hope, that he was not just an empty shell. Even though he rarely spoke and had no memories of my childhood, I still nurtured the hope and belief that there was something more to him. After having a vivid dream about my father one night, I knew it was time to write and ask all the questions I had asked him in my dream:

Dear Dad,

Although we have met a couple of times recently, I don't know who you are. Time is short, and I have waited so long. I can't begin to know you unless you write to me. Tell me about yourself. When were you born? What was your childhood like? Tell me about your meeting with our mother, about the war, about your accident. I was so excited when I got your phone call a few years ago, right out of the blue, a call I'd given up on long ago. I was excited you wanted to meet me after all these silent years, but I have to admit I was also a little nervous. It was something I had longed for since I can remember, and now it was about to happen. I was going to meet my dad. The dad I hadn't seen since I was six years old. I didn't know what you'd look like. I had seen a black and white photograph taken on your and my mother's wedding day, and another one of us as a family with Pattie and Colin just after I was born. But that's all. And yet when we met, you had nothing to say. No memories of us as children, no photographs from the past. Nothing. I often find it is easier to write than to talk, and I once heard you had written poetry as a young man. So, I am asking you to write, write, write. Tell me about yourself.

With love

Jenny

I didn't really expect a response, but later that year I received a four-page letter describing his childhood, his love of horses at an early age, and to my surprise, an account of his accident in Malta.

'*I was Aerodrome Control Pilot, responsible for aircraft taking off in sequence. As the Germans and/or Italians were overhead all lights were forbidden, but a car with headlights full on drove up to me. I got out my revolver and told the passenger in no uncertain terms to switch off. To my astonishment out stepped the Air Officer Commanding, Air Vice Marshall H.P. Lloyd.*

A few nights later, on the 8th March 1942, with aircraft bombed up I got the okay to take off but unfortunately another aircraft was taxiing up the runway towards me, equally bombed up and the inevitable happened. My rear gunner was blown in his turret halfway up the runway and got out without a scratch. As the wings of the two aircraft collided, I remember seeing a sheet of flames shooting up from the trap door to my right, which hit my face and hands. Thinking I ought to move my next recollection is of sitting on the tarmac below the aircraft, a trip of about eight feet. Expecting bombs to arrive from the enemy overhead I hurried into a bit of a ditch I'd spotted beside the runway and lay there while the bombs from both aircraft blew up.

After some time, the ambulance crew eventually arrived and took what they had collected to hospital to mix with the many naval casualties from their convoy work. I was taken to hospital and never saw any of my crew again, though three survived. Replacing dressings of lint every other day on my forehead and hands produced quite a lot of blood and I was given a transfusion. A fortnight after being admitted and hands and face dressed, in came A.V.M Lloyd and asked me if there was anything I wanted. I said, 'Get me back to the UK,' and a fortnight later I was flown in a Hudson back to Hendon and driven to East Grinstead to the tender care of Archie McIndoe, a pioneering New Zealand plastic surgeon who worked for the Royal Air Force during World War II of whom I have the greatest admiration. Although my hands were infected with streptococci I was soon given skin grafts from my thighs onto my forehead and right hand, which took excellently, but my left, done a week later rejected the graft due to infection and contraction of the fingers on my left hand resulted after a further attempted skin graft.

The bliss of relaxing in a hot saline bath with the dressings peeling off after their bloody and painful removal in Malta was beyond relief. Being in ward 3, I met many badly burned Battle of Britain troops, including Richard Hilary and Bill Simpson. We would be in hospital for an operation grafting on some eyelashes and ears before being sent out to mix with the outside world. One of the greatest in this respect was the manager of Christopher and Latherly's Pub in East Grinstead who would always welcome everyone from hospital regardless of what they looked like. This was indeed a wonderful re-introduction to life....'

Jock Boyd

This felt like the beginnings of what it must be like to have a father. Now I was getting the real stuff, no more descriptions of his dogs and his garden. I had the feeling that this account of his accident had been kept behind locked doors, never to be brought out into the light of day. My dad was opening up! Maybe there was more. The extraordinary thing was he ended his story just after Pattie was born and there was nothing about his life in Kenya or about his other children. I thanked him and, feeling as if that was the best I would get, gave my brother and two sisters a copy of his four-page history, and left it at that.

Life carried on as usual, Cottonwood, the workshops and my yearly trips to Los Angeles, but on one of these visits, the summer of 2005, I went with Mick and his wife Lynn to visit our daughter, Amelia, in hospital. With her face beaming as she leaned her head against the pillow, a tiny little bundle by her side, she proudly introduced us to our new granddaughter, Izadora. Our LA family was growing, Mick and Lynn had given birth to their twins four years earlier, and now we had another little girl.

A year or so later, in 2007, my father called me unexpectedly.

"I've started writing again," he said. "I want to show you some of the old photographs I've found."

I got the train from Waterloo to Crewkerne, where he was now living with his partner Mary, but this time I felt peaceful, no longer excited. I didn't know how this meeting would go, but I was interested to hear what other memories had come to light.

We sat together at the round glass dining room table, but this time I was not fearful of his silence. We had a reason to communicate. He showed me two little red notebooks - on one was written 'Horses' and on the other 'Flying'. He handed these to me and watched as I opened them and studied his scrawled writing. He pointed out certain bits that were written in the margin, as if last minute memories had surfaced and needed to be included. I held these books with reverence. We laughed at certain bits - he likes to laugh, I discovered - and we have a similar sense of humor. While describing what he'd written about, I was free to ask him questions about his life.

I decided to take the plunge at one point, to tell him what I'd always wanted to say, but never thought I'd ever get the opportunity. I told him my belief that as a child I was very close to him and had felt his pain of isolation, his feelings of being locked inside, and had taken them on as my own. I told him that it had been my life's journey to find myself from behind those walls. These words sprung out of my mouth, not knowing what his response would be or if he'd even understand. He looked at me and nodded; he knew what I meant. As I spoke, I didn't know whether I was talking to him, or to myself with him as witness. In a way it didn't matter, just saying the words created a sense of connection. Then, in a soft voice he said:

"When you left Africa I never knew where you were living. I didn't know how to contact you."

I was astounded! It was a revelation to me. I hadn't been abandoned. All those years of searching and escapism because I had felt unwanted, not loved by my own father. Instead of believing he didn't want to contact us, I could tell myself he wasn't able to. Whether he would have or not doesn't really matter, and I will never know.

By asking him about himself he'd found distant memories lodged in the back of his mind, which were now vivid, frozen memories that had begun to thaw. This man had a youth and it was bubbling to the surface, crashing through layer upon layer of ice, ready to be expressed. This was a world he then tried to show me through old black and white photographs taken with a Brownie Box camera and pages of writing that looked as if a spider had walked mindlessly across the page after being dropped into a pot of ink. He'd found old photographs of himself in army uniform, and others while steeple chasing in Kenya. He had discovered an old brown leather attaché case filled with memorabilia from the war, including a faded logbook listing bombing raids he was part of, the dates of each raid recorded right up to the day of his near fatal accident. I looked at the lunch menu my father handed to me covered with signatures and at the top was written in black print, 'The Guinea Pig Club'. It was the name given to the pilots injured in the Battle of Britain who were treated by Archibald McIndoe at the burn unit of the Queen Victoria Hospital in West Sussex. The Guinea Pigs were given this name because McIndoe had no choice but to try out his ideas on the men, as he had no book to refer to or guide him. Reconstructive surgery was in its infancy at the time, and my father, I discovered, was one of the guinea pigs.

All these treasures he gave to me.

"Who else would want them?" he asked nonchalantly. "I don't need them anymore."

As we sat side-by-side at the table, I told him how brave he was, flying into the face of danger.

"Not brave," he said with a look of surprise. "I loved flying; I was doing what I loved."

I smiled and looked at the small leather case that lay open beside him, at the photographs poking out of pockets in the lid. A pile of notepapers had been neatly placed in front of him ready to show me another piece of the puzzle from the life of an eighty-nine-year old man I called 'Dad'.

I walked away with these priceless gifts, feeling elated. It was more than I had hoped for. The person hidden beneath what had seemed an empty shell had now emerged. Between us we had awakened his memories from long ago and released the prisoner from suspended animation.

After our memorable meeting, I saw my father on a number of occasions and every time the connection between us stayed strong and silent. Pattie and I went to his 90th birthday celebration with our nephew, Paula's son, Will. It was a small affair, just pre-lunch drinks one cold January morning. My father's companion, Mary, and a smattering of neighbors stood around the room chatting while he sat in his armchair with a drink in his hand, mostly silent. Little did we suspect that the rest of his family, including his two daughters, would be celebrating with them the following day. Even though his wife had died a few years previously, my father was still keeping us apart, an old secret long past its sell-by date!

On a cold winter's day in November 2008, a day I had hoped would never come, I stood with my family and friends outside the Guildford Crematorium, overwhelmed with grief, in front of Paula's coffin. She had died of an overdose. She had battled with addiction throughout her life, and no matter how many treatment centers she'd been to, no matter how good she was at talking the talk, it hounded her, biting at her heels, until it finally won. I had told myself over the years that if that ever happened, I wouldn't be surprised, but when it actually did the shock and disbelief were shattering. I looked up at one point and caught a glimpse of my father in the distance, looking frail and leaning on his walking stick, with Mary by his side.

The last time I spoke to my father before he died was when I went with Pattie to visit him in hospital. As we walked in and stood beside his bed, I knew he recognized me for a fraction of a second before zoning out.

"What are all those rabbits doing over there?" he asked, his shaky finger pointing towards the bed opposite. "What are they doing running around?"

We sat with him for a short while and then gave each other the nod. Pattie got up, kissed him on the cheek, and said goodbye. I did the same, but after saying goodbye, without thinking I said, "See you soon." Two days later, on February 23rd, 2012, he died.

Two years later, when Ron Welch's son replaced him as CEO, the change in leadership gave me the push I needed to retire. I wanted to spend more time on my writing. I continued to bring Rokelle Lerner to London for her workshops three times a year, but apart from that I let go of my involvement in other workshops.

Musicians in Tune was finally published in the UK in 2014, under a different title, *It's not only Rock 'n' Roll*. I was asked to speak at the Whitstable Festival in Kent; Andy Miller, an author and music buff, was to interview me about my book. As I waited in the Green Room with my husband, David, I could hear the audience laughing and clapping next door. The speaker was obviously doing well.

I had recently given a talk at The Barnes and Noble bookstore in Hollywood, with Mick and a couple of other musicians, but this was my first experience of speaking on my own at a literary festival and to this number of people.

There was a friendly atmosphere backstage, people walking in and out of the room, asking if we'd like a cup of tea, or anything a little stronger. They were very grateful I'd cut short my trip in the US to speak at their first three-day festival, organized by a woman called Victoria Falconer. I was to be the last-but-one speaker on the Sunday.

After hearing the applause from next door and looking at my watch, a larger-than-life woman burst in through the door holding a glass of wine. I gathered she was the speaker, an established author and the cause of all this clapping. Her eyes rested on me for a second before saying something to Andy. She bustled around the sofa, gathered her things and then walked towards the door. As she gulped back the last of her wine and placed the glass down on the table, she looked at me again.

"Are you nervous?" she asked.

I stared at her for a second, trying to work out whether I was nervous.

"No," I replied, probably more surprised than she was.

"Oh, thought you'd be nervous." Then she opened the door and was gone.

Five minutes later I walked from the back of the hall to the front, trying not to look at the two hundred or more people on my left. It was a full house. Once we were seated in armchairs, each with a microphone in front of us, Andy introduced me as Dr. Jenny Boyd. For the first time I looked out at the sea of faces, and then smiled.

"What inspired you to write this book?" Andy asked.

I leant forward, facing the audience, and started to talk. As I did this an overwhelming sense of relief ran through me. I wasn't nervous. Instead of feeling nervous, I wanted to tell the listeners what inspired me, how I found the musicians to interview, and how I believed we all had the ability to be creative. Andy asked one question after another, good questions, questions that gave a lot of scope. After more conversation back and forth with Andy, the time came for the audience to ask questions. Hands shot up as members of the audience asked about the book or the musicians and my life in the rock and roll world.

I pointed to a hand waving above the crowd.

"What inspired you to organize all these workshops?"

Andy had mentioned the workshops when he'd introduced me. A picture of myself from long ago flashed through my mind. I leant closer to the microphone; the image of that young woman so lost and unhappy hovering around me.

"During a low point in my life," I said, "while I was living in LA, my marriage to Mick in tatters and on the verge of a breakdown, I had nowhere to go for help. And so, without realizing it until recently, I created the kind of workshops for others that I would have given anything to have gone to myself. It would have saved me from drowning, and it would have lessened the years it took me to turn my ship around."

As I drove home with David that evening, my mind wandered back to all the workshops I'd organized since relocating to England twenty-two years ago. I had spent all those years building a platform for dynamic speakers, cutting-edge treatment centers and inspiring facilitators of workshops for both individuals and families. I had brought people together; I had found others who shared my beliefs. On that drive back to London I realized something had changed. I had found my voice.

What I have learned from this extraordinary journey is that when I listened to my heart, when I finally followed George's advice to "Just be yourself", that's when things would work out. Through trusting my judgment and intuition, I found myself in the right place at the right time. I realize now that it was essential for me to do things my way, to be true to myself. I was not a traditionalist. I didn't follow the status quo. I did what intuitively felt right for me, whether it was dancing along catwalks, taking a chance and buying a one-way ticket to San Francisco, or interviewing musicians about their creative process with no idea that it would one day become a book. When I trusted my gut, I found skills I never knew I had. My many years of working in the addiction field and being instrumental in helping people to find the road to recovery, to finding themselves, allowed me the insight into my own path of sobriety.

But when I went against my intuition, when I fell into the trap of hiding behind drugs or alcohol, that's when I'd lose the connection to myself and that's when my life would spiral out of control. No one was at the helm. Drugs and alcohol didn't suit me, and I knew it, but it took a long time for me to really know it and take it on board. It hadn't helped when the whole circus was on its way down the rabbit hole, so to speak, when the band started to take off and my relationship to Mick began to falter. And it didn't help me stay grounded when everything and everyone around me was flying high. There was something larger than Mick that I was fighting against that hit me to the core. This wonderful, talented, and exciting band was hurtling towards my darkest and deepest fears that their fame, money, and drugs, as seductive as they were, would pull our family apart. Along with this fear, and what lay deeper inside me was the knowledge that my sense of self was under threat.

It was only once I stopped trying to escape from the sadness, loneliness or fear that I was able to get back in touch with my own creativity, my spirituality, and could finally be myself. There were wonderful times on this journey of mine; there were also hard times as I fought against my demons and what was going on in my life. But I feel extremely lucky and grateful for the life I've led, and especially for the people who are and have been part of it.

Despite struggling for years with our relationship when the balance of power, control or influence was out of kilter, Mick and I are to this day and always have been very dear to each other and the best of friends. We usually meet up once a year with our children and grandchildren, either at his house in Mau, in Los Angeles, or at a Fleetwood Mac concert when they come to London.

My yearly visits to LA continue so I can spend time with Amelia, Lucy, our grandchildren - Wolf and Izzy - friends and other members of my or Mick's family. I am in constant touch with my family here in England, my siblings, nephews, nieces and great-nephews and nieces. Because of my twenty-four years with David, I have inherited a large and wonderful extended family as well, many members of whom I have known since birth.

Life feels grounded and steady, with good health and good friends, but true to form I am still finding my own way to reach for the stars, to express myself; writing, public speaking, composing songs and singing in a choir, but above everything, enjoying what it feels like to... "Just Be Myself."

THE END

A journey beyond the muse

:

285

ACKNOWLEDGEMENTS

There are so many people I wish to thank for their help and encouragement throughout the writing of this book. First, I would like to give thanks to Victoria Falconer for introducing me to Matthew Smith and Kerry-Jane at Urbane Publications. Their confidence in me, and my story, was deeply appreciated. Warmest thanks go to Claudia Riemer Boutote of Raven Studio. It was a privilege and a joy to work with Claudia, and her support and editorial insight was a huge contribution. Many thanks go to Richard Blakely, an old friend from our Maharishi ashram days, for his invaluable help, encouragement and reminiscences.

Thanks go to Maddie Miller, Sally Bradforth and Roz Perrott for their help, and to Larry Vigon for art direction and design, along with Barbara Leung Larson. I give heartfelt thanks and gratitude to family and friends who have been so supportive throughout this whole process, including Sandra Vigon, Annie Lionnet and Liz Kalinowsaka. My thanks and appreciation goes to my husband, David Levitt, for his ongoing encouragement and his ability to find the perfect word when needed!!

I would like to give a special thanks to all the photographers and people who have generously given photographs, including those I was unable to locate: Karl Ferris, Eric Swayne, Ron Traeger, Sharon Weisz, Herbie Worthington, Sally Fleetwood, Roderick Delroy, Paul Saltzman, Oliver Ferrand, Mary Torry Devito, Annabel Mehran, John Cole, The Beatle Story, Liverpool and Pattie Boyd.

www.thejennyboyd.com

As a young fashion model with Mick Fleetwood as her boyfriend and Beatle George Harrison as her brother-in-law, Jenny found herself immersed in the pop culture of the Swinging 60s. She moved to San Francisco for six months in 1967 where she inadvertently found herself at the centre of "Flower Power." On her return to England Jenny became the inspiration for Donovan's famous song, "Jennifer Juniper." She accompanied her sister and The Beatles to Maharishi's ashram in India to study meditation. Despite being attuned to the spiritual bloom and innocence of the 60s, Jenny also experienced the turmoil and decadence of the 70s. Her two marriages to Mick Fleetwood, founder member of Fleetwood Mac, brought her to the forefront of the rock and roll world — constant touring coupled with fame, money, drugs and heartbreak. Jenny later married drummer Ian Wallace that, after ten years, ended in divorce. Struggling in the dark to find and develop her own voice and identity, Jenny went to college, achieving a Masters in Counselling Psychology followed by a Ph.D. in Humanities. She wrote a book on musicians and the creative process called, 'Musicians in Tune', which was later retitled, 'It's Not Only Rock'n'Roll'. For the next twenty years Jenny worked in the addiction field, both in the States and the UK, as well as creating her own very successful company offering workshops in London, facilitated by therapists from the US, for people in need of help with recovery, relationship issues or just support. Jenny is a writer and public speaker. She divides her time between London, where she lives with her husband, and Los Angeles with her family.

INDEX

URBANE

Urbane Publications is dedicated to
developing author voices, and publishing
books that challenge, thrill and fascinate.
From page-turning memoirs to essential reference,
our goal is to publish what
YOU want to read.

Find out more at
urbanepublications.com